T0041537

THE LEGO® ZOO

50 EASY-TO-BUILD ANIMALS

JODY PADULANO

no starch press
San Francisco

This English edition is co-published by No Starch Press, Inc. and Nuinui.

Printed in China
Third Printing

26 25 24 23 22   3 4 5 6 7

ISBN-10: 1-59327-922-1
ISBN-13: 978-1-59327-922-6

Publisher: William Pollock
Production Editor: Janelle Ludowise
Cover Design: Mimi Heft
Interior Design: Clara Zanotti and Maison adv, with Mimi Heft
Developmental Editor: Annie Choi
Proofreader: Lisa Devoto Farrell
Compositor: Kim Scott, Bumpy Design

For information on distribution, bulk sales, corporate sales, or translations, please contact No Starch Press, Inc. directly at info@nostarch.com or:

No Starch Press, Inc.
245 8th Street, San Francisco, CA 94103
phone: 415.863.9900
www.nostarch.com

Library of Congress Cataloging-in-Publication Data:
Names: Padulano, Jody, author.
Title: The LEGO zoo : 50 easy-to-build animals / Jody Padulano.
Other titles: Zoo LEGO. English
Description: First edition. | San Francisco : No Starch Press, Inc., [2018] |
Translation of: Lo zoo LEGO : 50 modelli di animali.
Identifiers: LCCN 2018024733| ISBN 9781593279226 (print) | ISBN 1593279221
(print) | ISBN 9781593279233 (epub) | ISBN 159327923X (epub)
Subjects: LCSH: LEGO toys. | Animals--Models.
Classification: LCC TS2301.T7 P33 2018 | DDC 688.7/25--dc23
LC record available at https://lccn.loc.gov/2018024733

[PRHPS]

In memory of Joe Dever

Acknowledgments

Thank you to everyone who has helped me and made this book possible. First, my thanks go to my publisher NuiNui; ItLug, who's been a great resource for all kinds of information for LEGO fans in Italy; RomeBrick, whose members provide inexhaustible sources of inspiration; and Chiara, who helped in every way possible (and more). Many thanks to my friends, my mother, Kenny, Aurora, Edwin, Gloria, Ethan, Ryan, and Emily—you're my family and the main reason why this 40-year-old can still play with LEGO!

About the Author

Born and raised in Rome, author Jody Padulano is a happy AFOL (Adult Fan of LEGO). He works as an IT engineer in telecommunications, but his passion is in creating games and video games. He likes to travel, play role-playing games, and, of course, collect LEGO, which has been a hobby from an early age. An active member of ItLug and RomaBrick, important LEGO communities in Italy, Jody has exhibited his works across Italy and abroad.

CONTENTS

CHAPTER 3 54

CHAPTER 4 110

CHAPTER 5 152

Terminology

LEGO builders have come up with special names for their bricks. Without a standard way to refer to different LEGO parts, it would be really hard to understand building instructions or share techniques with other people. Let's go over some terminology we'll use in this book.

Stud

Studs are the little buttons on top of a brick that fit into other parts. We count studs like a unit of measurement.

Brick

Bricks are the most common part. Their sizes are based on how many studs they have. For example, a 1×1 brick has only one stud, while a 2×2 brick has two studs on each side for a total of four studs, and so on.

Round Brick

A round brick is similar to a brick except its edges are rounded.

Modified Brick

This is a special type of brick that can have a stud on the side, a bent shape, or even a clip.

Plate

Plates are like bricks but shorter. You need to stack three plates together to make one brick. They're useful for smaller structures.

Round Plate

A round plate is a plate with rounded edges.

Modified Plate

This is a special type of plate with modifications like an eyelet, a clip, or a handle.

Tile

Tiles are like plates except they don't have studs on top. You can use their smooth surface to build floors and more.

Round Tile

This is a tile with rounded edges.

Modified Tile

This is just like a tile, but it has something extra, like a clip.

Wedge

Wedges are similar to bricks, but they have a diagonal edge.

Wedge Plate

This is a plate with diagonal edges that are neither round nor square in shape.

Slope

A slope is a brick with a slanted surface. We use numbers in degrees (45, 33, 65, 75, 30, and so on) to describe how slanted it is. Slopes always have fewer studs on top than on the bottom. For example, slope 45 2×2 can take four studs below but only two on top.

Inverted Slope

This is an upside-down slope that has more studs on top than below.

Cone

This is a cone-shaped brick that's wider at the base than it is on top.

Bracket

A bracket is a plate that's bent at a 90-degree angle with studs on the top and on the side.

Hinge

Hinges come in brick or plate versions, and you can use them to add motion to your models.

Antenna and Lever

These parts are often used to create the antennae of animals.

Dish

Unlike round plates, dishes have a stud on top and are slightly convex, like a tiny umbrella.

Of course, there are many other parts like doors, windows, and Technic pieces, and I won't go over all of them here. But this list is a good first step. Knowing basic LEGO terminology will help you become a better builder as well as make it easier to shop for parts online.

Introduction

In this book, you'll learn how to build 50 awesome animals! The models are organized into five levels in order of difficulty, so you can gradually build up your skills. The book includes a handy list of LEGO terminology as well as tips for organizing your parts, how to get help, and where to buy parts you don't have. You'll also learn how other builders approach their projects.

Sorting Your Bricks

Every builder has their own way of sorting pieces, but here are some tips to get you started. Although you may be tempted to sort by color, this is usually not a good idea. Unless you're building something in just one color, the best way is to sort by type.

For example, suppose you have a bunch of 1×1 and 1×2 bricks. You should first group all the 1×1 bricks together and then sort by color. This way, when you need a brick of that size, you can find it easily. Trying to find a black 1×1 brick in the middle of other black bricks is too hard!

Also, if you have lots of pieces of the same color and type, try to keep them together. But if you have only a few parts of a certain type, you can put them close to others you think might go together. **Generally, you should sort by type, not by color.**

Using What You Have

Keep in mind that you don't have to follow the instructions in this book exactly. Your imagination is more important! So if you feel like using another part, or if you have parts in different colors that fit, go for it!

For example, if you have to use a 2×2 brick in a model, but you only have two 1×2 bricks of the same color, you can use those two instead—it will work just fine! Sometimes you may need to use parts you already have in creative ways. But most of the parts used in this book are easy to find, so you shouldn't have too much trouble. **Remember, there are many different ways to build the same thing!**

Buying Parts You Don't Have

There are many ways to find the parts you need.

LEGO sets You can find many different types of bricks in these sets.

Pick a Brick You may be able to find what you need at *https://shop.lego.com/en-US/Pick-A-Brick-11998*. You'll need a LEGO account to buy bricks on this site, so ask an adult to help you make purchases online.

LEGO Stores Visit a LEGO Store to look for what you need—they usually have walls with a selection of bricks.

BrickLink Last but not least, you can try the BrickLink website at *https://www.bricklink.com*. This is one of the largest brick building sites in the world, so you'll probably find what you're looking for here. Get help from an adult to complete your purchases.

To place an order on BrickLink, just select the bricks you want and add them to your cart. After choosing a payment and shipping method, you should get an email from the seller with instructions to complete the purchase.

You can create a Wanted List on BrickLink that will look for a store that has all the pieces in your Wanted List. This way, you save money and avoid the hassle of buying from multiple sellers.

Building Techniques

You'll see that some animals in this book are harder to build than others—this is because they use different building techniques. In this book you'll learn how to build vertically (stacking bricks on top of each other) as well as horizontally (attaching to the sides) using the *Studs Not On Top (SNOT)* technique. We'll use some Technic pieces as well to make the elephant's trunk, for example.

After building these 50 animals, you'll be able to use what you learned to make even more amazing things! Imagine what you want to build and **think in bricks**! What color will it be? What parts will you need? Don't worry about messing up—if you make a mistake, you can just start over!

CHAPTER 1

Welcome to LEGO Zoo! In this book, you'll learn how to make all kinds of animals to add to your zoo.

Here are six animals you can build in no time at all. You won't need too many bricks for these.

Let's get started!

(See page ix for tips on where to find parts!)

CATERPILLAR

A small insect that crawls on the ground, the caterpillar is one of the easiest animals you can build in this book. You can create this little animal in just a few steps.

If you don't have all the pieces, try using similar bricks.

PARTS LIST

DIFFICULTY

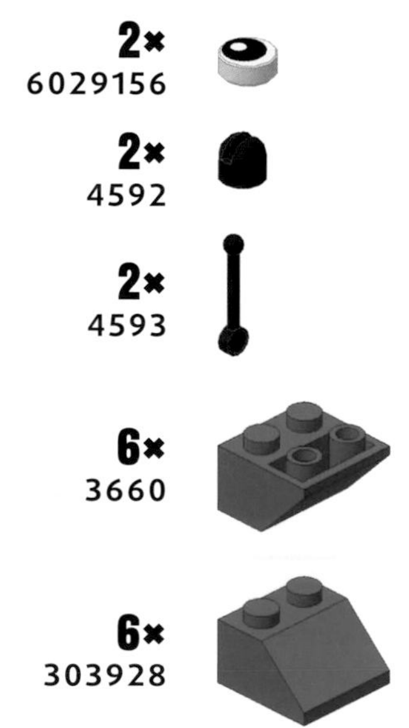

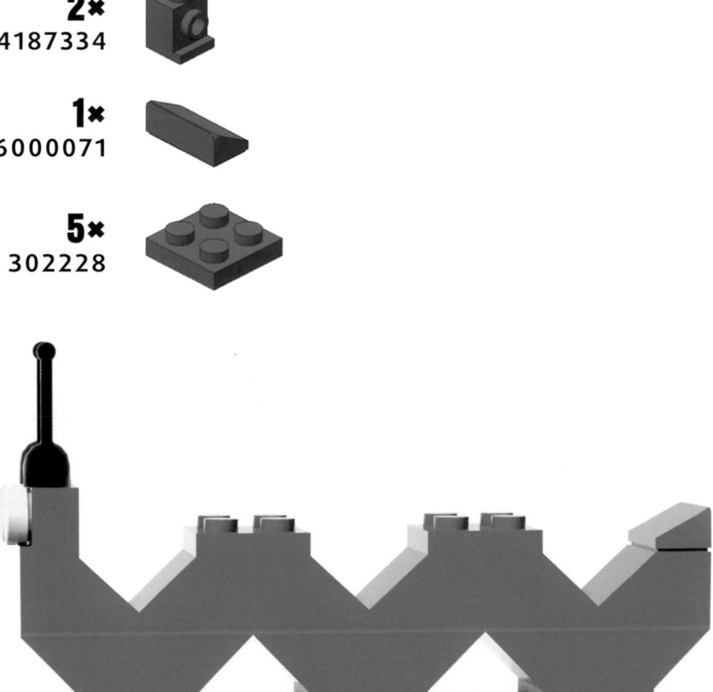

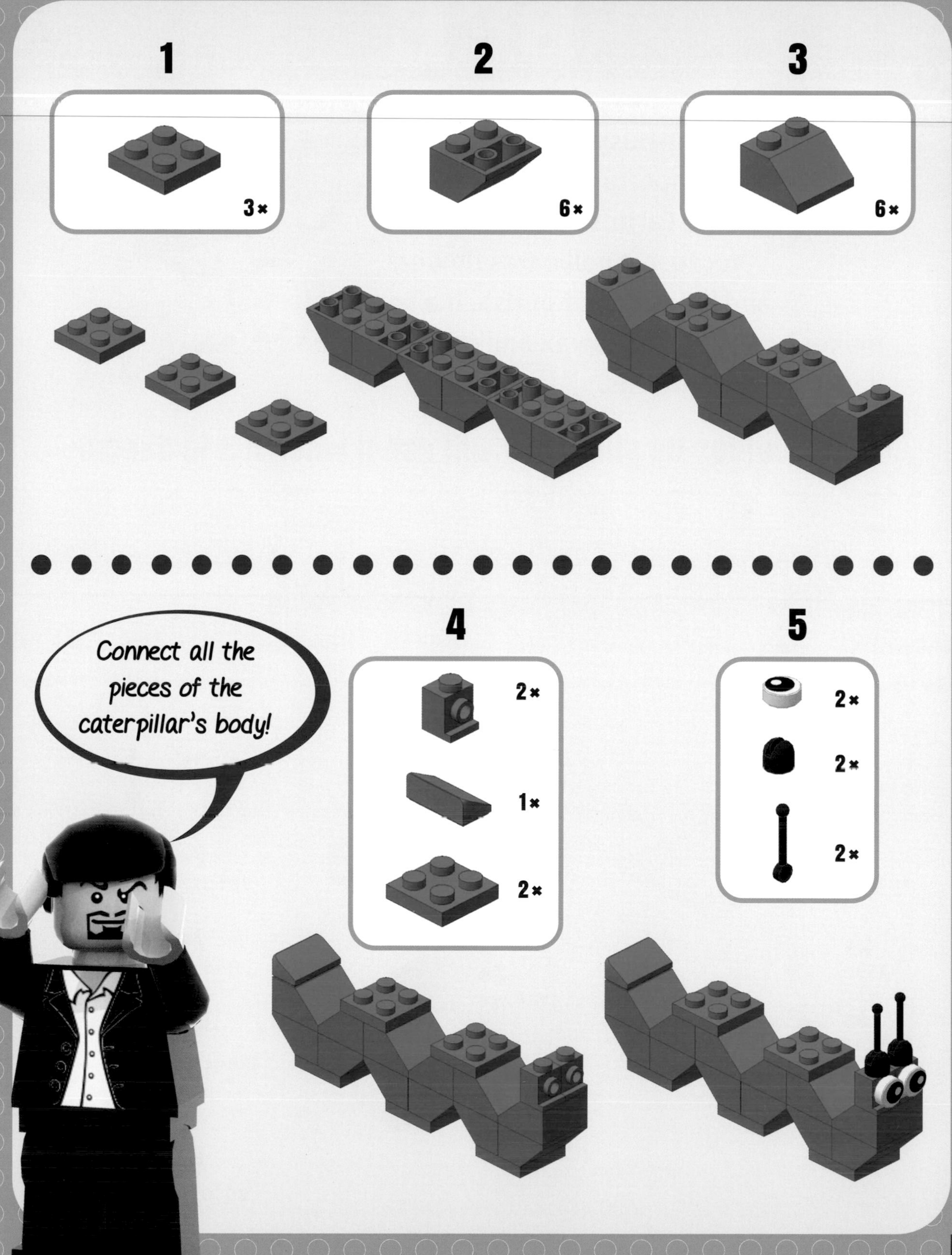
1
3×
2
6×
3
6×
4
2×
1×
2×
5
2×
2×
2×
Connect all the pieces of the caterpillar's body!

BEE

The busy bee is an important animal for the Earth's ecosystem because it pollinates flowers and helps them flourish. It also makes honey and beeswax and can dance in cool patterns.

Watch out for its stinger! It will use it when it's in danger.

PARTS LIST

DIFFICULTY

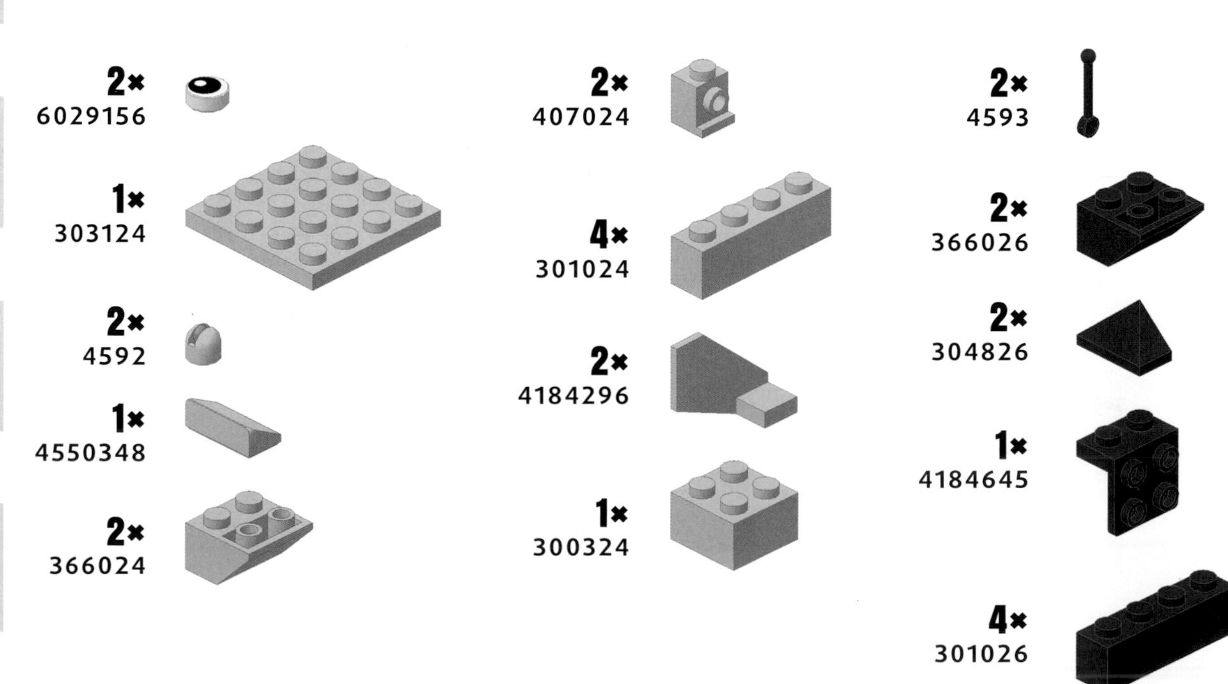

1
1×
2
2×
1×
3
1×
2×
4
3×
3×
5
2×
1×
1×
6
2×
1×
2×
7
2×
2×
2×
Here's how you build the stinger.

CANARY

What do you call a little yellow bird that sings beautifully? A canary, of course! This canary is also easy to build.

Use red or brown bricks to create another type of bird like a robin or a sparrow.

PARTS LIST

DIFFICULTY

2× 4624985 

1× 304024 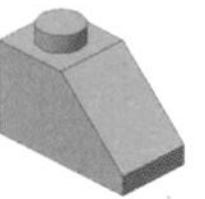

2× 303924 

2× 300524 

2× 2450 

2× 302324 

4× 302424

5× 302124 

3× 300424 

3× 362324 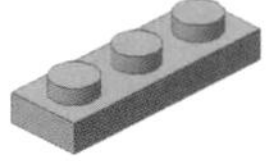

6× 362224 

2× 82357 

5× 300124 

1× 300224 

2× 4173805 

2× 4188450 

1× 6020106 

1

2×

2

1×

2×

3

1×

1×

4

4×

5

1×

1×

1×

6

2×

2×

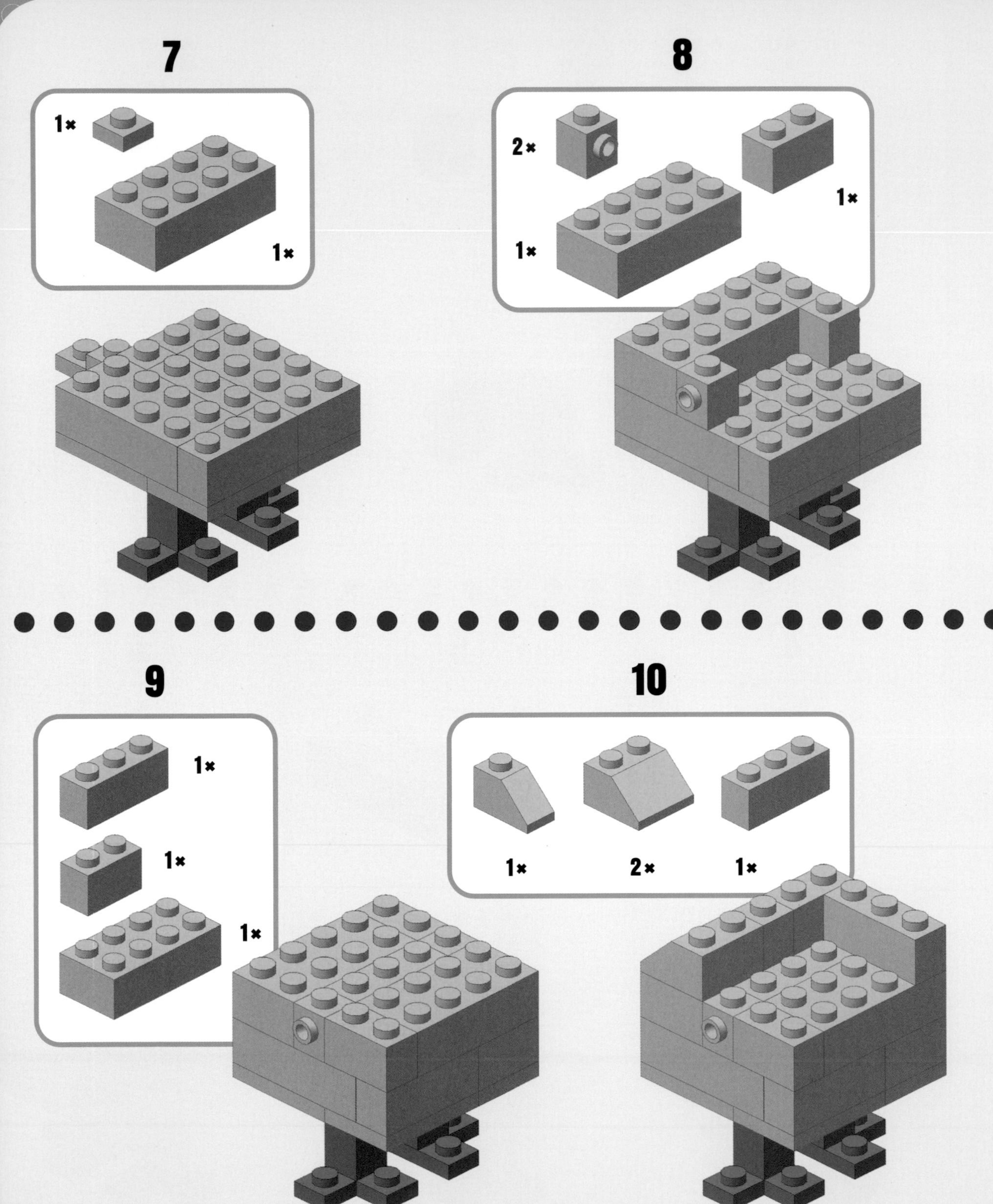
7
1×
1×
8
2×
1×
1×
9
1×
1×
1×
10
1×
2×
1×

11
1×
1×
1×
12
2×
1×
Remember to put the wings on both sides.
13
2×
1×
1×
14
1×
1×
2×

CROCODILE

The crocodile is a peculiar animal with powerful jaws. Its jaws are so big that it often has to turn on its side to open its mouth!

This is a fun model you can try right away.

PARTS LIST

DIFFICULTY

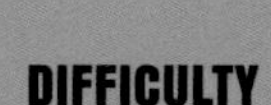

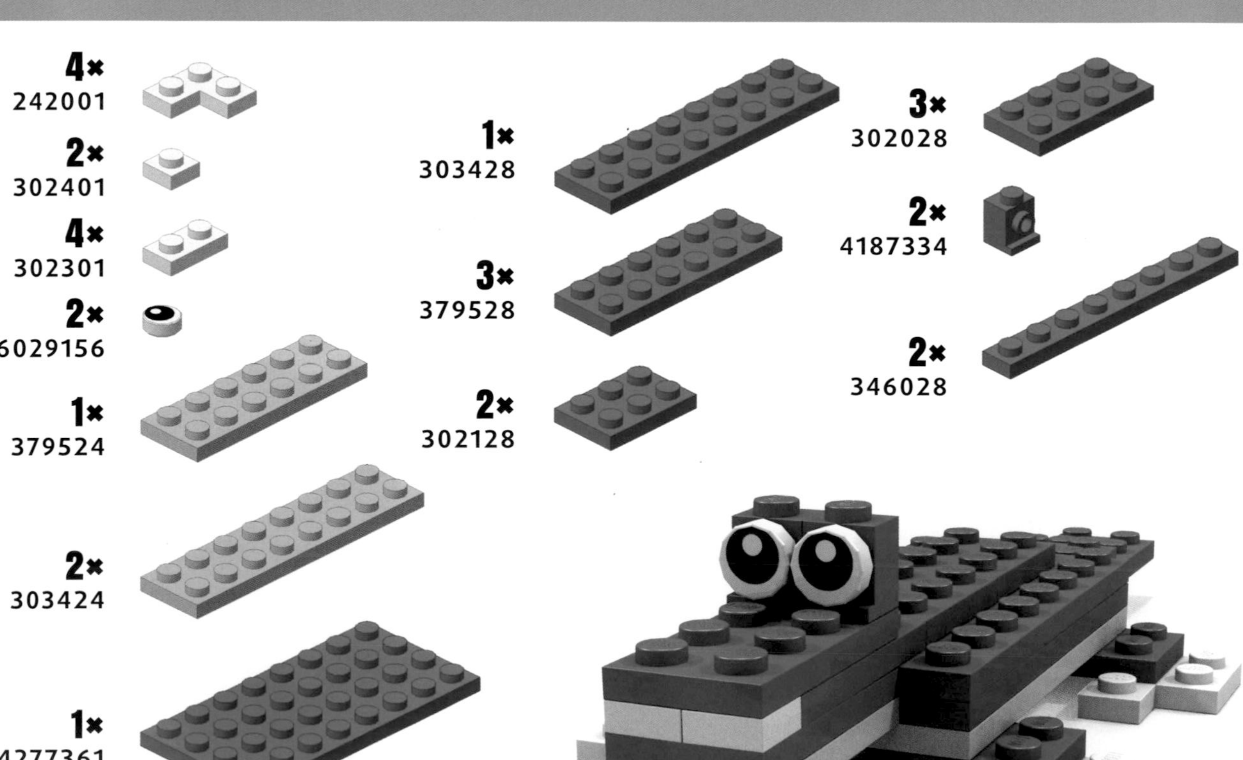

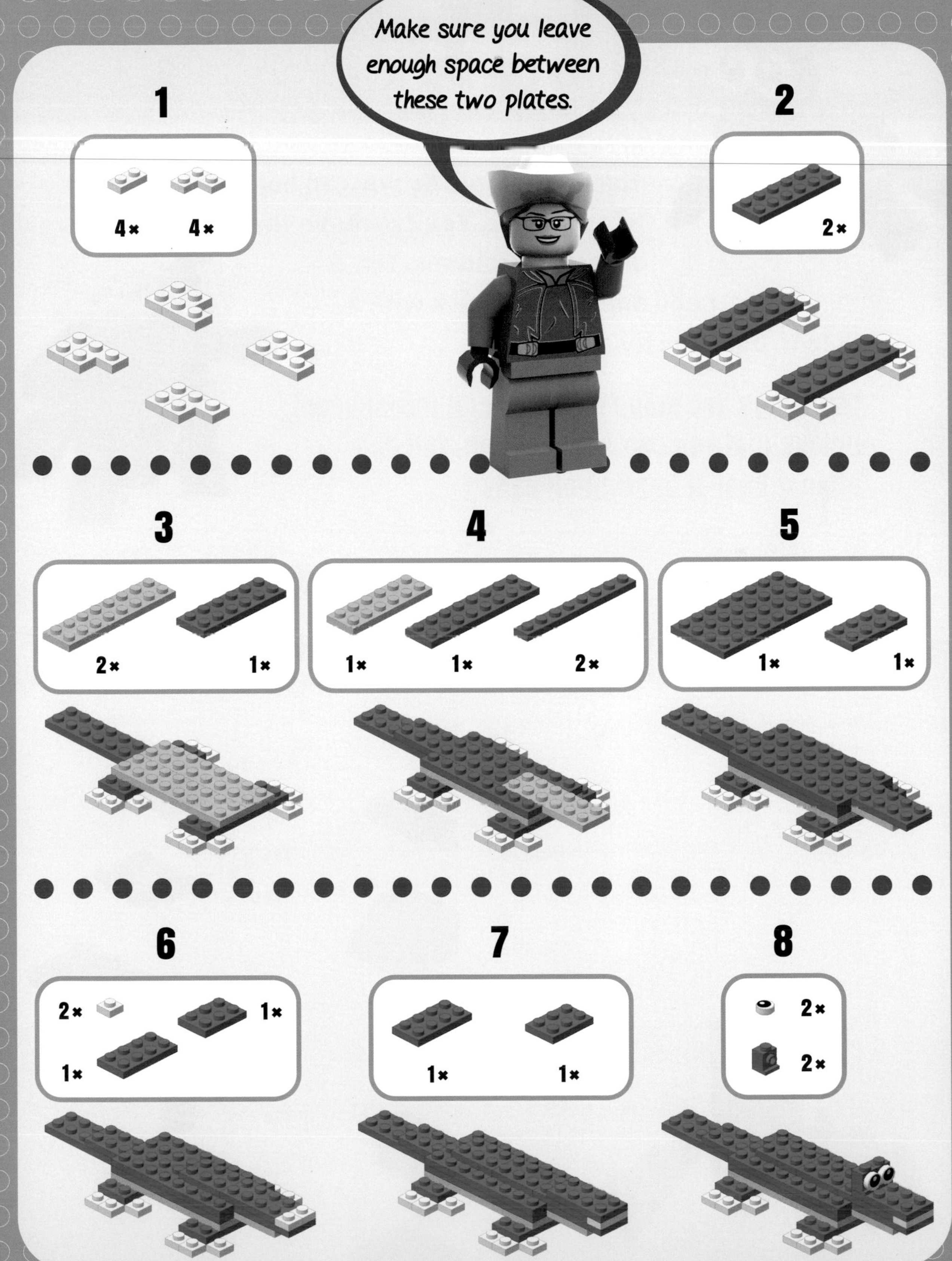
Make sure you leave enough space between these two plates.
1
4×
4×
2
2×
3
2×
1×
4
1×
1×
2×
5
1×
1×
6
2×
1×
1×
7
1×
1×
8
2×
2×

FLY

Here's a simple fly you can build using only a few pieces. You can move the legs into different positions. You'll need one Technic brick with a hole to build the fly's head.

The wings are made up of special transparent bricks that you can see through. You can almost hear it buzzing already!

PARTS LIST

DIFFICULTY

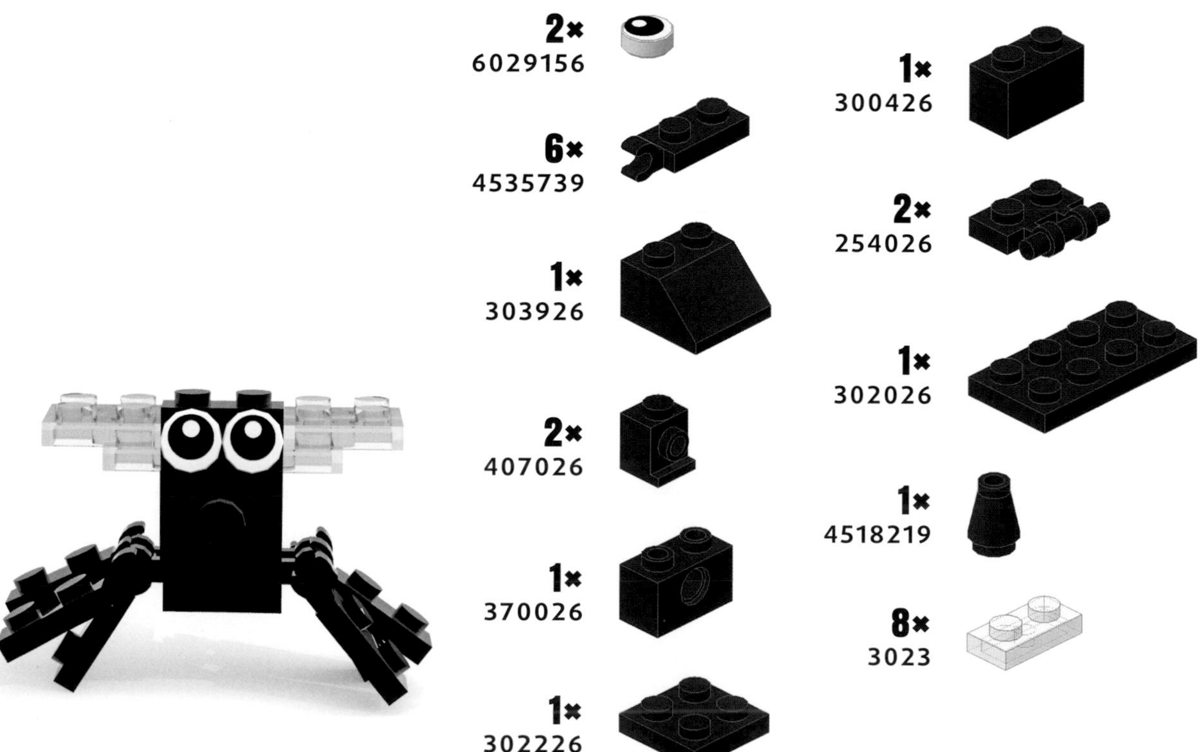

1
1×
2
2×
3
6×
Hinges let you position the legs at different angles.
4
1×
5
1×
1×
1×
6
2×
4×
1×
7
2×
4×

MOUSE

Always hungry for cheese, this clever rodent would do anything for its favorite food. This mouse has whiskers and a long tail that you can move around.

Try building your mice in different shades of gray or brown.

PARTS LIST

DIFFICULTY

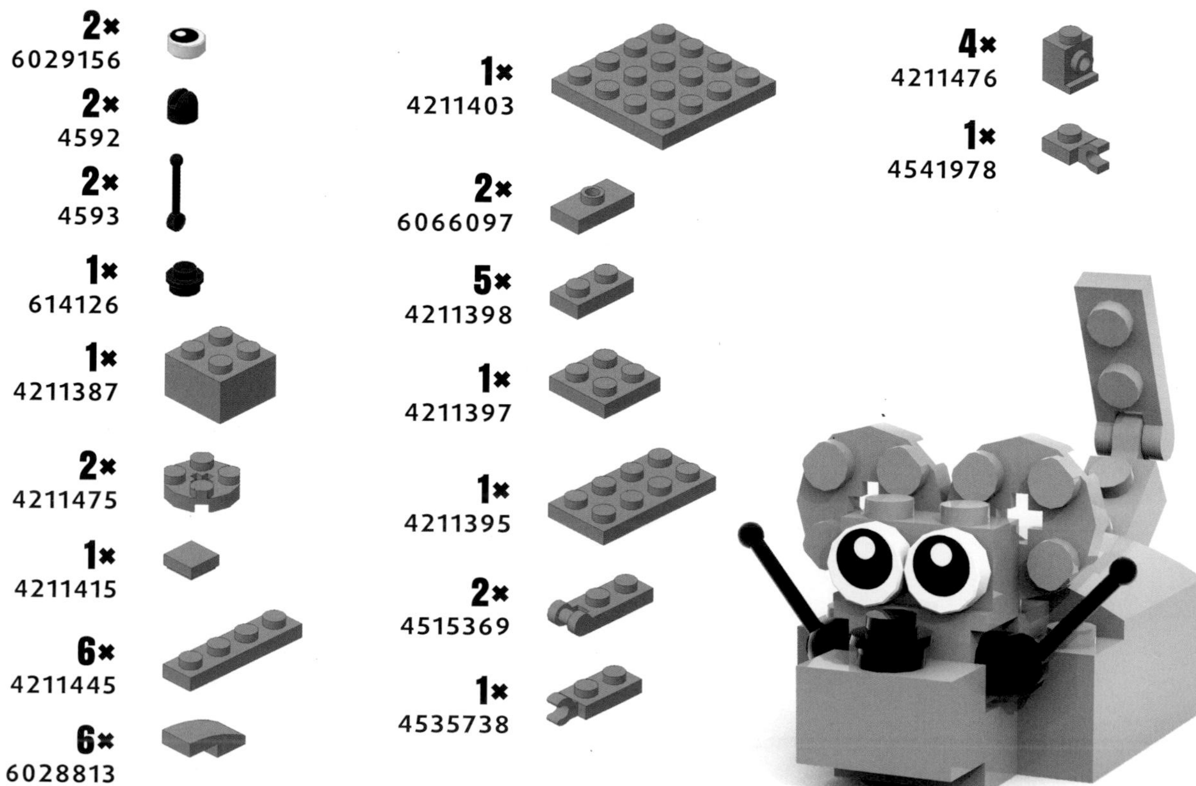

1
1×
1×
2
2×
1×
1×
3
2×
2×
4
1×
2×
1×
5
1×
1×
2×
2×
2×
Mini antennae make great whiskers!
6
1×
1×
1×
1×
7
1×
2×
1×
8
6×
9
2×
1×
10
2×
1×

CHAPTER 2

You'll need a few more parts to build the animals in this level, but they're still quite simple and fun to make.

Try them right now!

(See page ix for tips on where to find parts!)

MOUNTAIN GOAT

These goats live on steep mountains and are great climbers. They use their big horns to scare away predators. You can even use their milk to make delicious cheeses.

When you build this goat, pay attention to how the head sticks out horizontally from the body.

PARTS LIST

DIFFICULTY

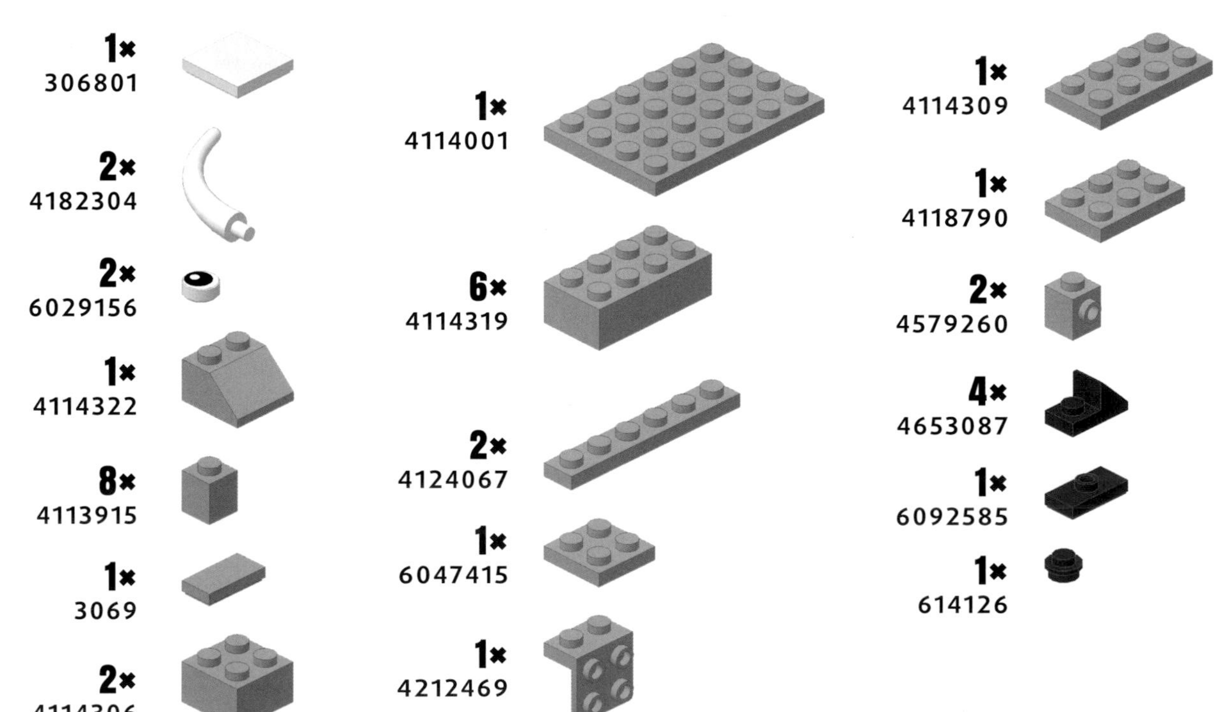

1
4×
4×
2
4×
3
1×
3×
4
3×
5
2×
1×
1×
6
1×
1×
7
1×
1×
A
1×
B
1×
1×
2×
C
2×
1×
1×
A
B
C
8
1×
9
2×
1×
1×
Add horns to make this goat complete!

BEAVER

Beavers use their big teeth to cut down trees and shape them into logs for building dams. Learning to make this brick beaver will help you build more complicated animals later.

Try making other toothy animals like an otter or a marmot.

PARTS LIST

DIFFICULTY

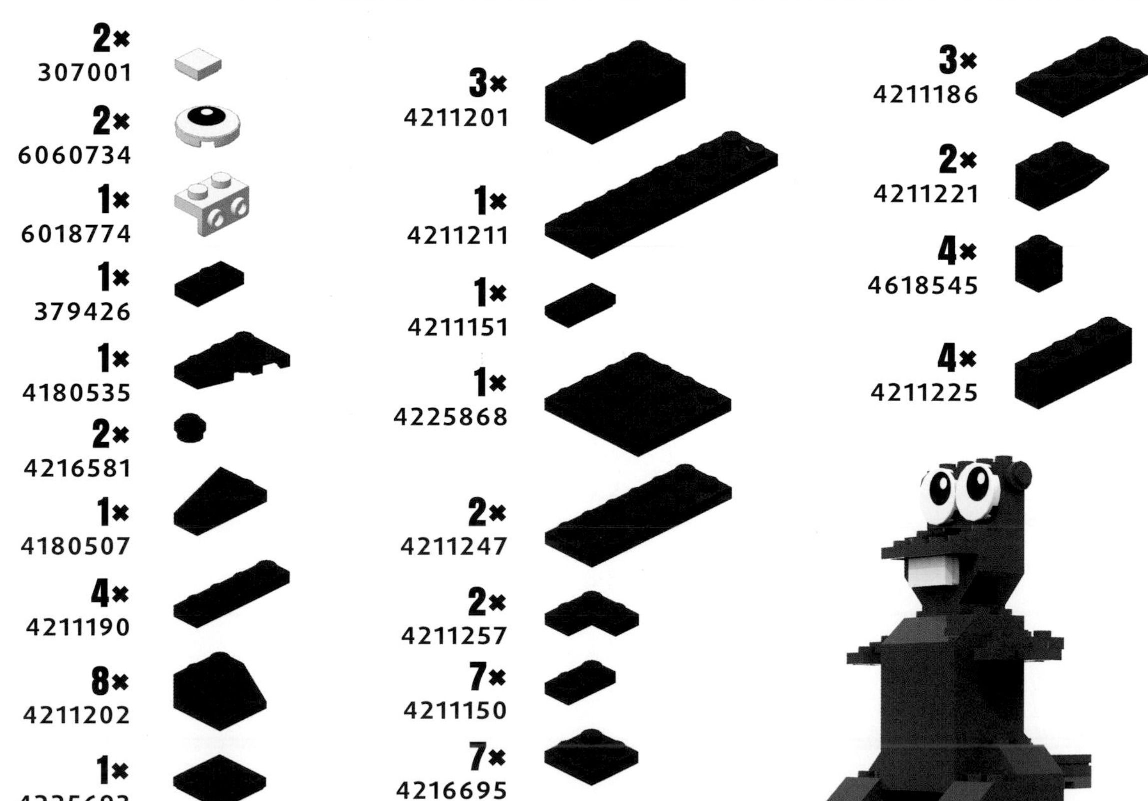

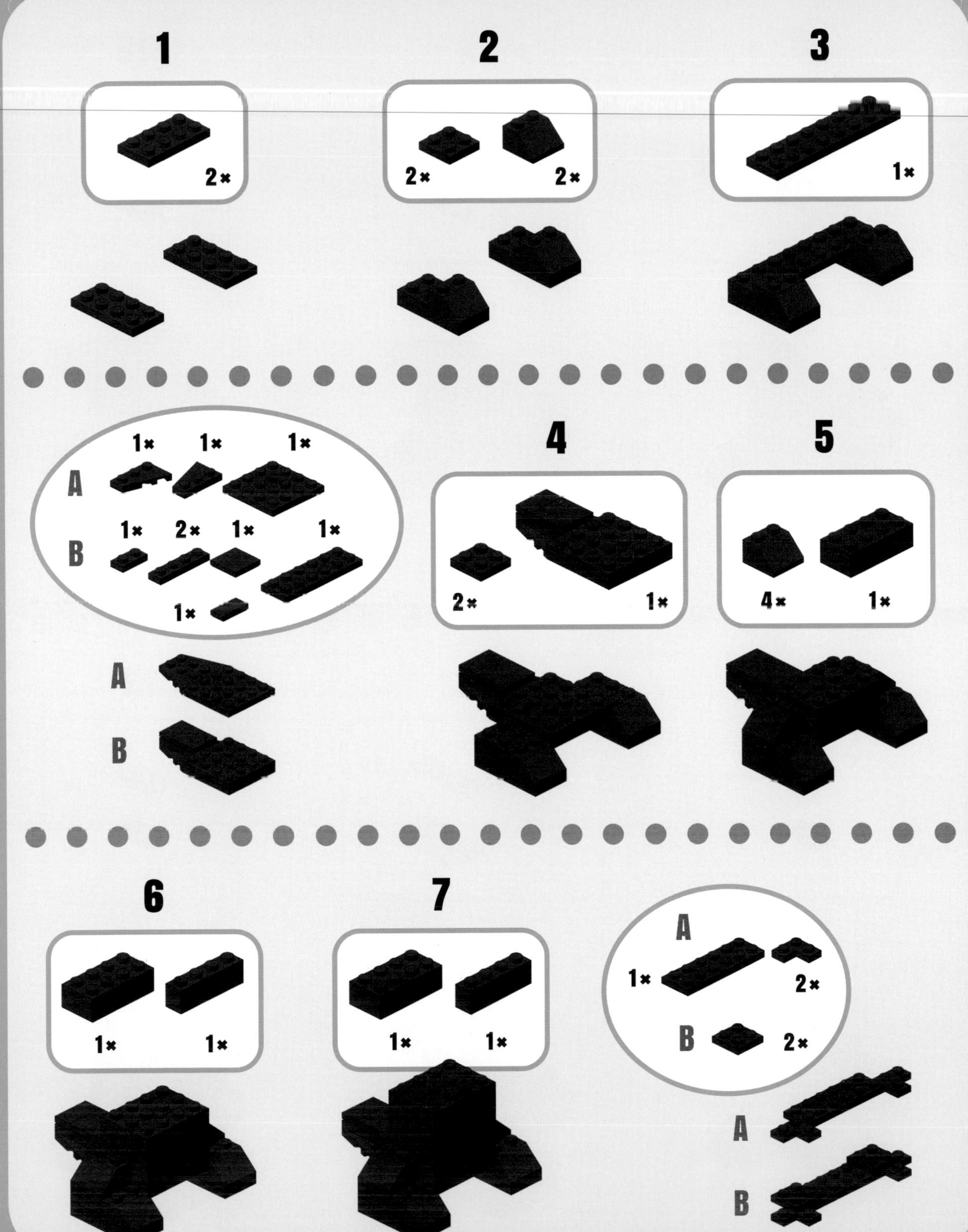

1
2×
2
2×
2×
3
1×
1×
1×
1×
A
1×
2×
1×
1×
B
1×
4
2×
1×
5
4×
1×
A
B
6
1×
1×
7
1×
1×
A
1×
2×
B
2×
A
B

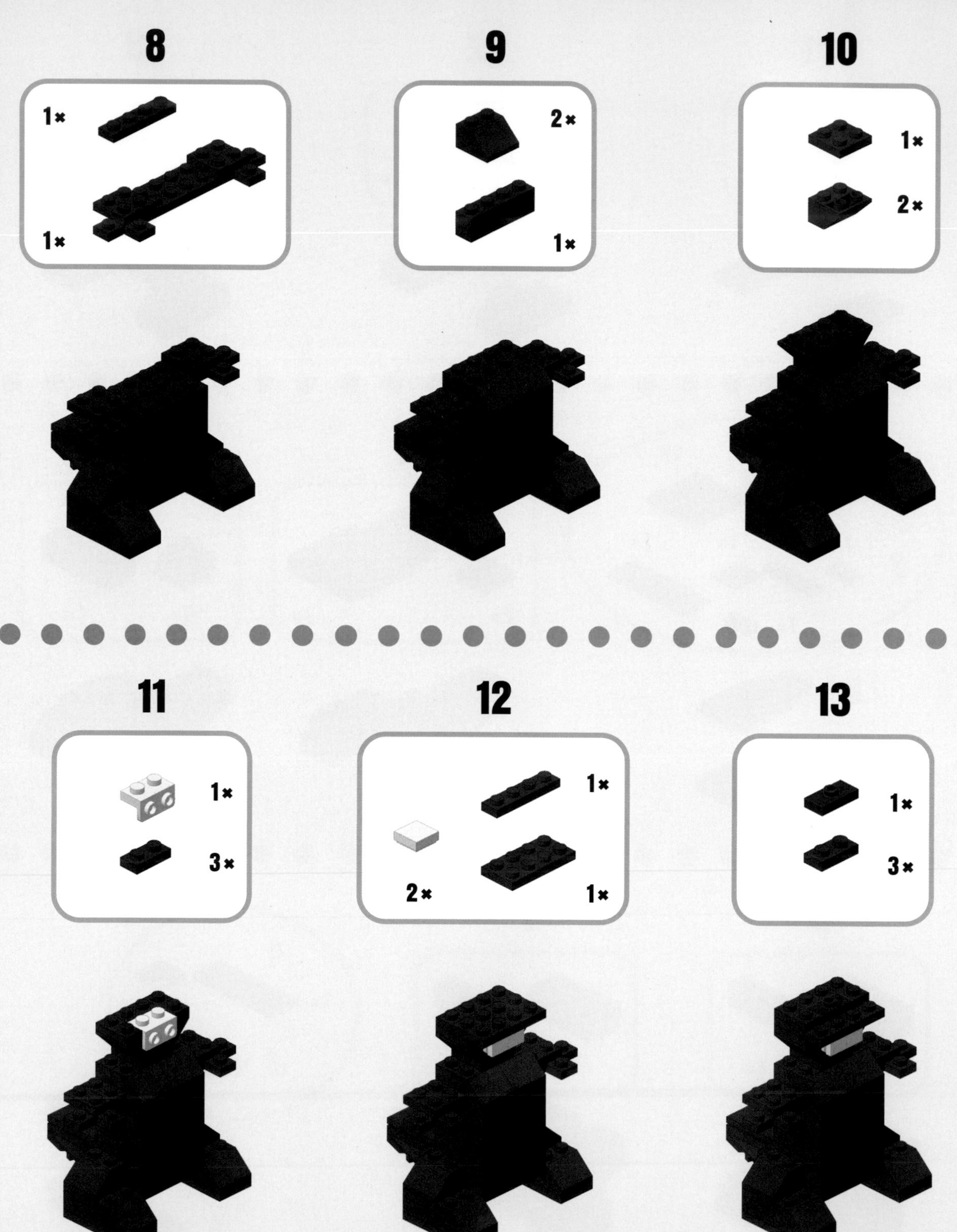
8
1×
1×
9
2×
1×
10
1×
2×
11
1×
3×
12
1×
2×
1×
13
1×
3×

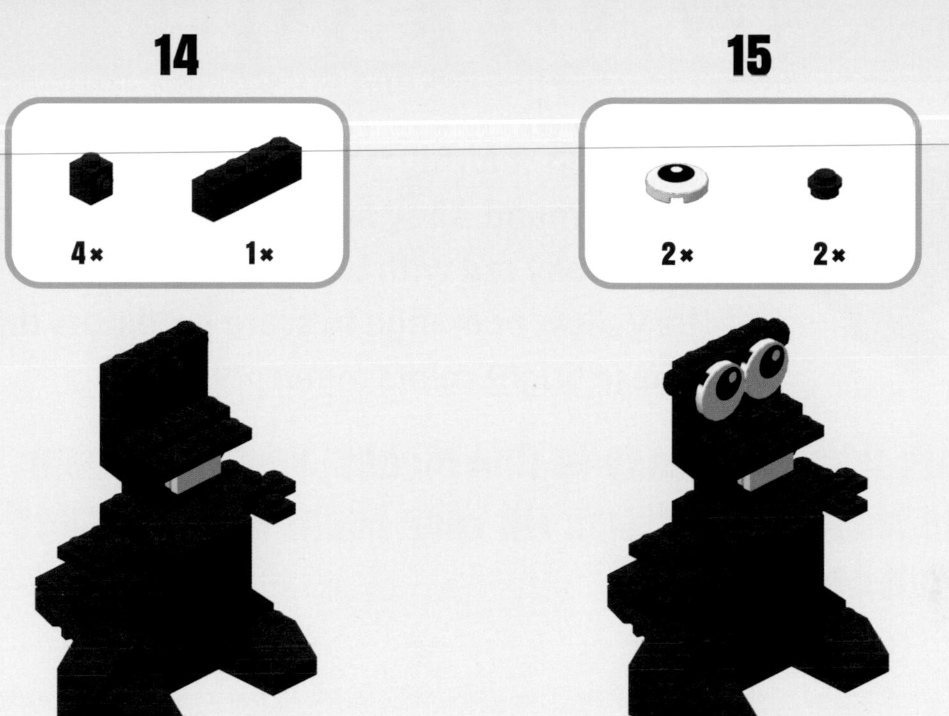
14
4×
1×
15
2×
2×

Nice job putting on the beaver's teeth!

LADYBUG

Small and colorful, ladybugs are the cutest bugs around. They have a round shell, which is usually red with black spots, but it can also be yellow or orange to scare predators that think these bright colors mean poison.

With just a few easy-to-find pieces, you can create the ladybug's pattern. Fill your room with ladybugs of all colors!

PARTS LIST

DIFFICULTY

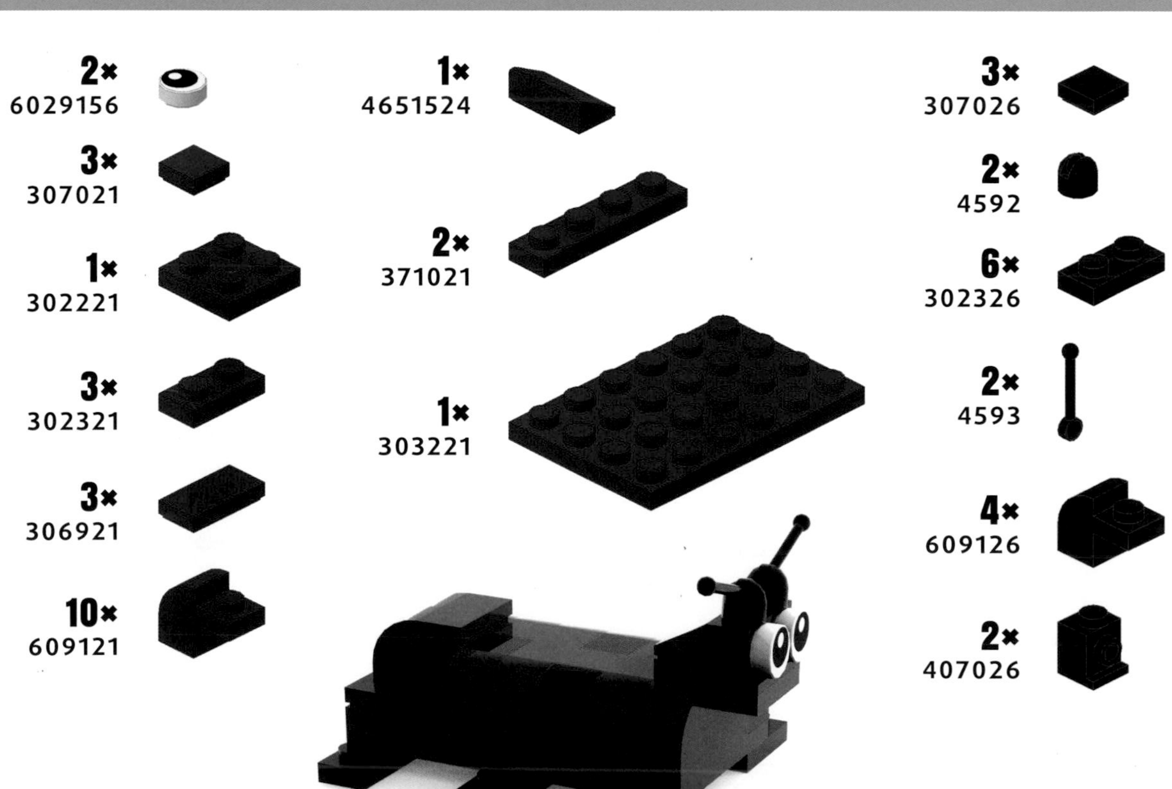

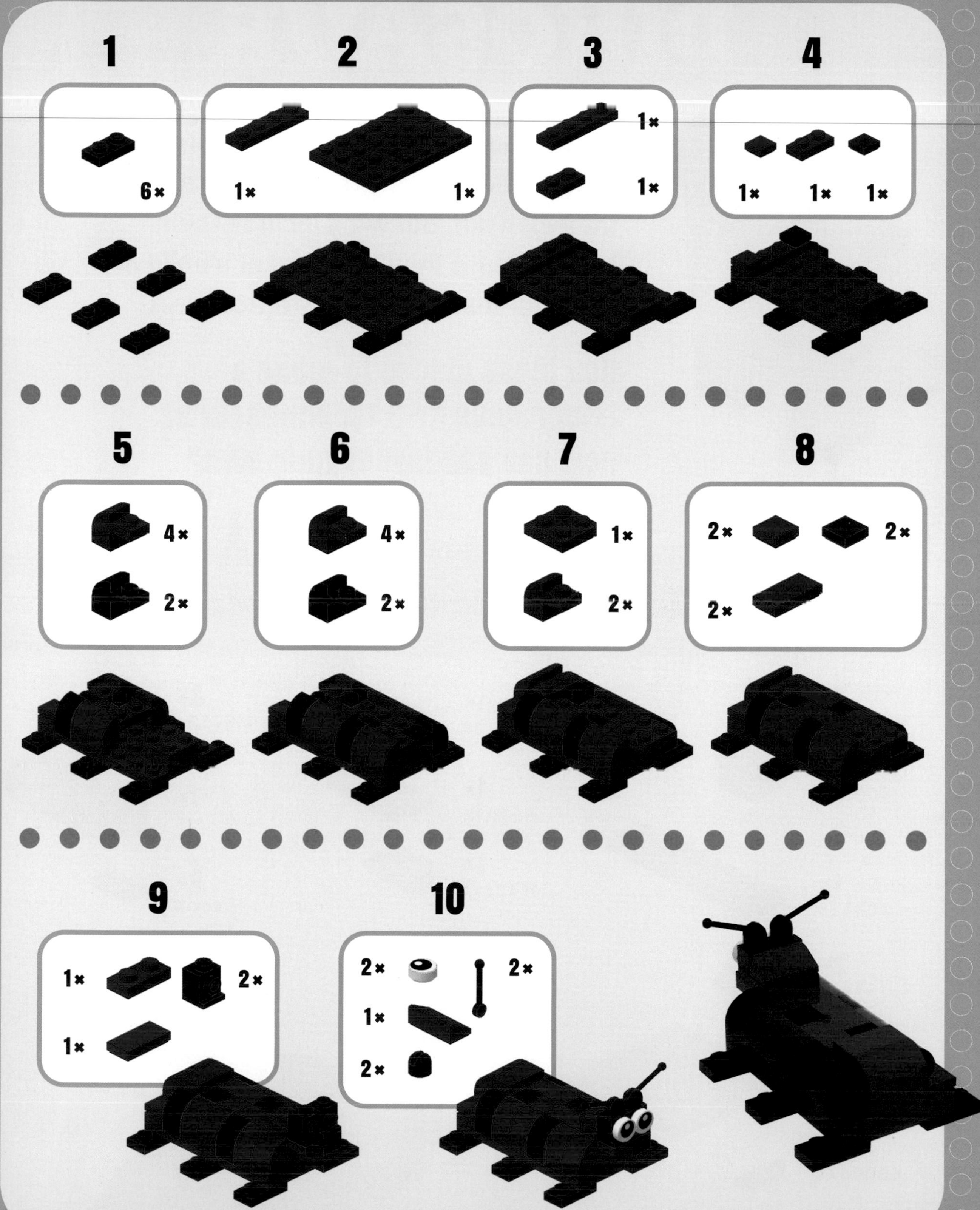

1
6×
2
1×
1×
3
1×
1×
4
1×
1×
1×
5
4×
2×
6
4×
2×
7
1×
2×
8
2×
2×
2×
9
1×
2×
1×
10
2×
2×
1×
2×

DINOSAUR

Sadly, you won't see this animal in a zoo. Dinosaurs are extinct, which means they died out. But we'll include them here because they're cool. Let's build a dinosaur that looks like Brontosaurus!

Use these pieces to make a Triceratops or a Tyrannosaurus rex. Can you invent your own?

PARTS LIST

DIFFICULTY

2× 6029156

27× 300328

1× 303428

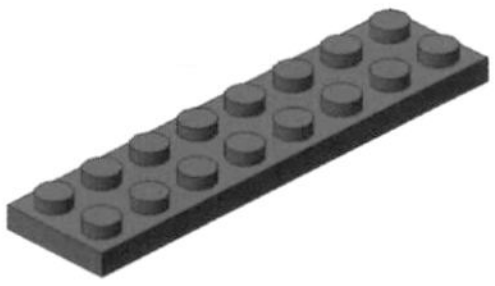

2× 303928

1× 6097194

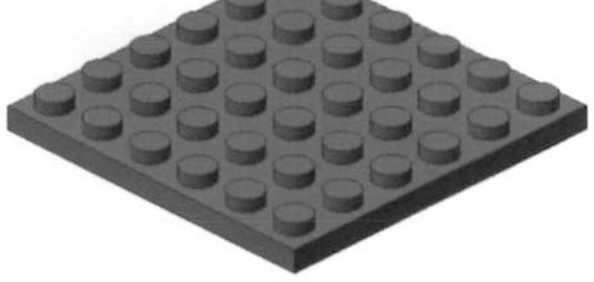

3× 6000071

2× 302328

1× 302128

1× 302028

1× 4142717

4× 4187334

1× 4181135

8× 4264404

Watch the distance between these pieces, which will be the dinosaur's feet and tail.
1
2×
1×
2
8×
3
4×
4
1×
1×
1×
1×
5
3×
1×
1×
6
1×
1×
3×
7
6×
8
6×
9
4×
10
1×
1×
11
2×
1×
1×
12
2×
1×

CHICKEN

Look who just laid an egg! This chicken is quite simple to build—the only tricky part is its tail and wings that you need to position properly.

Can you try building the eggs using white bricks?

PARTS LIST

DIFFICULTY

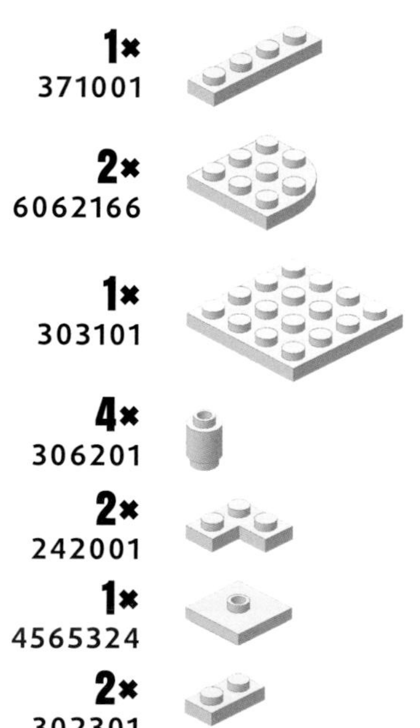

- 1× 371001
- 2× 6062166
- 1× 303101
- 4× 306201
- 2× 242001
- 1× 4565324
- 2× 302301
- 1× 300401
- 4× 4558952

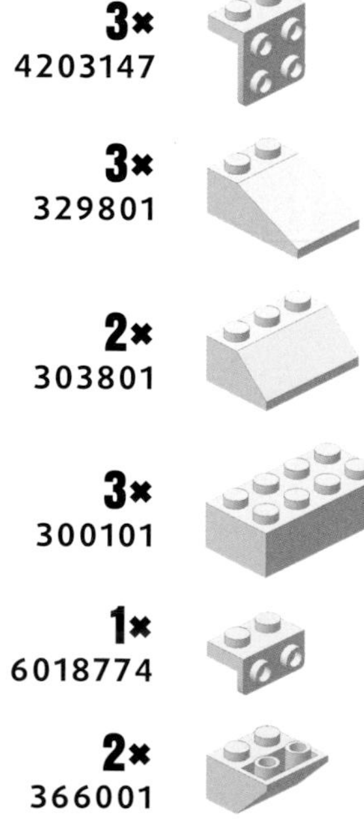

- 3× 4203147
- 3× 329801
- 2× 303801
- 3× 300101
- 1× 6018774
- 2× 366001
- 3× 302001

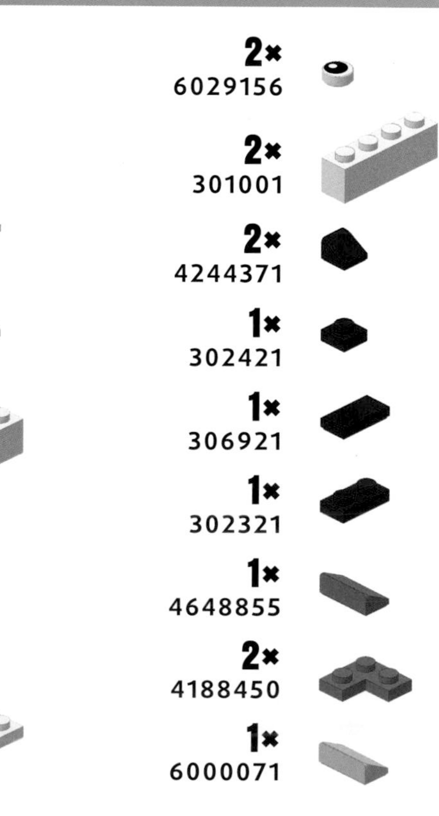

- 2× 6029156
- 2× 301001
- 2× 4244371
- 1× 302421
- 1× 306921
- 1× 302321
- 1× 4648855
- 2× 4188450
- 1× 6000071

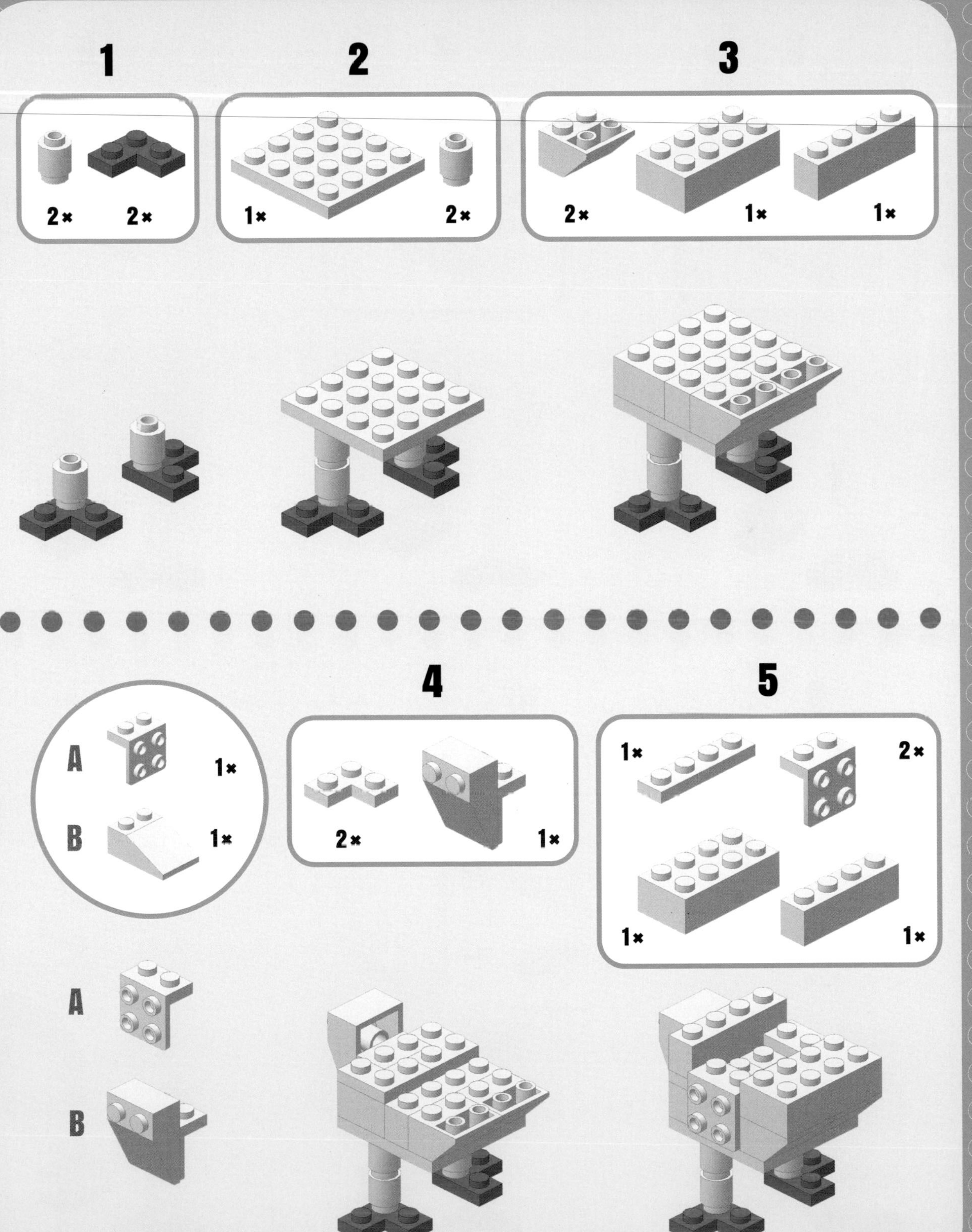
1
2×
2×
2
1×
2×
3
2×
1×
1×
A
1×
B
1×
4
2×
1×
5
1×
2×
1×
1×
A
B

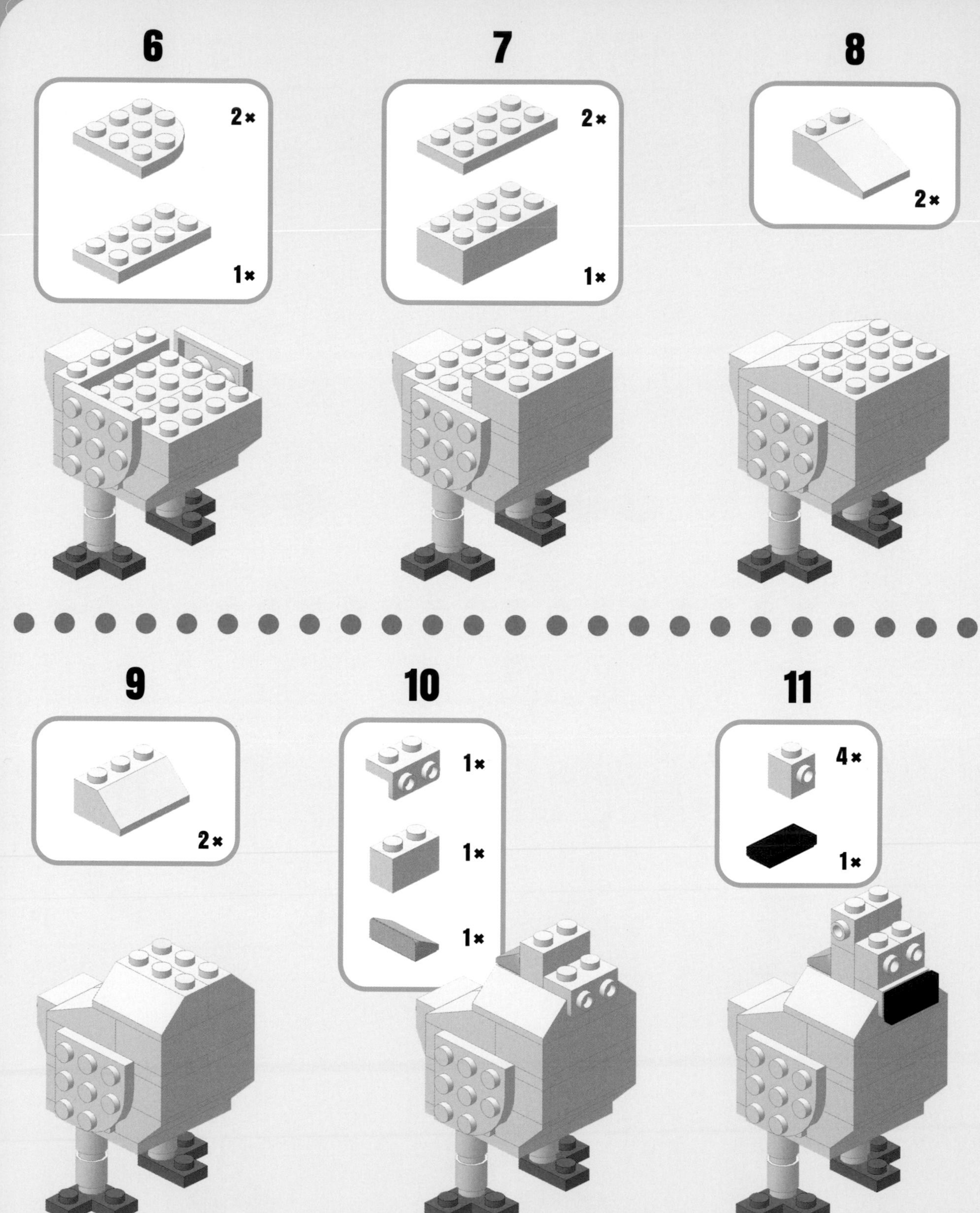

6
2×
1×
7
2×
1×
8
2×
9
2×
10
1×
1×
1×
11
4×
1×

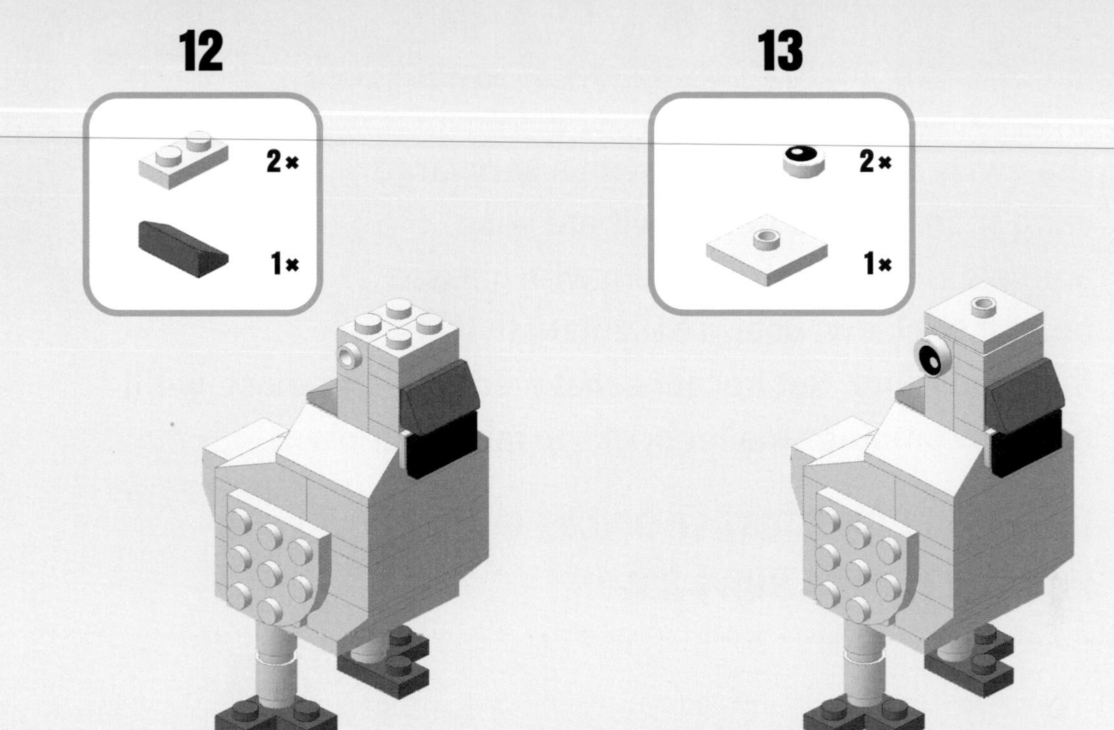
12
2×
1×
13
2×
1×

14
2×
1×
1×
Make the hen's crest.

OWL

The owl is a nocturnal bird with a very large wing span. People think owls are wise animals and often draw them with glasses on. Our brick owl uses a baseplate that is five studs long. But because that piece doesn't exist, we'll have to combine smaller bricks to make our own.

Try combining smaller bricks in other ways to make parts you don't have!

PARTS LIST

DIFFICULTY

- 3× 371001
- 2× 300201
- 2× 242001
- 4× 302301
- 5× 302101
- 4× 300101
- 4× 302001
- 2× 362301
- 2× 301001
- 2× 302124
- 4× 302426
- 1× 4282860
- 6× 4211190
- 4× 4211150
- 1× 4618545
- 5× 4211225
- 1× 4211220
- 2× 6075212
- 3× 4211247
- 4× 4211201
- 2× 4225693
- 1× 4271874
- 4× 6035291
- 2× 4221590
- 8× 4211186
- 6× 4211152
- 4× 4211149

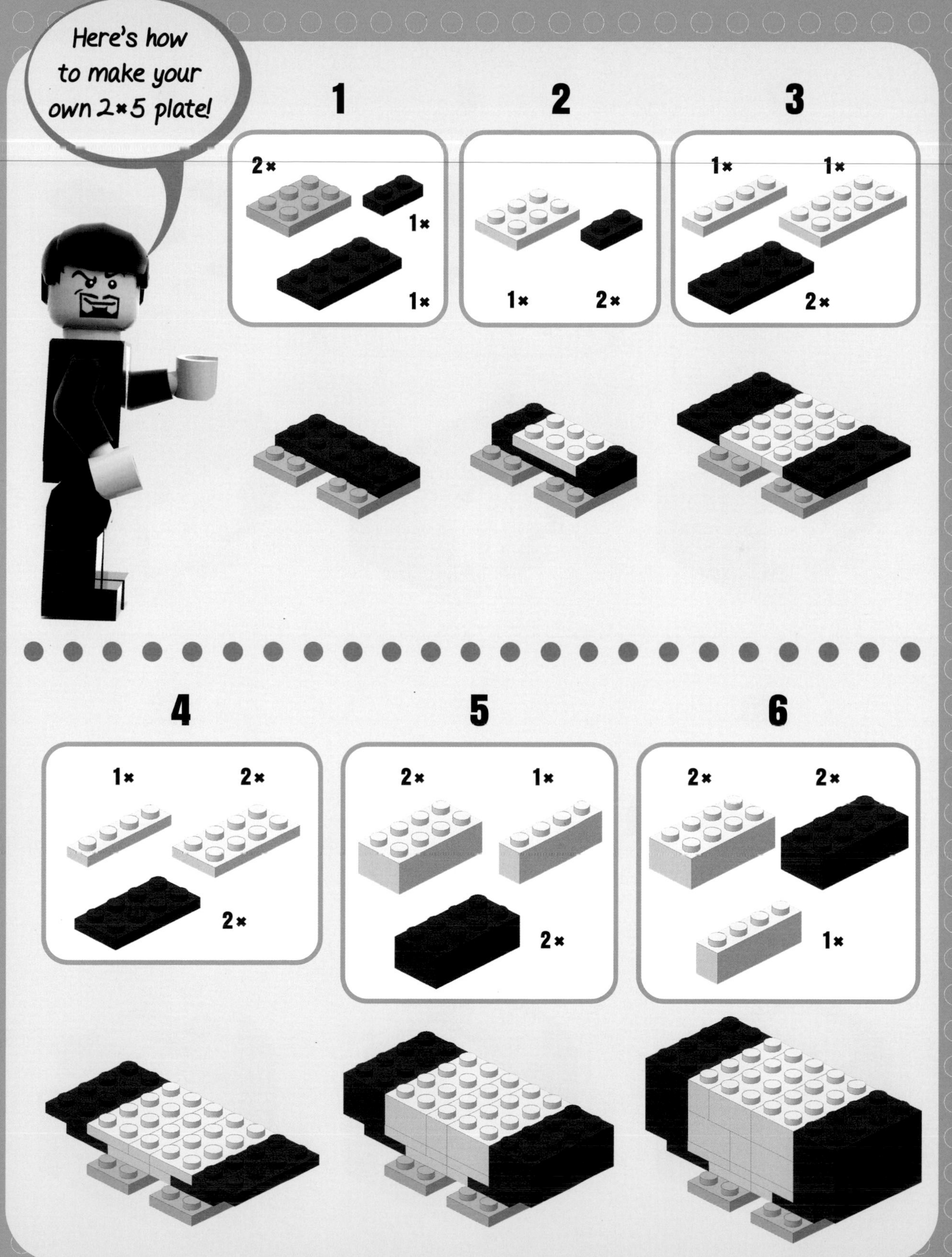
Here's how to make your own 2×5 plate!
1
2×
1×
1×
2
1×
2×
3
1×
1×
2×
4
1×
2×
2×
5
2×
1×
2×
6
2×
2×
1×

7

1×
2×
1×
2×

8

1×
1×
2×
2×
2×

9

1×
2×
2×

10

2×
2×
2×
1×
1×

11

2×
1×

12

2×
2×
2×

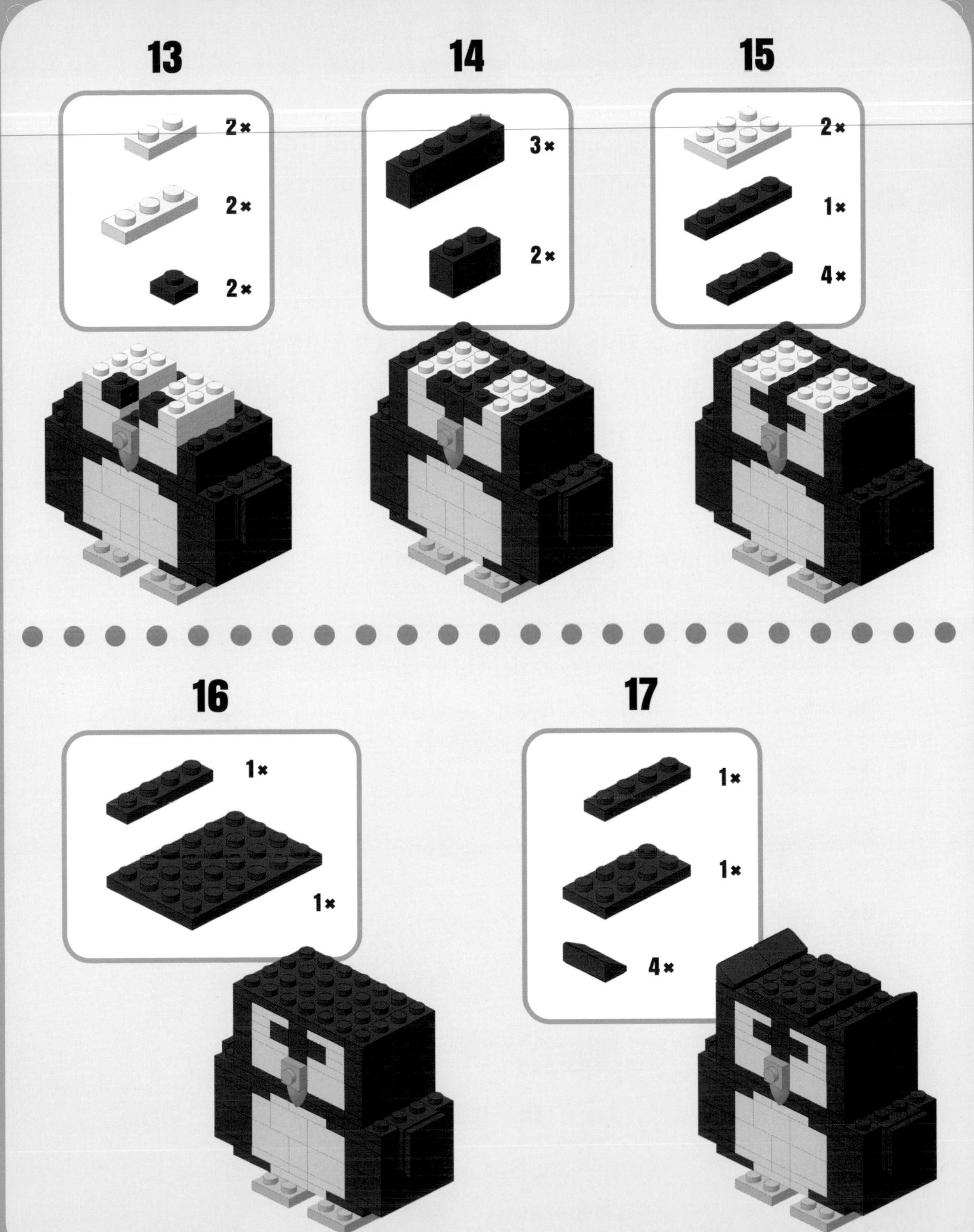
13
2×
2×
2×
14
3×
2×
15
2×
1×
4×
16
1×
1×
17
1×
1×
4×

PIG

What's a portly farm animal that loves to roll around in the mud? You guessed it—it's a pig!

To build this little pig, you'll use a building technique called SNOT (Studs Not On Top), which lets you add bricks sideways and even upside down. Without this handy technique, the ear flaps wouldn't look as real.

PARTS LIST

DIFFICULTY

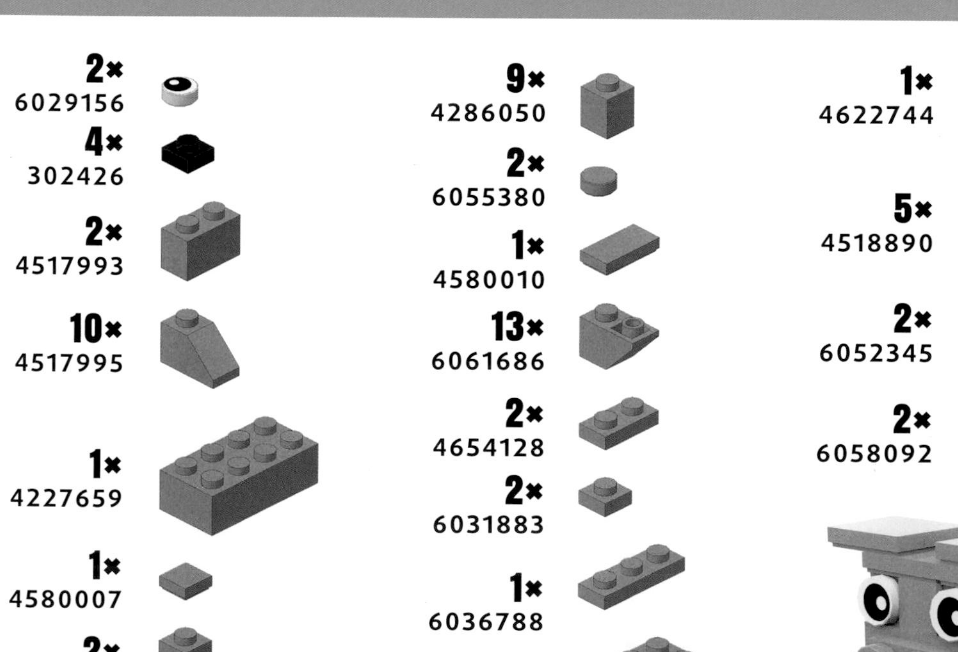

1
4×
2
4×
Use the 1×2 plate to hold two 3×3 plates together.
A
1×
B
2×
A
B
3
1×
1×
4
1×
5×
5
5×

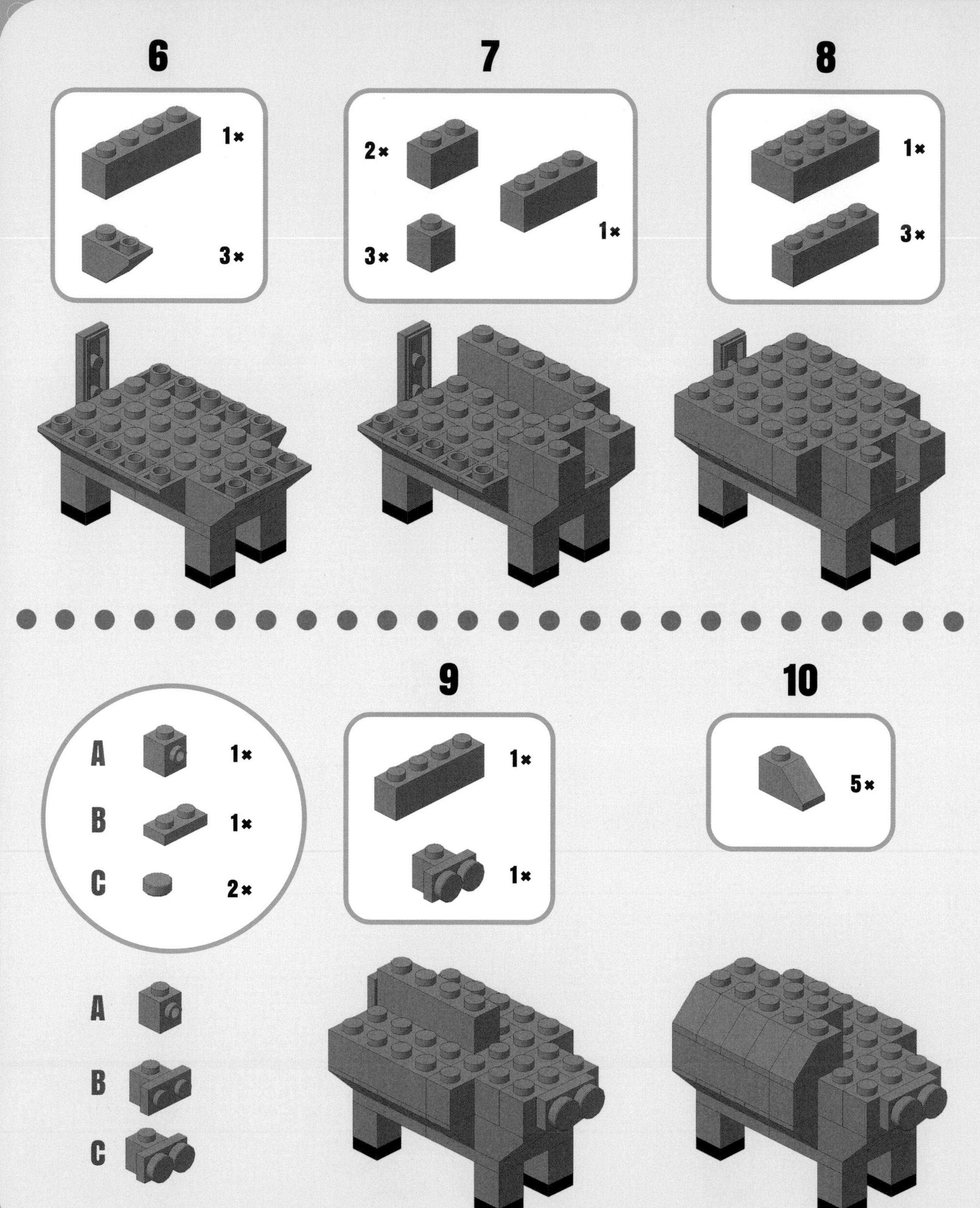
6
1×
3×
7
2×
1×
3×
8
1×
3×
9
1×
1×
10
5×
A
1×
B
1×
C
2×
A
B
C

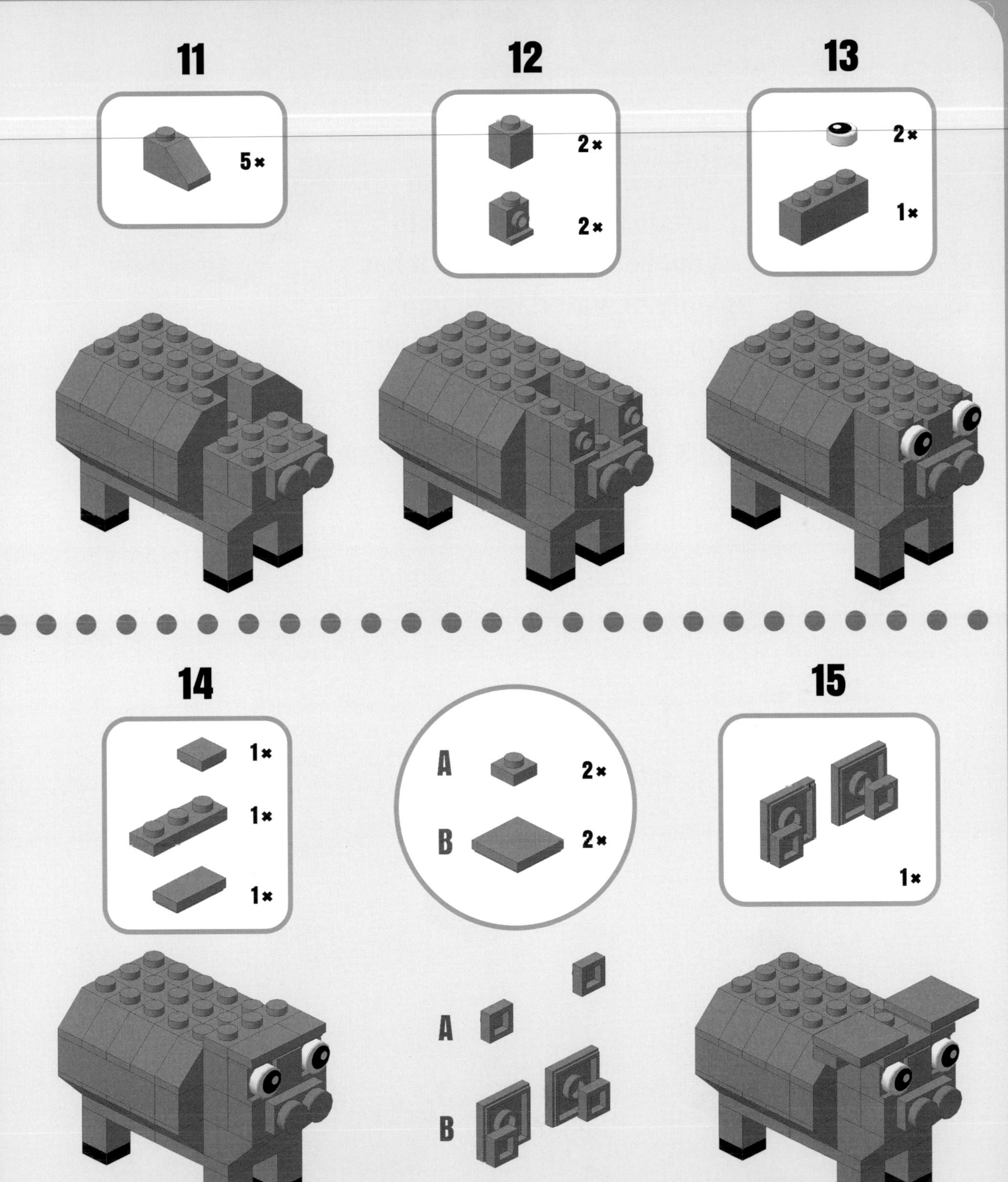
11
5×
12
2×
2×
13
2×
1×
14
1×
1×
1×
A
2×
B
2×
15
1×
A
B

FISH

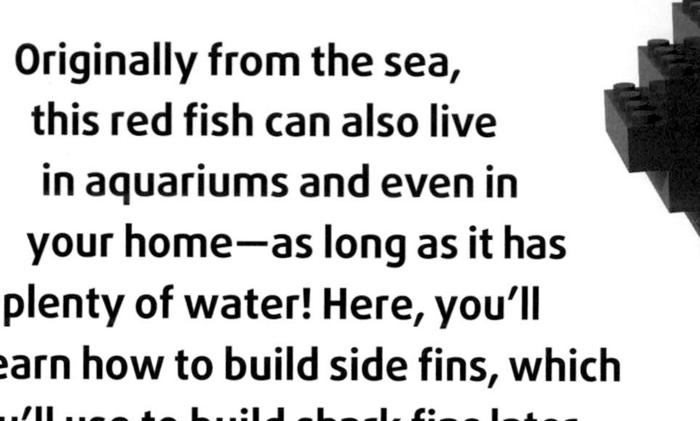

Originally from the sea, this red fish can also live in aquariums and even in your home—as long as it has plenty of water! Here, you'll learn how to build side fins, which you'll use to build shark fins later.

Use other colors to create different fish species!

PARTS LIST

DIFFICULTY

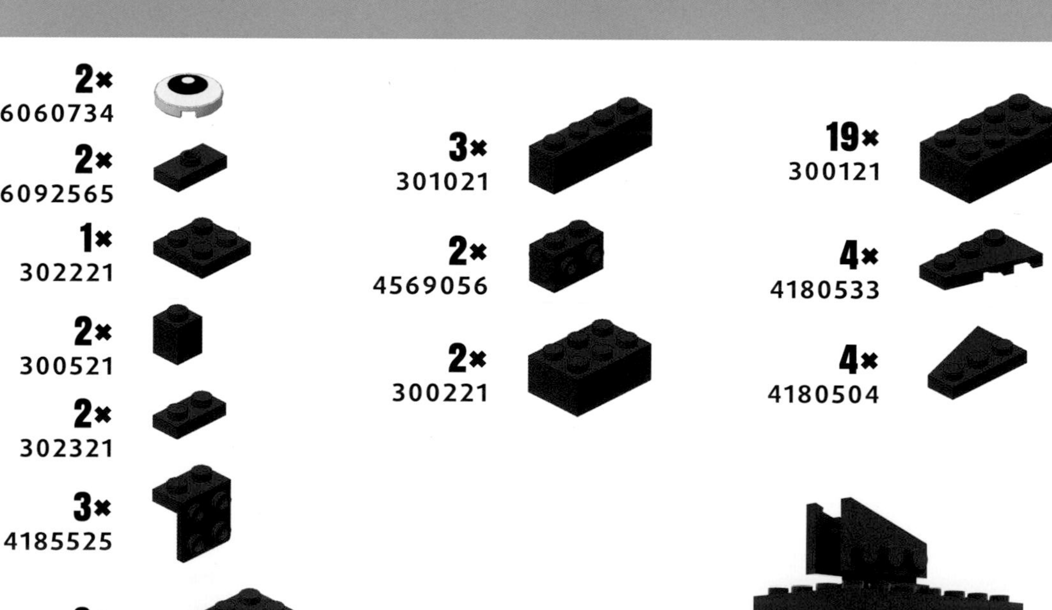

- 2× 6060734
- 2× 6092565
- 1× 302221
- 2× 300521
- 2× 302321
- 3× 4185525
- 2× 302021
- 2× 6092565
- 2× 4558886
- 3× 301021
- 2× 4569056
- 2× 300221
- 19× 300121
- 4× 4180533
- 4× 4180504

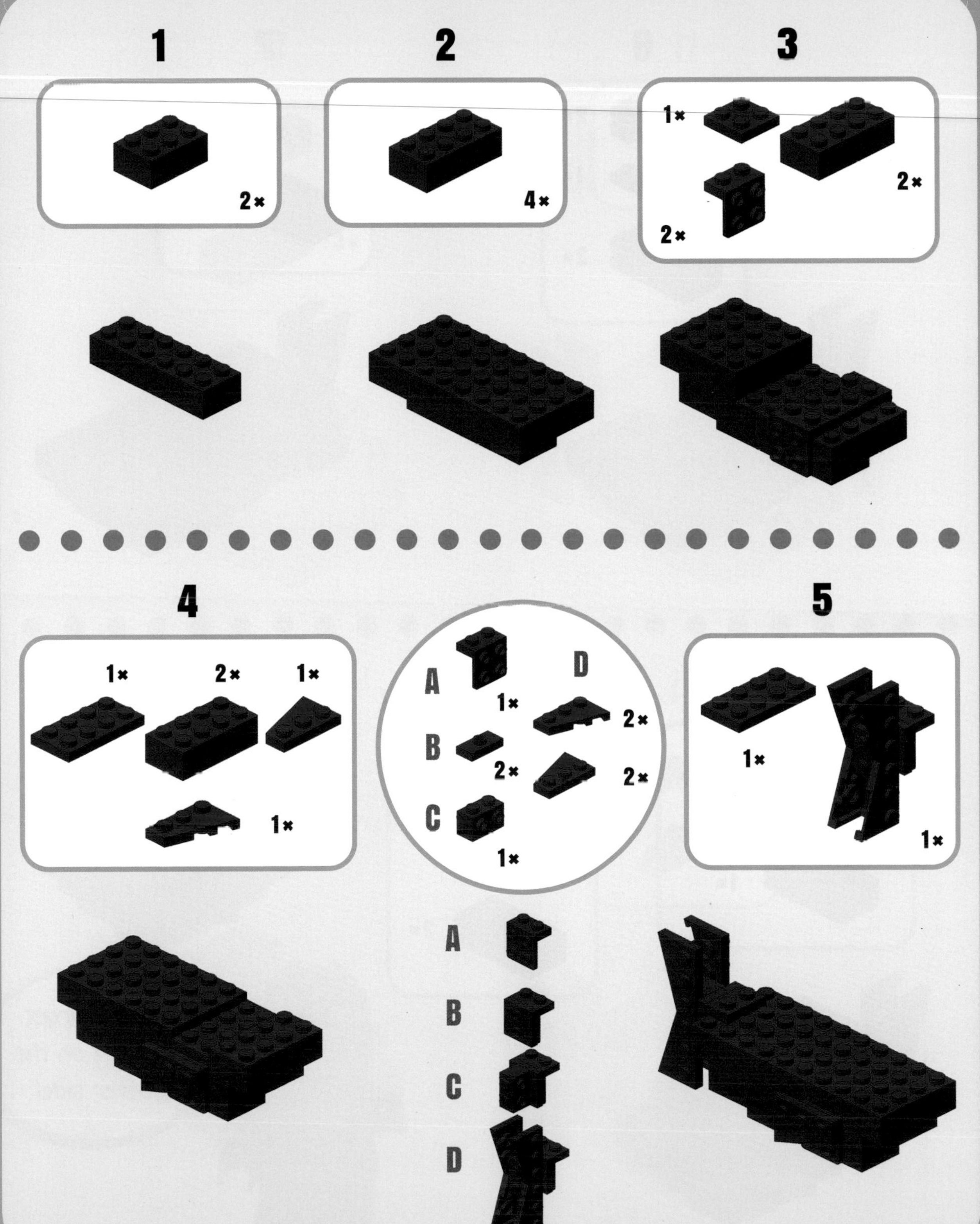
1
2×
2
4×
3
1×
2×
2×
4
1×
2×
1×
1×
A
1×
B
2×
C
1×
D
2×
2×
5
1×
1×
A
B
C
D

RHINOCEROS

The rhinoceros is a stout, muscular animal that feeds mainly on grass. It lives quietly in its natural environment (in Africa and southern Asia). But watch out—when it gets annoyed, it can tackle anything in its path!

This endangered animal is at risk of extinction.

PARTS LIST

DIFFICULTY

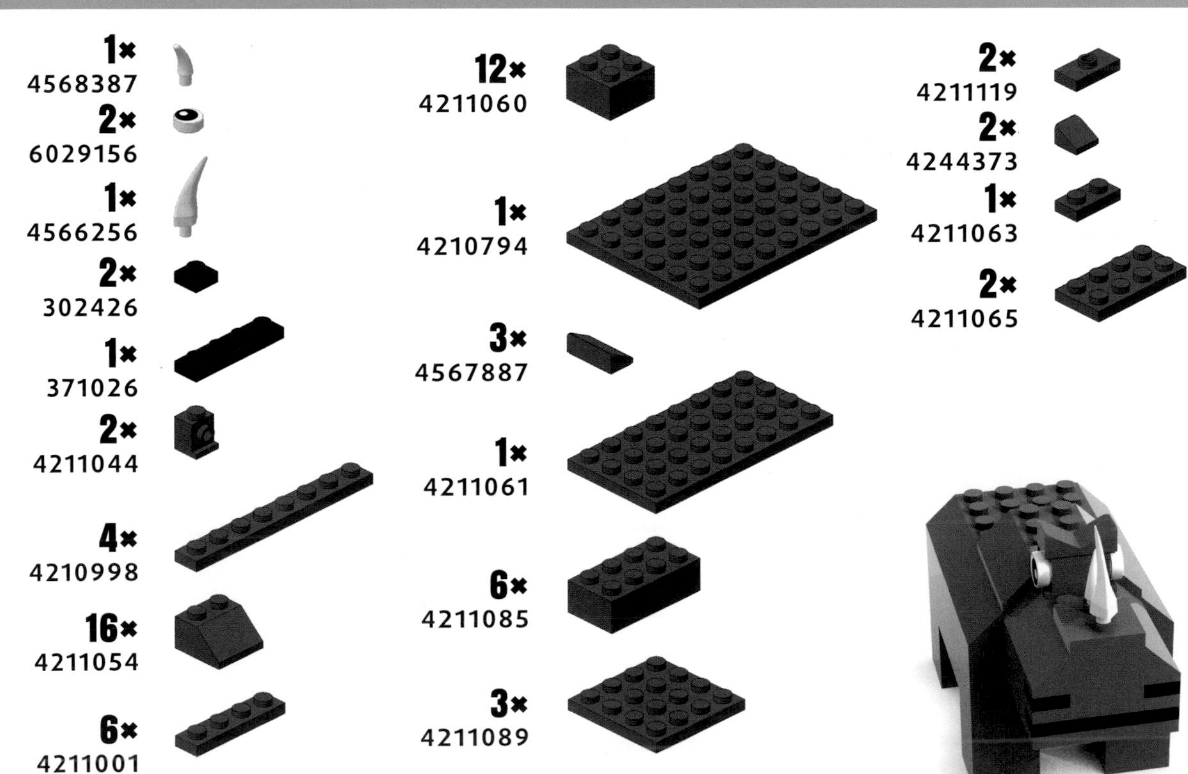

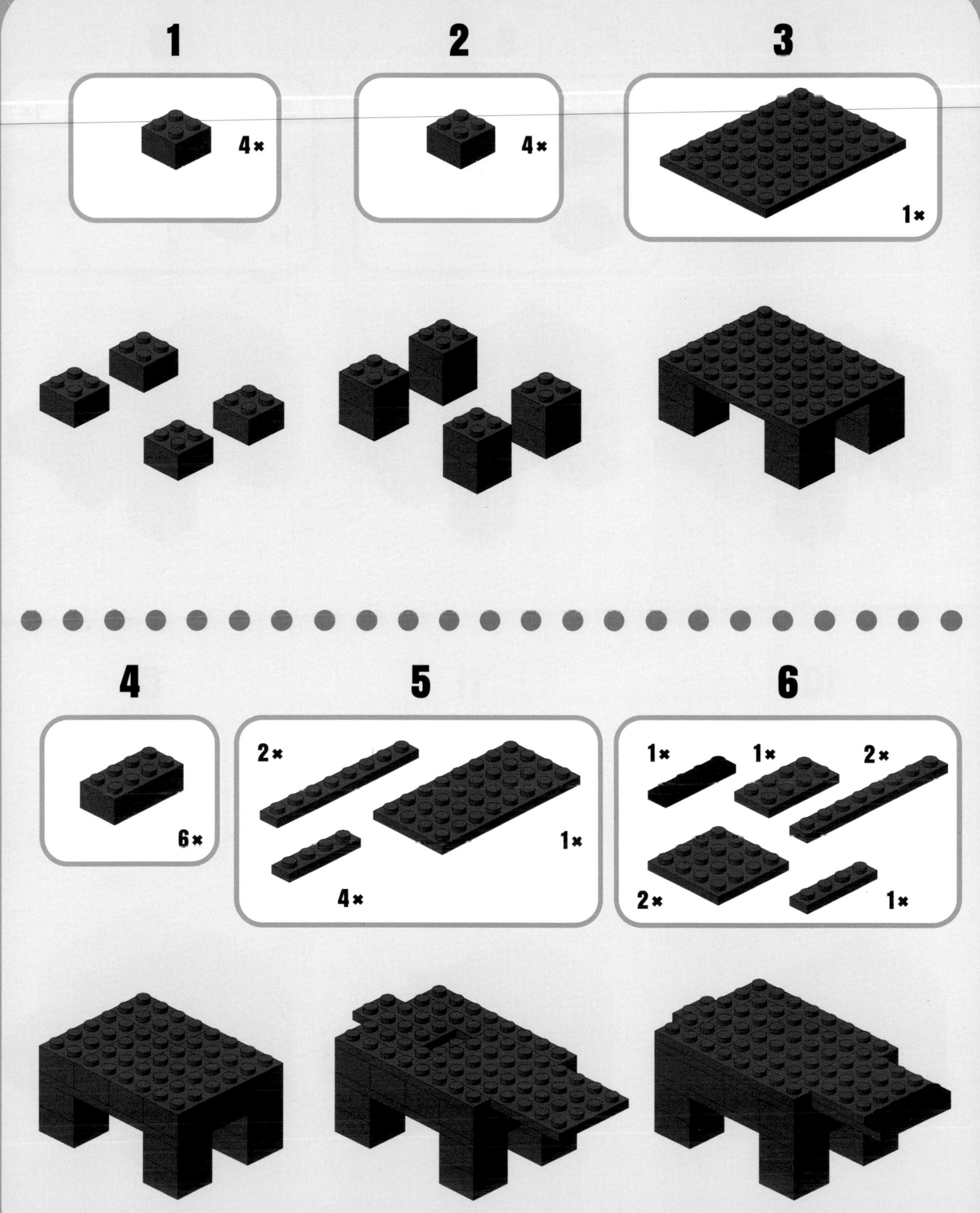
1
4×
2
4×
3
1×
4
6×
5
2×
1×
4×
6
1×
1×
2×
2×
1×

FROG

This slimy little creature lives in wetlands and marshes because it's an amphibian, an animal that lives on land and water. It uses its long tongue to feed on insects. This brick frog is about to take a big leap!

Have fun changing the color of the frog.

PARTS LIST

DIFFICULTY

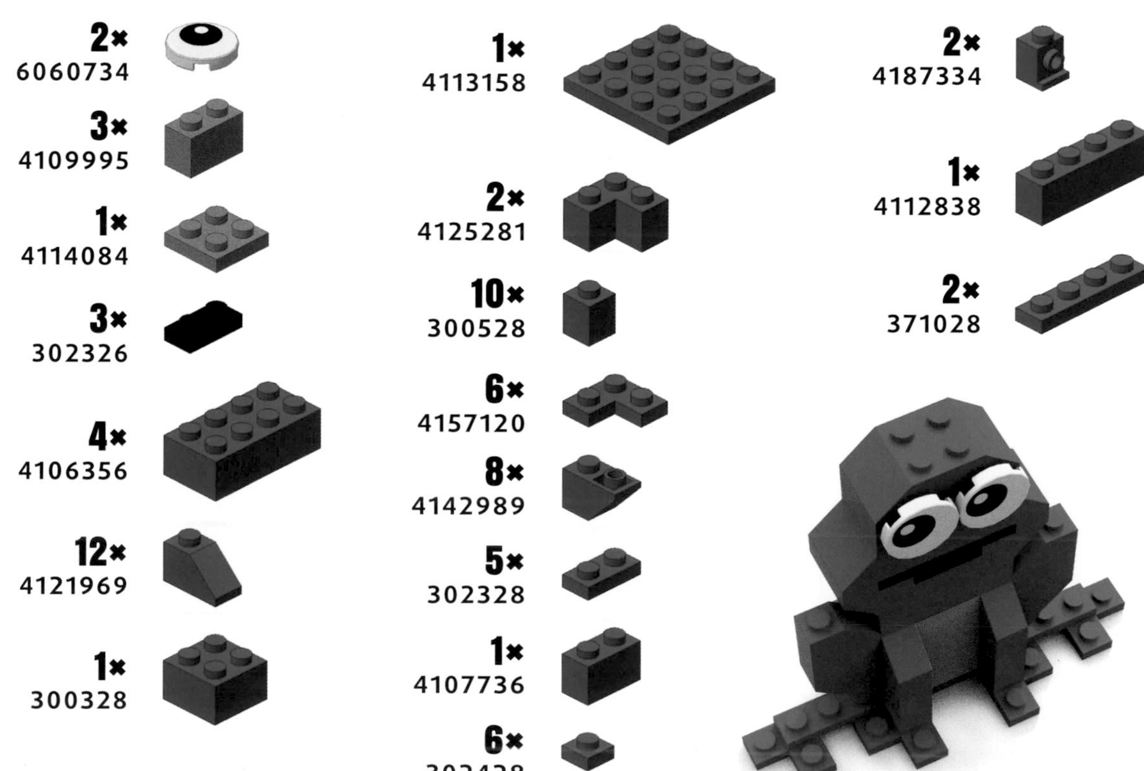

1
Pay attention to where you place the outside feet.
2
3
1×
4×
2×
2×
1×
2×
4
5
6
1×
1×
2×
2×
1×
1×
2×
2×
4×
2×

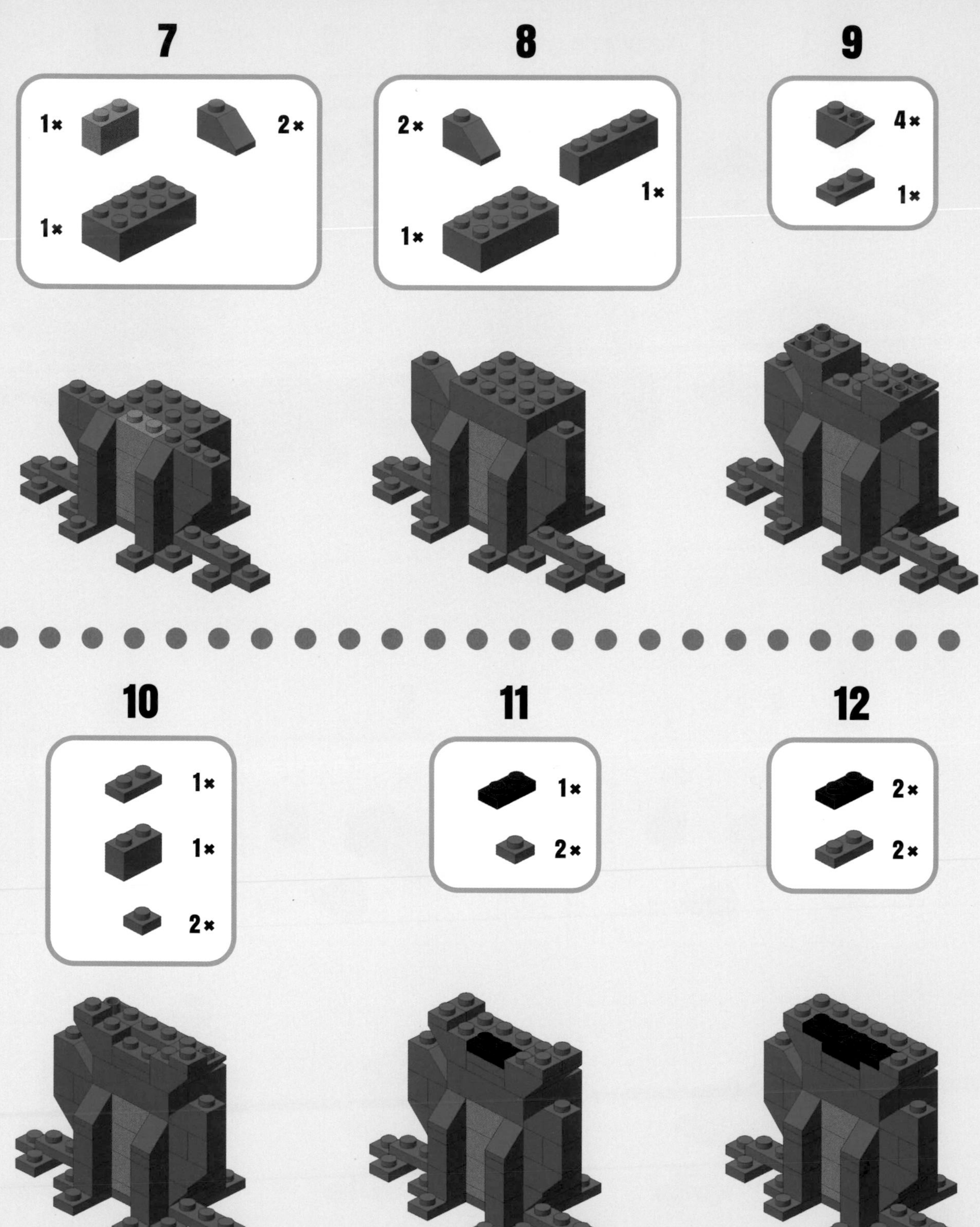
7
1×
2×
1×
8
2×
1×
1×
9
4×
1×
10
1×
1×
2×
11
1×
2×
12
2×
2×

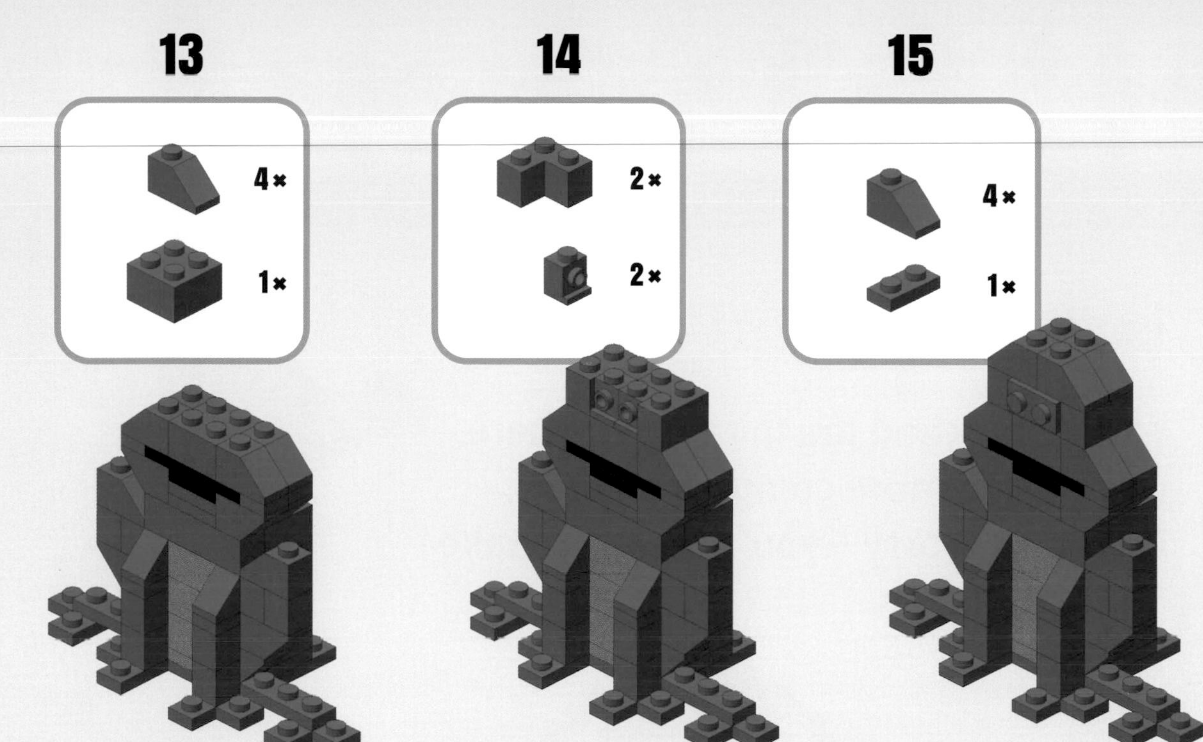

16

2×

CHAPTER 3

Congratulations!

You've reached the third level where you'll build more complex animals. But don't worry—you're ready to take them on.

(See page ix for tips on where to find parts!)

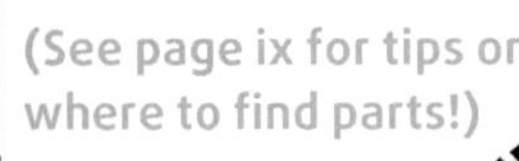

DONKEY

Donkeys help us with difficult tasks like carrying heavy objects and tilling the ground, making them exceptionally useful animals.

Here's how you build this cute donkey.

PARTS LIST

DIFFICULTY

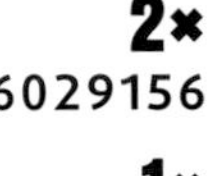
2× 6029156

1× 4109995
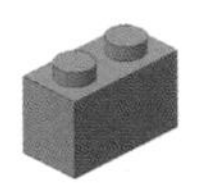
1× 4114084

1× 4113917

2× 4118793
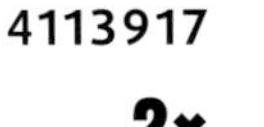
4× 4653087

1× 306826

5× 4548180
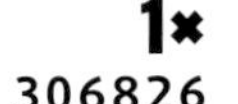

1× 302126
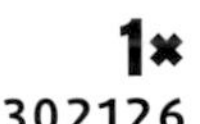

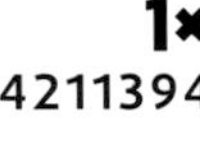
1× 4211394

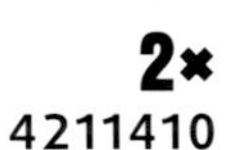
2× 4211410

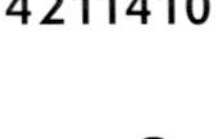
3× 4211356

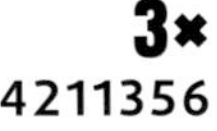
10× 4211389
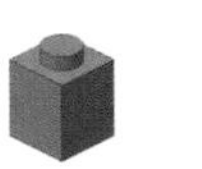

7× 4211385

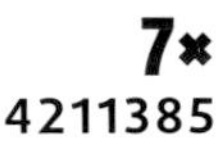

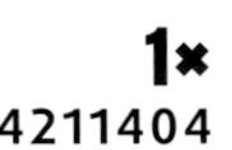
1× 4211404

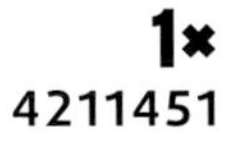
1× 4211451

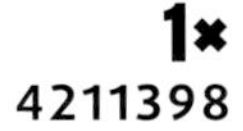
1× 4211398

2× 4211399
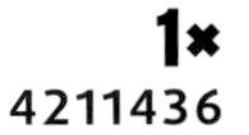
1× 4211436

14× 4211476

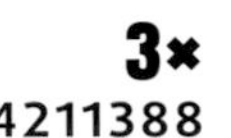
3× 4211388

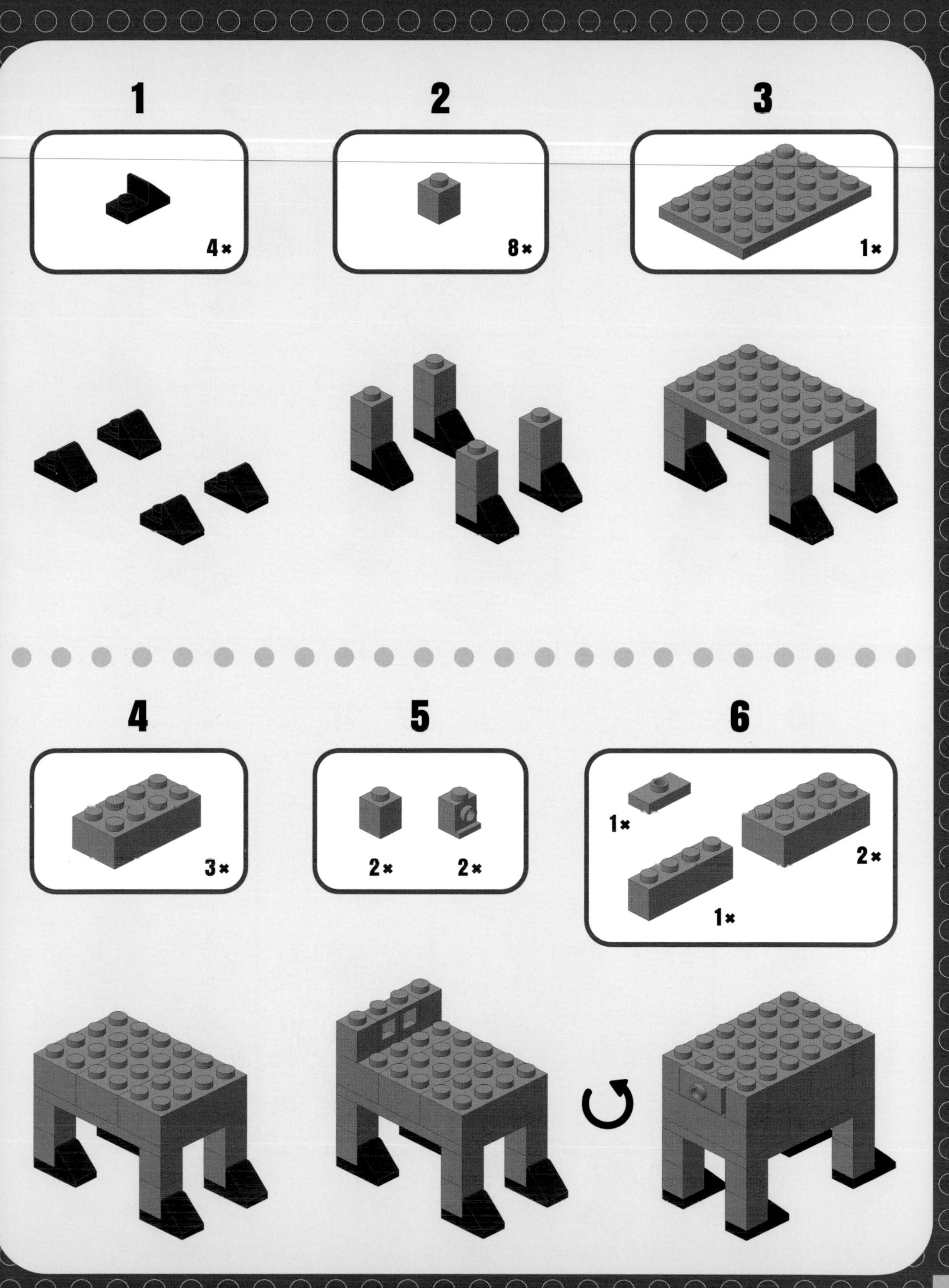
1
4×
2
8×
3
1×
4
3×
5
2×
2×
6
1×
2×
1×

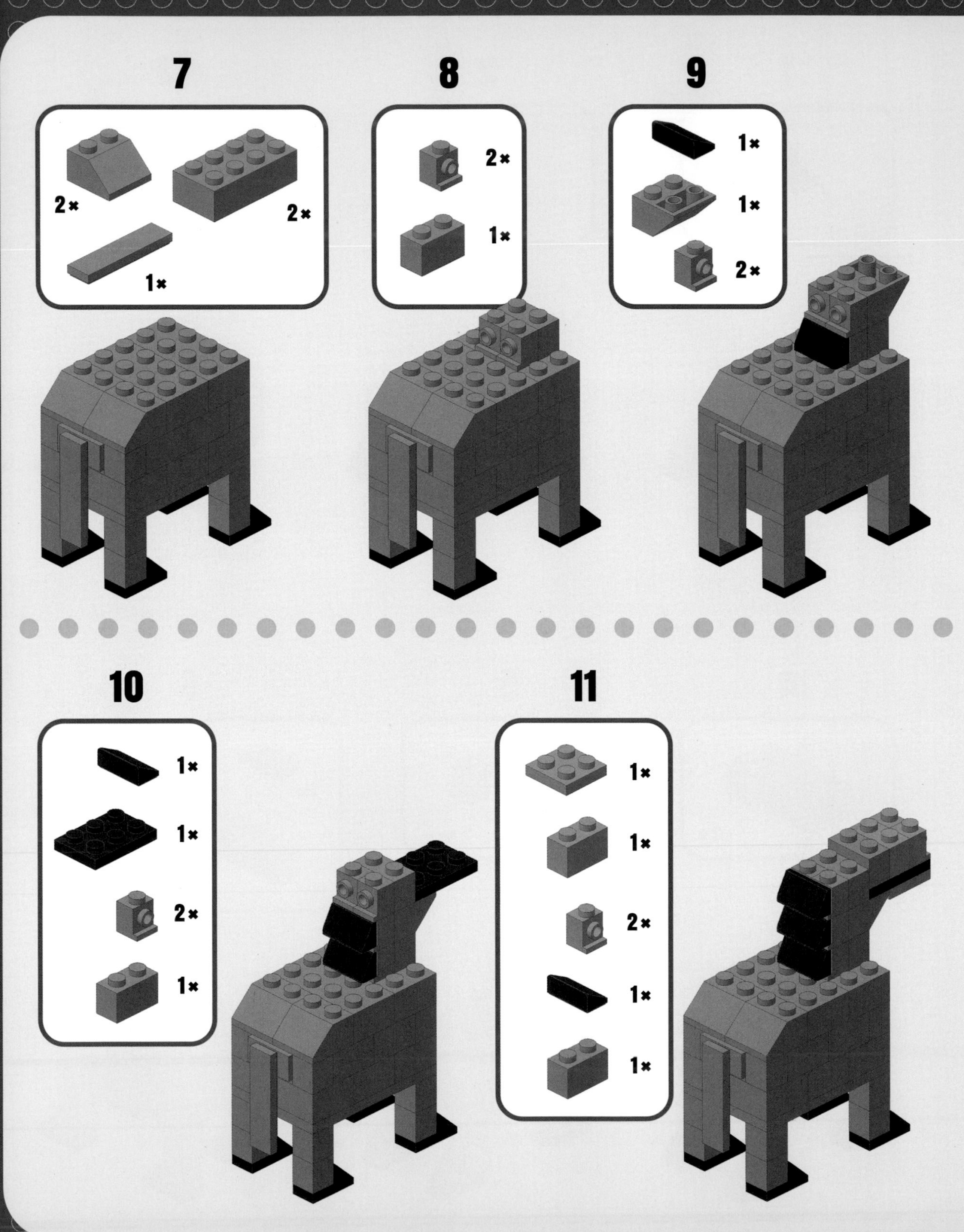

7
2×
2×
1×
8
2×
1×
9
1×
1×
2×
10
1×
1×
2×
1×
11
1×
1×
2×
1×
1×

12
1×
4×
13
1×
1×
1×
2×
14
2×
1×
1×
15
1×
2×
You can change the position of the donkey's ears as you wish.

CAMEL

This hump-backed animal lives in the desert and can survive for a long time without water. Can you name this animal? You guessed it—it's the camel! Let's add it to your zoo.

Did you know that the camel has two humps while the dromedary has only one? With some minor changes you could build both.

PARTS LIST

DIFFICULTY

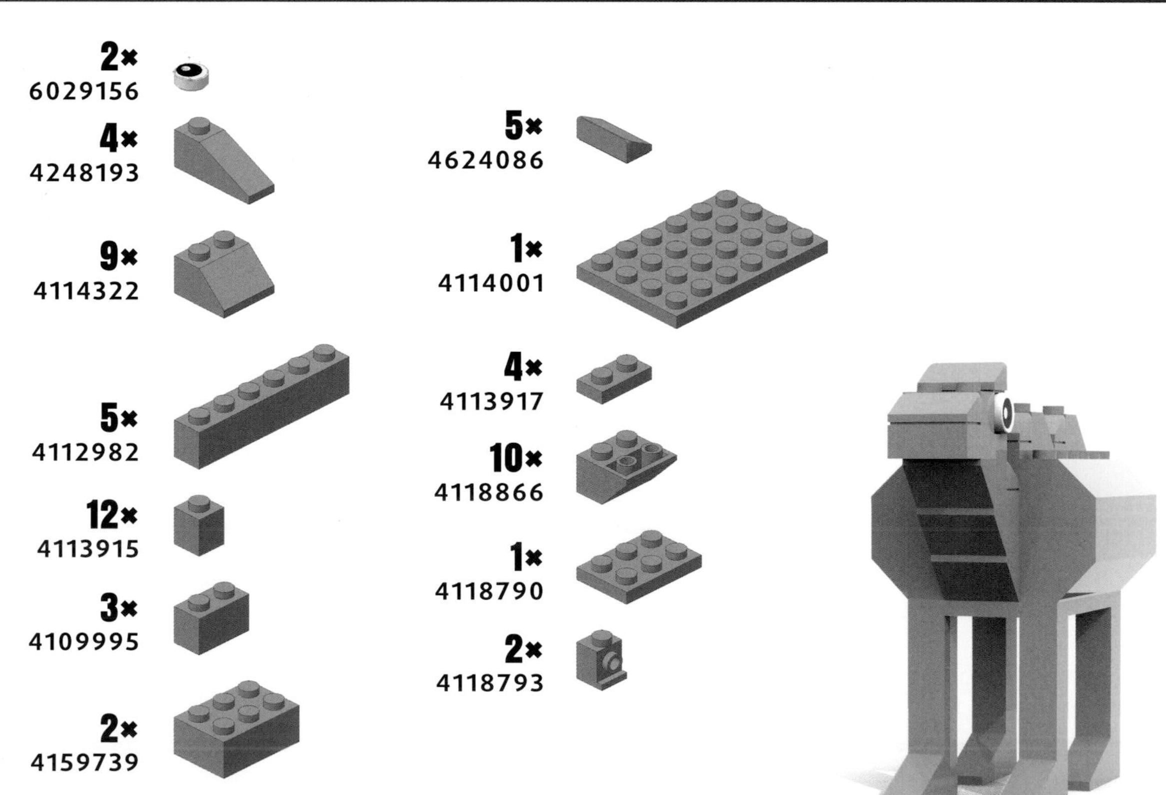

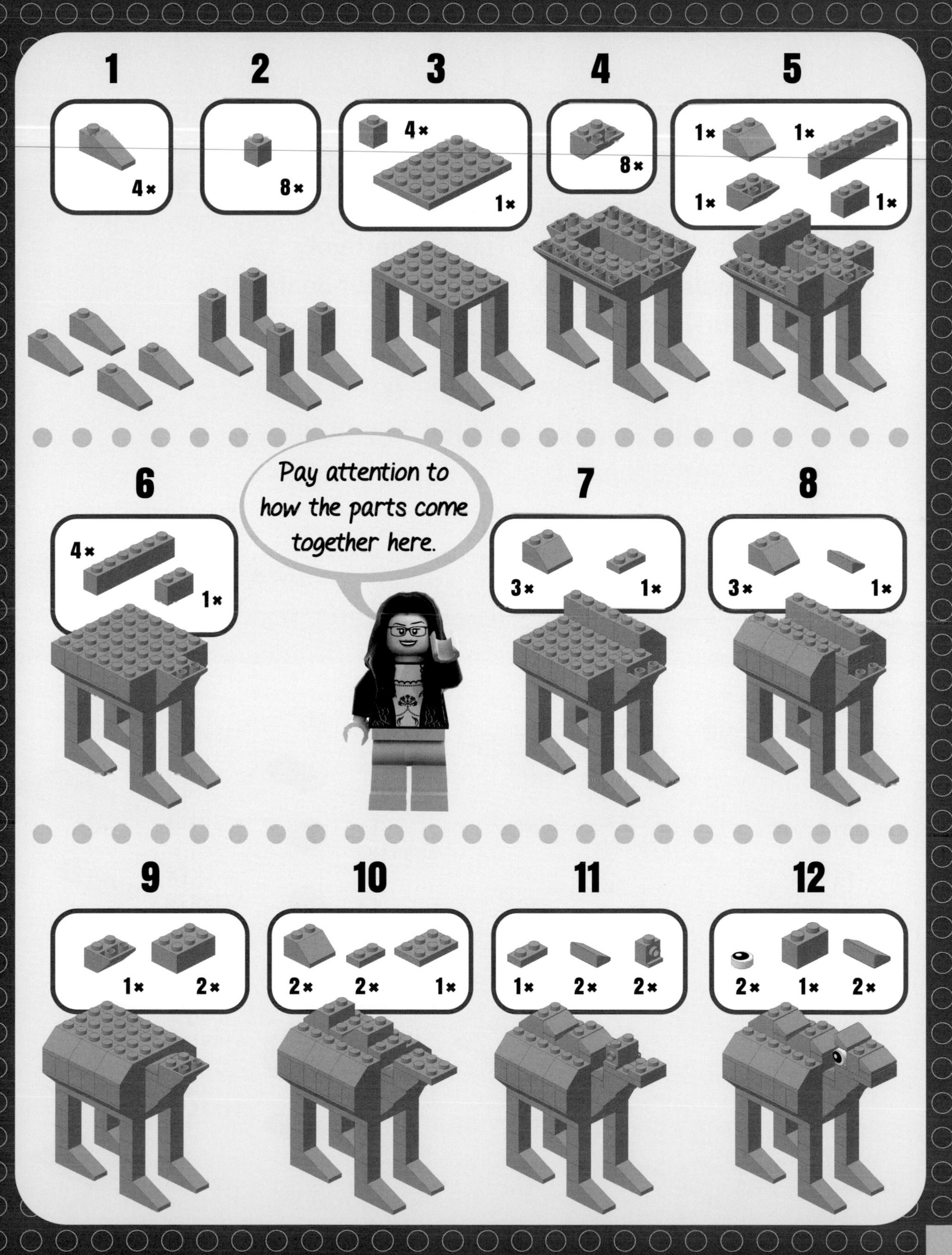
1
4×
2
8×
3
4×
1×
4
8×
5
1×
1×
1×
1×
6
4×
1×
Pay attention to how the parts come together here.
7
3×
1×
8
3×
1×
9
1×
2×
10
2×
2×
1×
11
1×
2×
2×
12
2×
1×
2×

DOG

Loyal and sweet, dogs are always ready to play with us. No wonder we call them a man's best friend! This zoo certainly wouldn't be complete without our dear four-legged friend.

There are many different types of dogs, but this one is a Harrier. Try building other breeds too.

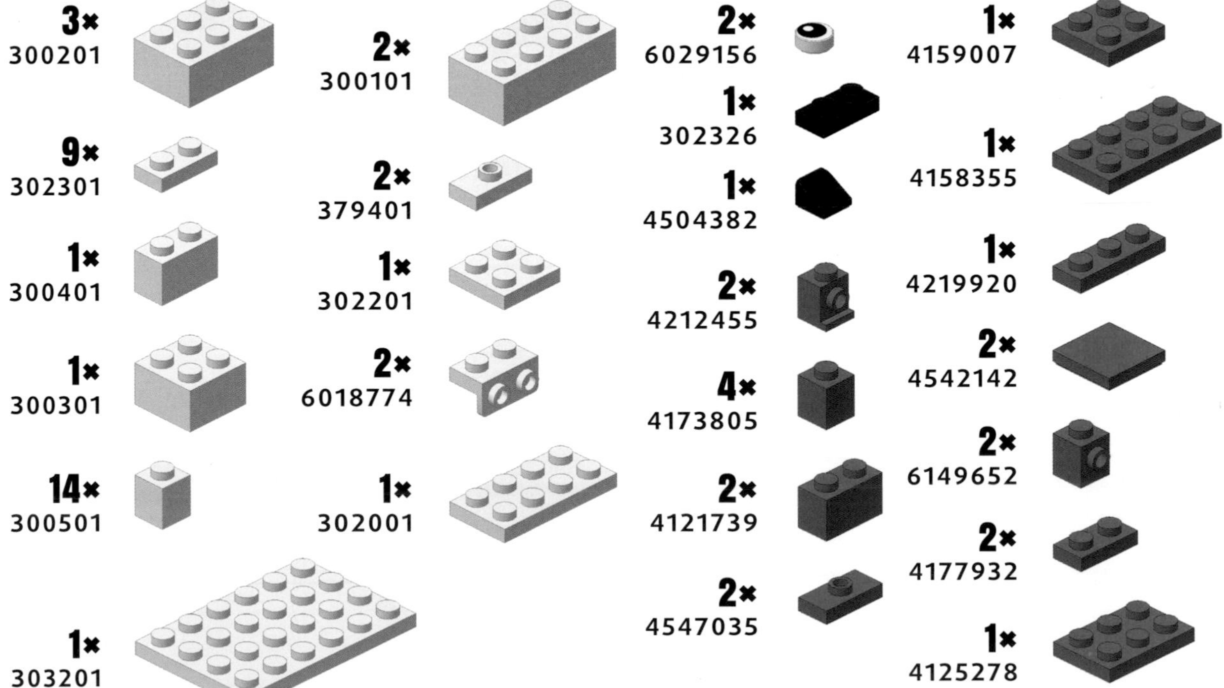

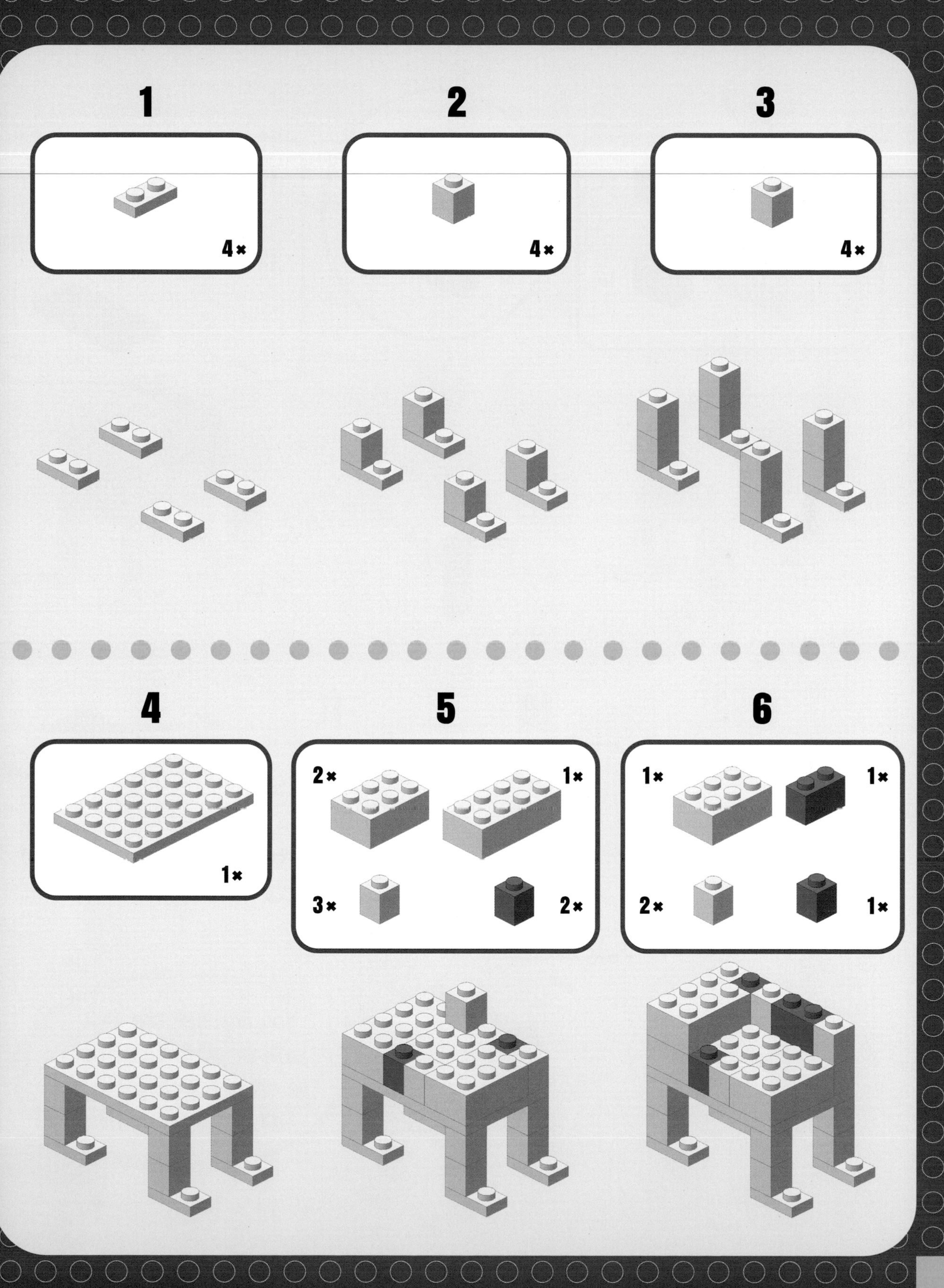
1
4×
2
4×
3
4×
4
1×
5
2×
1×
3×
2×
6
1×
1×
2×
1×

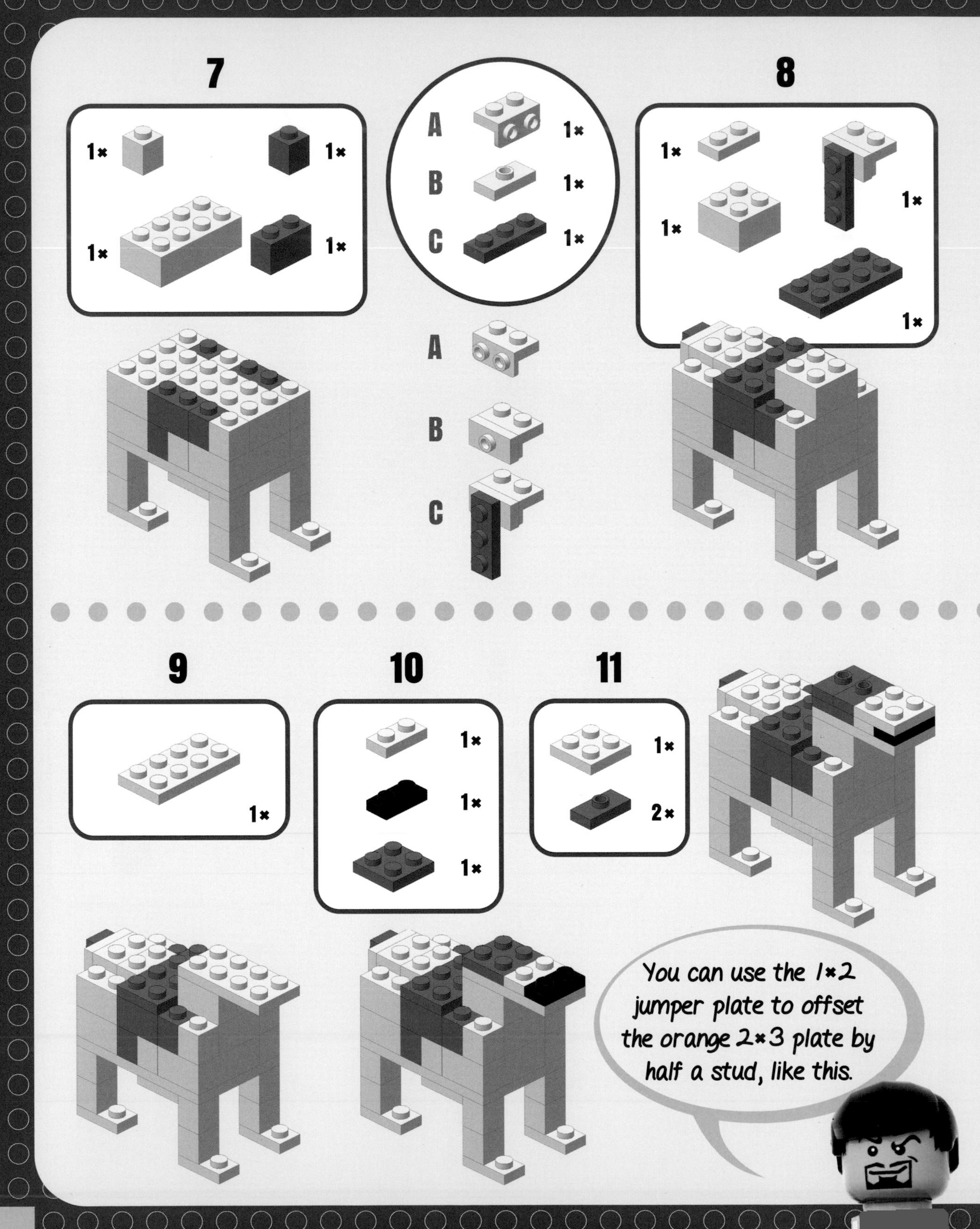
7
1×
1×
1×
1×
A
B
C
1×
1×
1×
8
1×
1×
1×
1×
A
B
C
9
1×
10
1×
1×
1×
11
1×
2×
You can use the 1×2 jumper plate to offset the orange 2×3 plate by half a stud, like this.

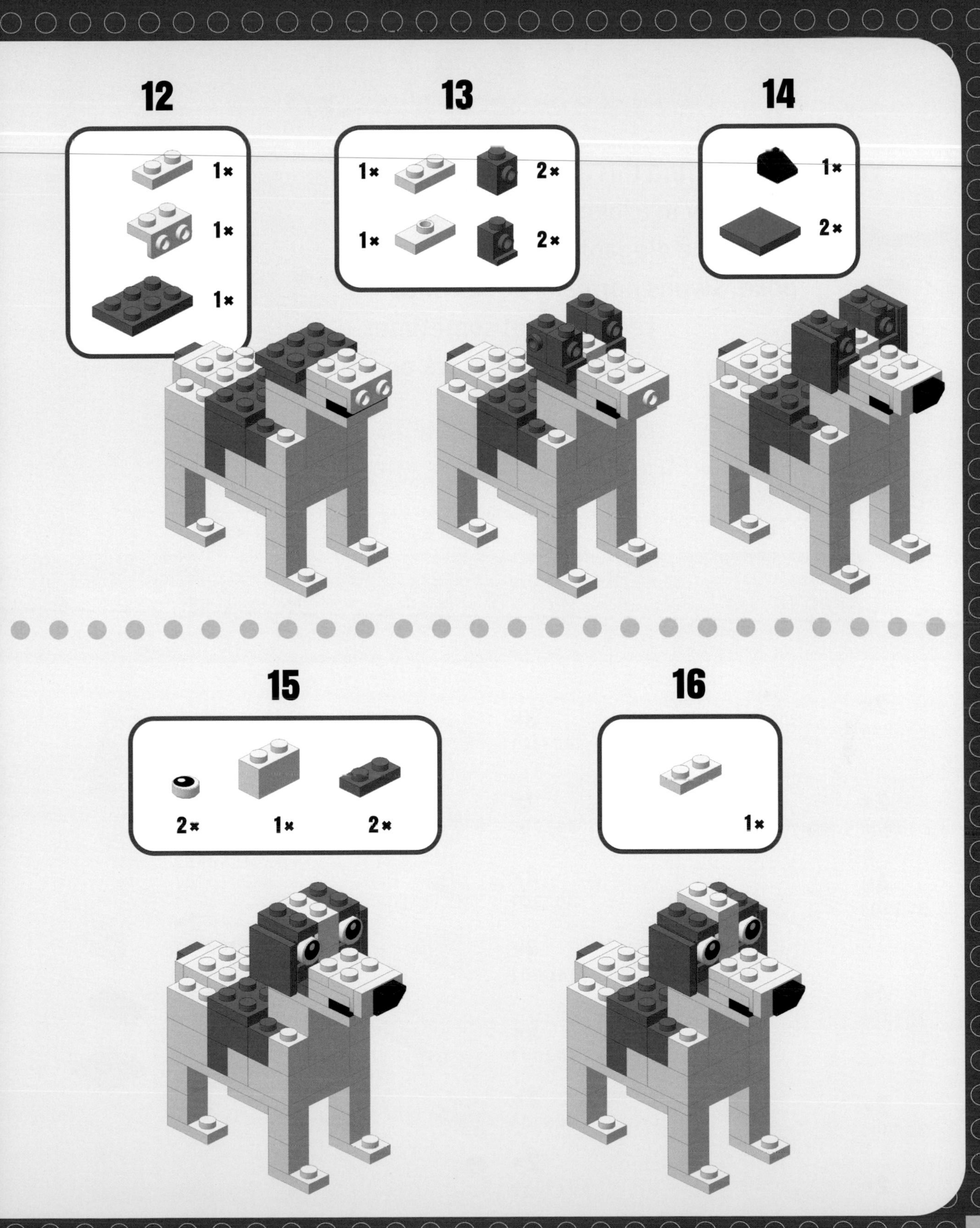
12
1×
1×
1×
13
1×
2×
1×
2×
14
1×
2×
15
2×
1×
2×
16
1×

SWAN

You'll probably find this animal swimming gracefully in a lake or pond. This model shows the elegant swan in a classic pose. Swans normally have white feathers, but sometimes you can find black ones.

DIFFICULTY

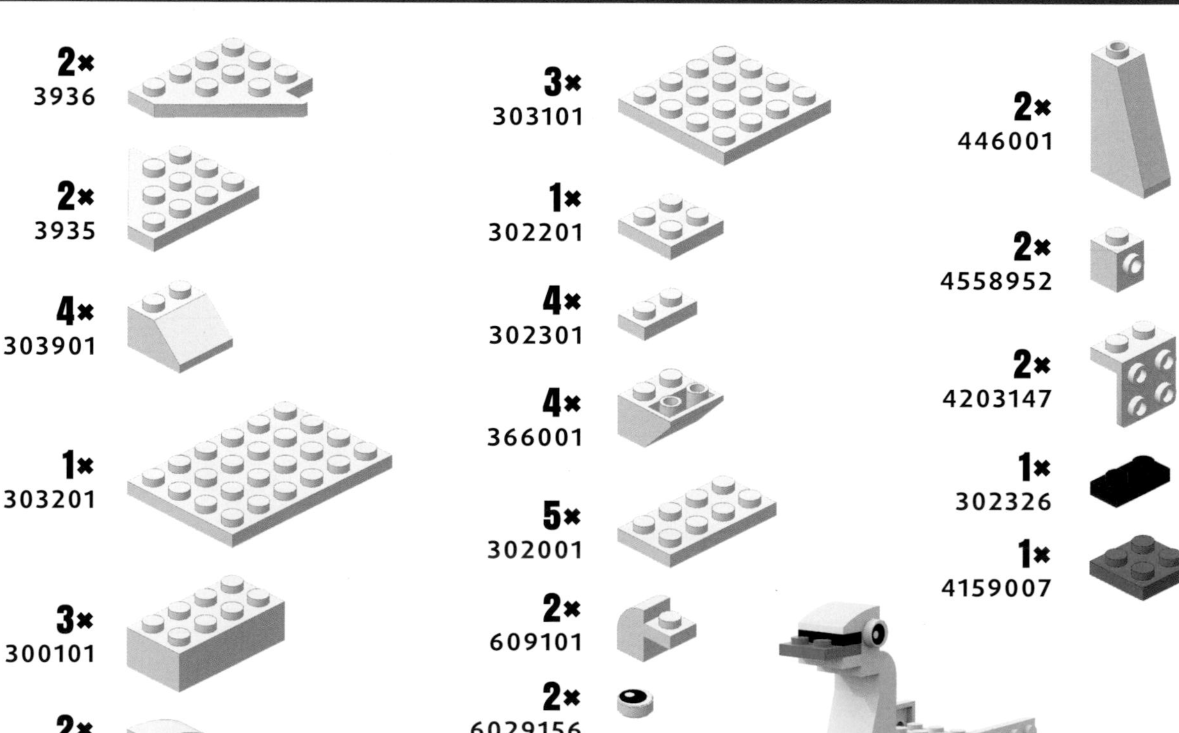

1
2×
1×
2
2×
2×
3
2×
1×
2×
4
2×
5
2×
3×
2×
6
4×
1×
7
1×
1×
2×
Pay attention to the position of the wings.
8
1×
1×
1×
2×
9
2×
1×
1×
10
2×
2×

ELEPHANT

The elephant is a pachyderm, which is an animal with very tough skin like the hippopotamus or the rhinoceros. ("Pachyderm" means "thick skin.") Elephants also have big ears and a proboscis, which is a fancy word for a long, moveable nose!

Just like a real elephant, this model has an adjustable nose made of ball joints and sockets that can move 360 degrees. Pretty neat!

PARTS LIST

DIFFICULTY

2× 6032360
2× 6029156
2× 4211103
2× 4211044
14× 4211135
2× 4210652
3× 4211001
1× 4498096
4× 4211060
17× 4211085
2× 4619760
8× 4558955
2× 4211119
2× 4210794
1× 4567887
1× 4211115
1× 4581225
2× 4211094
2× 4211063
1× 4210660
8× 4211065
1× 4211043
3× 4211088

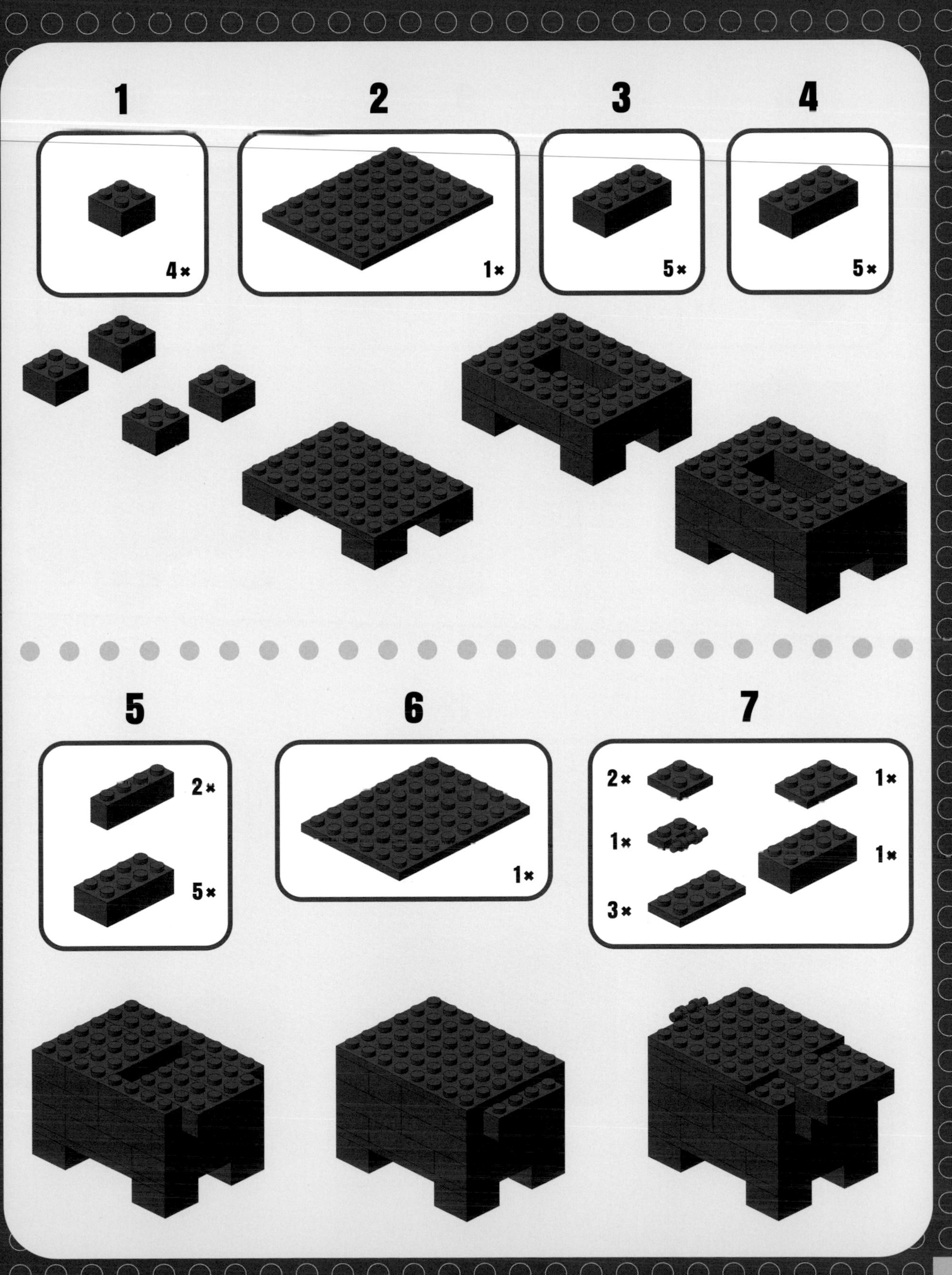
1
4×
2
1×
3
5×
4
5×
5
2×
5×
6
1×
7
2×
1×
1×
1×
3×

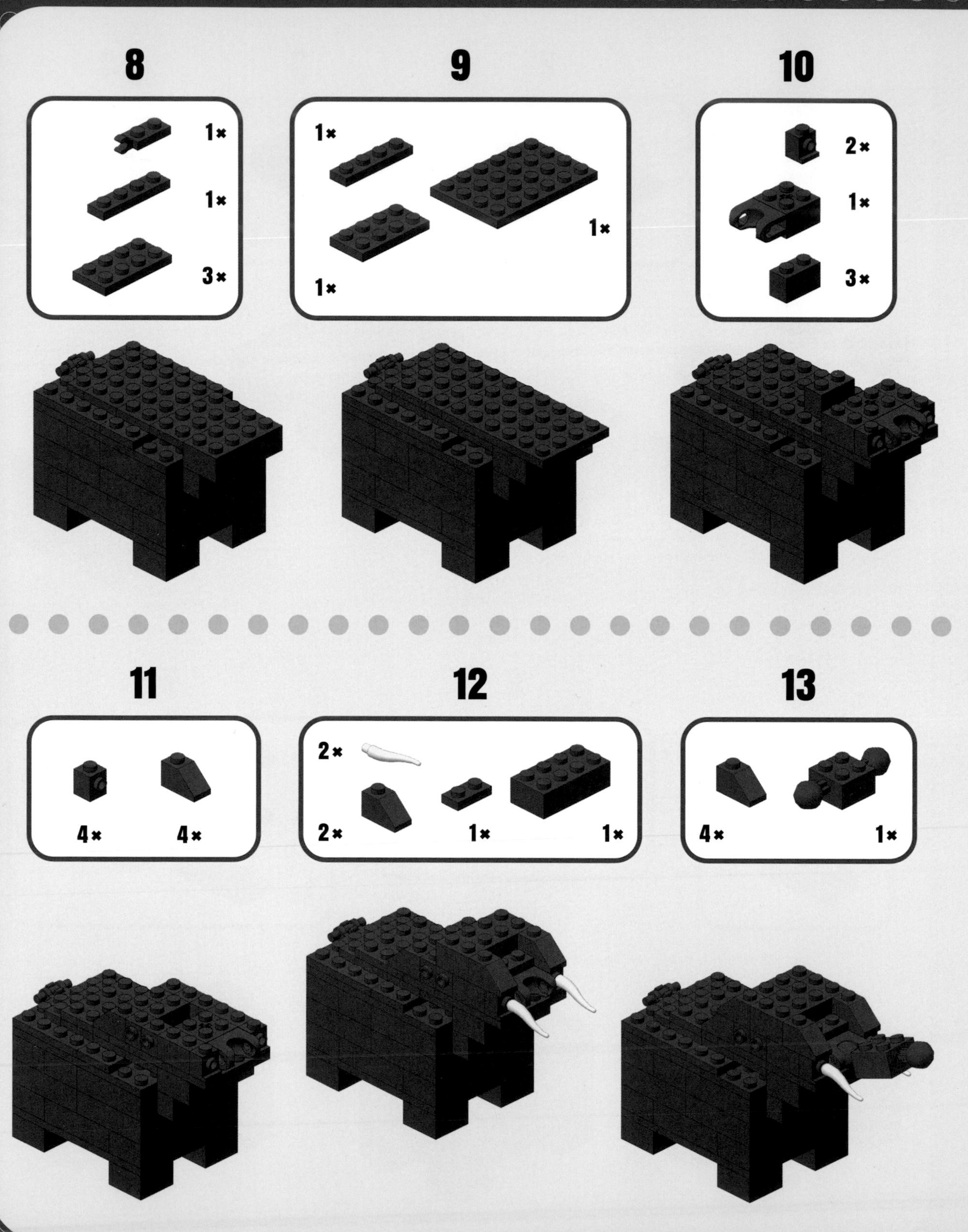
8
1×
1×
3×
9
1×
1×
1×
10
2×
1×
3×
11
4×
4×
12
2×
2×
1×
1×
13
4×
1×

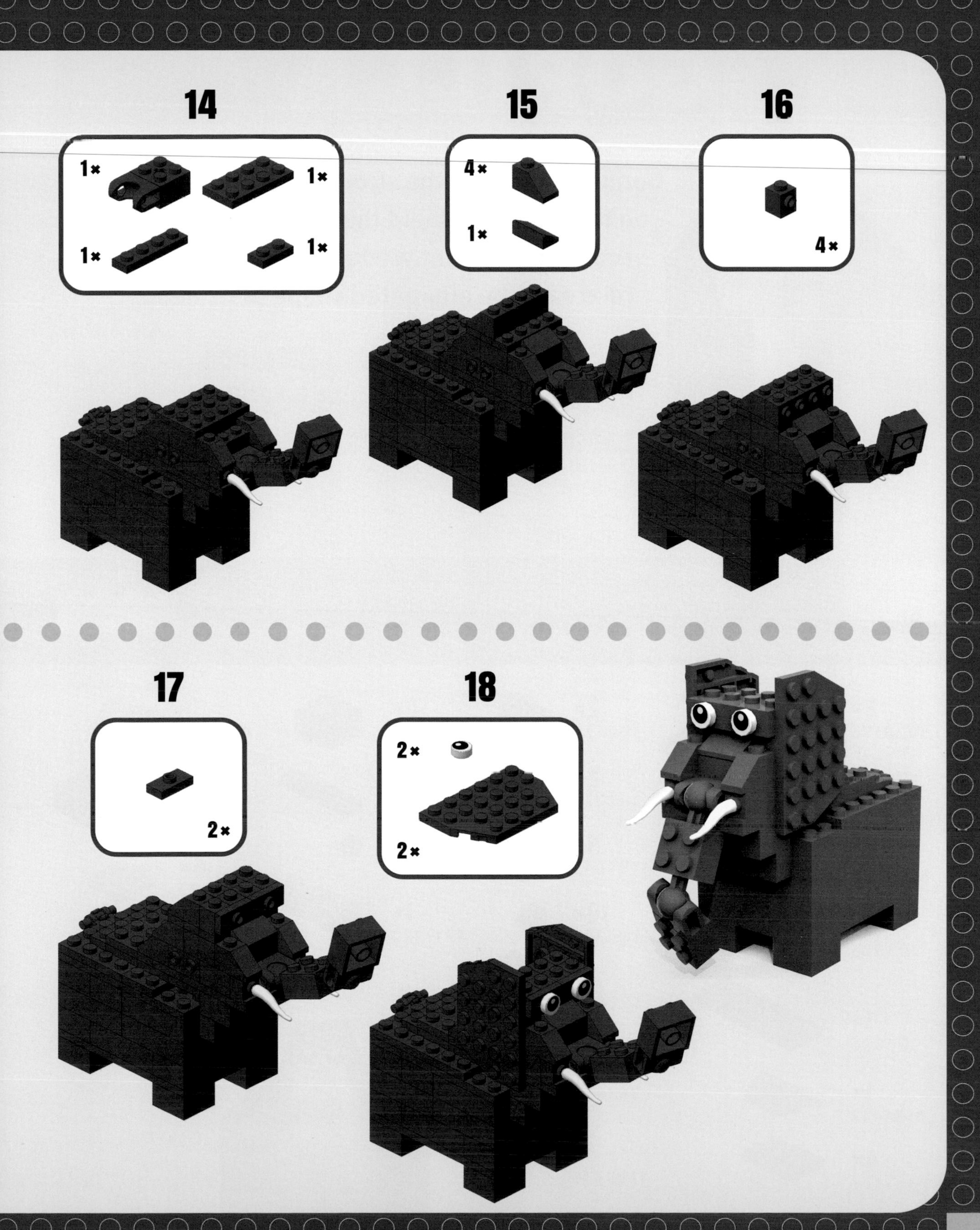
14
1×
1×
1×
1×
15
4×
1×
16
4×
17
2×
18
2×
2×

GORILLA

Gorillas are one of the strongest animals on the planet. To build this gorilla, you'll combine different wedge plates to re-create the elongated shape of its head.

This animal has always inspired much curiosity and has been the subject of many films, like King Kong!

PARTS LIST

DIFFICULTY

Qty	Part
2×	6029156
1×	303426
1×	4180508
8×	303926
1×	379526
1×	4531412
4×	302126
2×	300426
2×	302226
1×	4184645
10×	4504382
4×	329826
1×	301026
1×	4180536
10×	300326
3×	371026
2×	614126
1×	4211394
1×	4211410
1×	4211385
4×	4211397
1×	4211411
6×	4211570

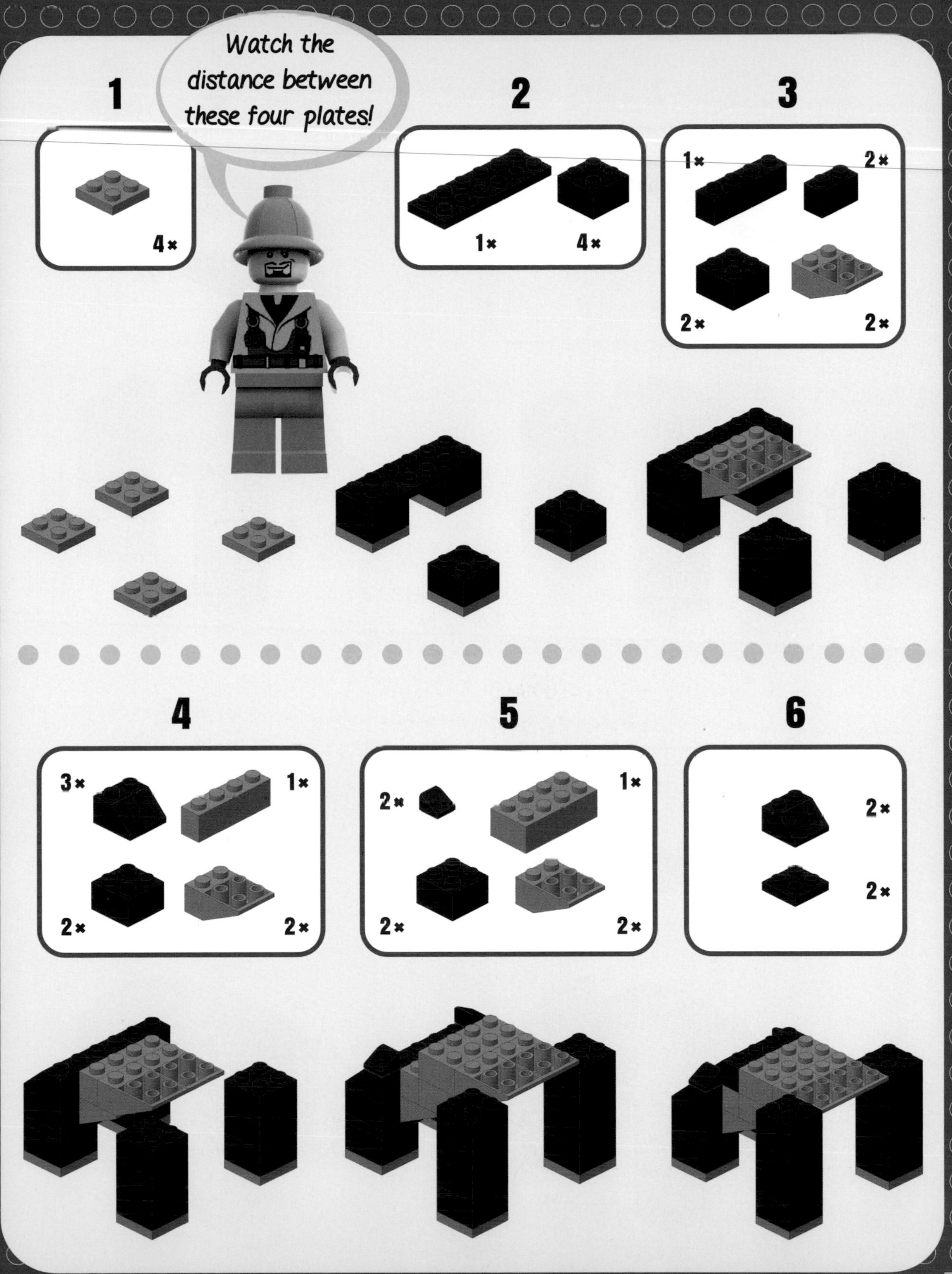
1
Watch the distance between these four plates!
4×
2
1×
4×
3
1×
2×
2×
2×
4
3×
1×
2×
2×
5
2×
1×
2×
2×
6
2×
2×

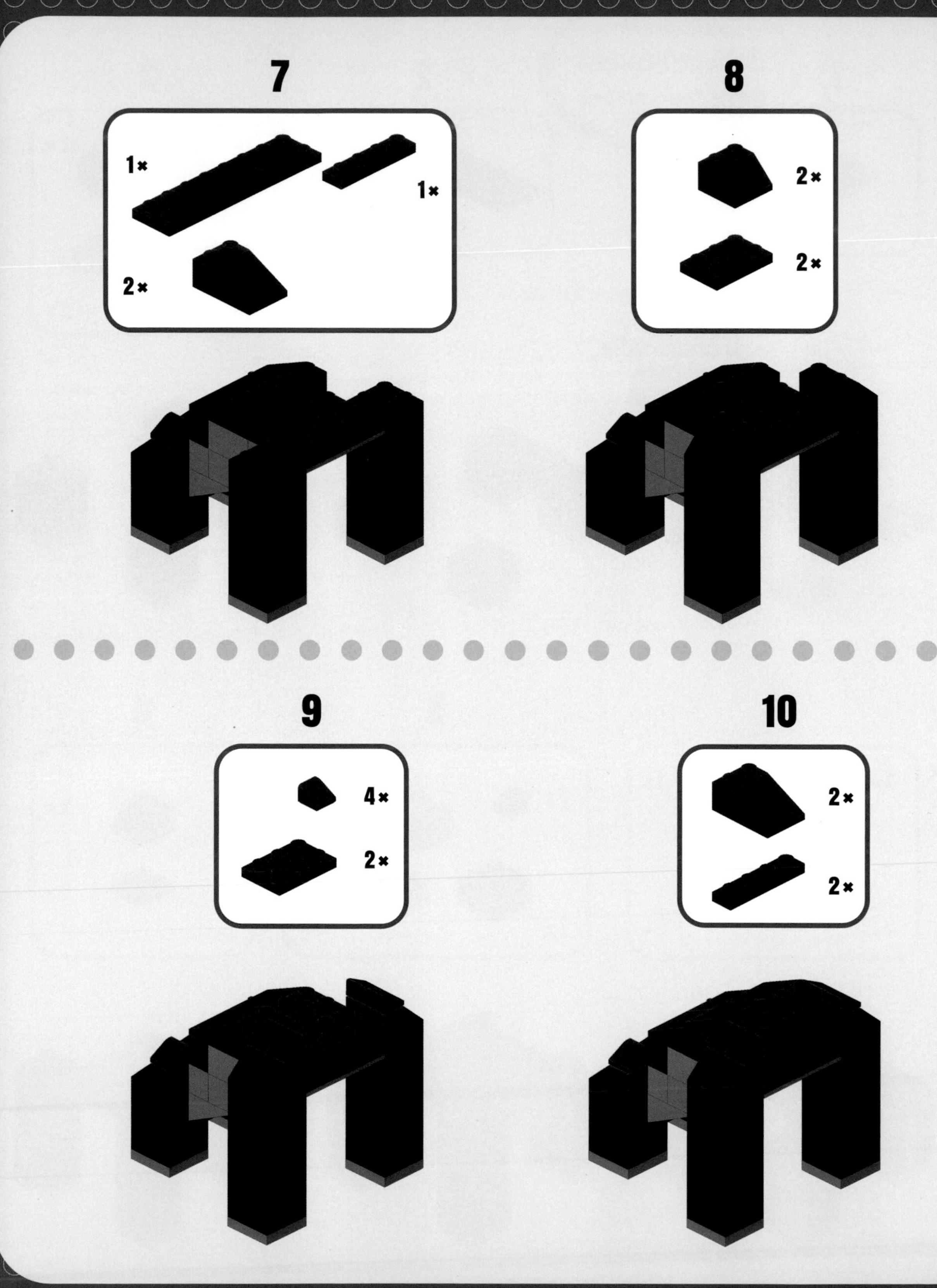
7
1×
1×
2×
8
2×
2×
9
4×
2×
10
2×
2×

11
1×
2×
1×
1×
1×
A
B
1×
1×
C
2×
2×
A
B
C
12
13
1×
1×
2×

CAT

This animal certainly needs no introduction. You've probably seen hundreds of them already! This brick cat is lounging. It's a gray cat, but you can change its color if you'd like. You just have to be careful when building the base.

This cat is not so simple to build, since you'll need lots of small parts as well as special jumper plates that let you attach bricks between two studs.

PARTS LIST

DIFFICULTY

2× 6029156
1× 4504382
2× 4521921
1× 4211398
6× 4211399
3× 4211133
2× 4210848
5× 4211001
3× 4211119
2× 4567887
1× 4211089
3× 4527082
1× 4211002
4× 4244373
8× 4211063
1× 4211043
2× 4211115
1× 4211104
2× 4211044
1× 4211135
1× 4211098
3× 4211085
2× 4211056
3× 4210719
2× 4211065

1
1×
3×
1×
1×
The first two steps are tricky, so be sure to check the positions of these parts!
2
1×
2×
3×
3
3×
2×
1×
4
1×
1×
1×
1×
5
1×
1×
1×
1×

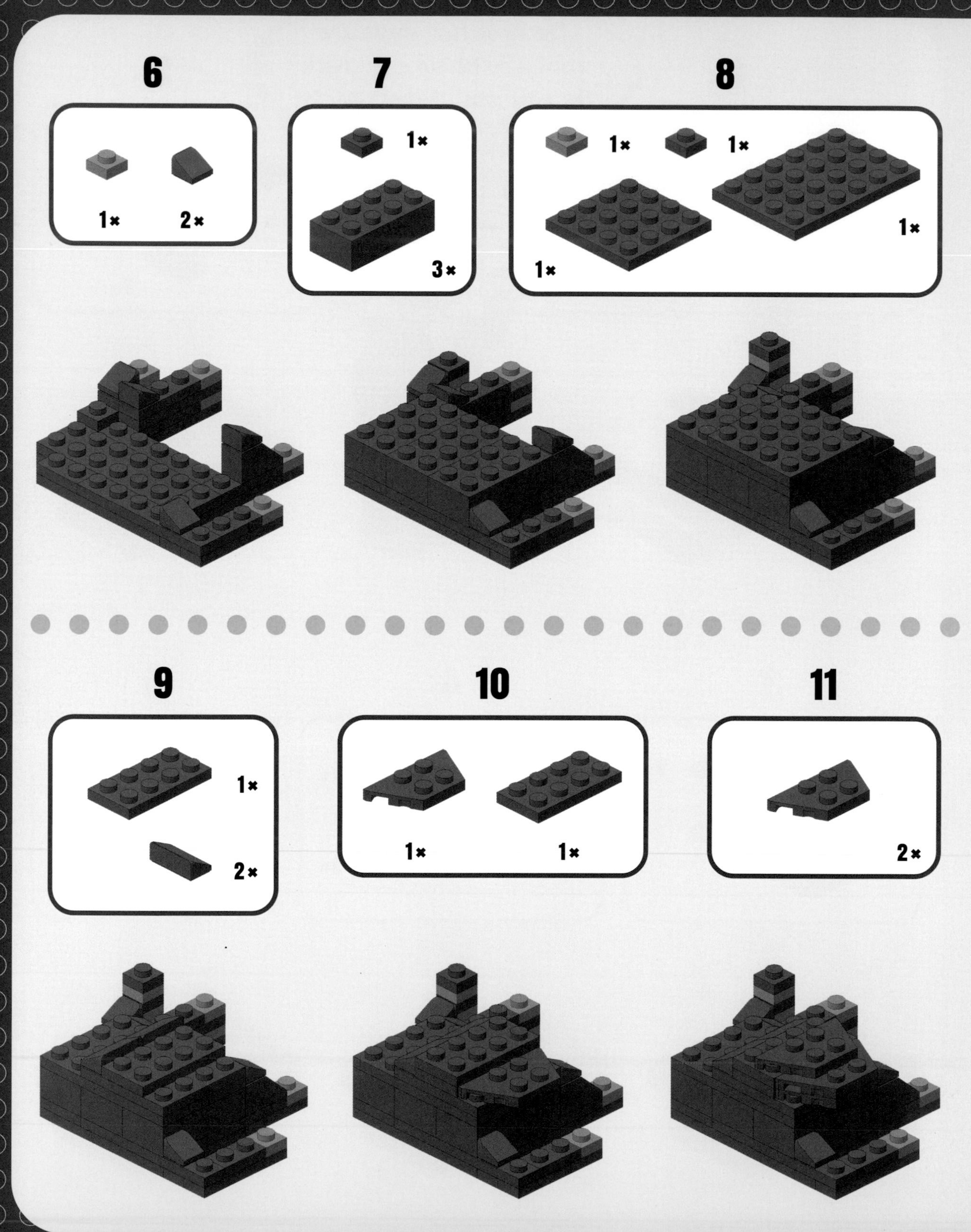

6
1×
2×
7
1×
3×
8
1×
1×
1×
1×
9
1×
2×
10
1×
1×
11
2×

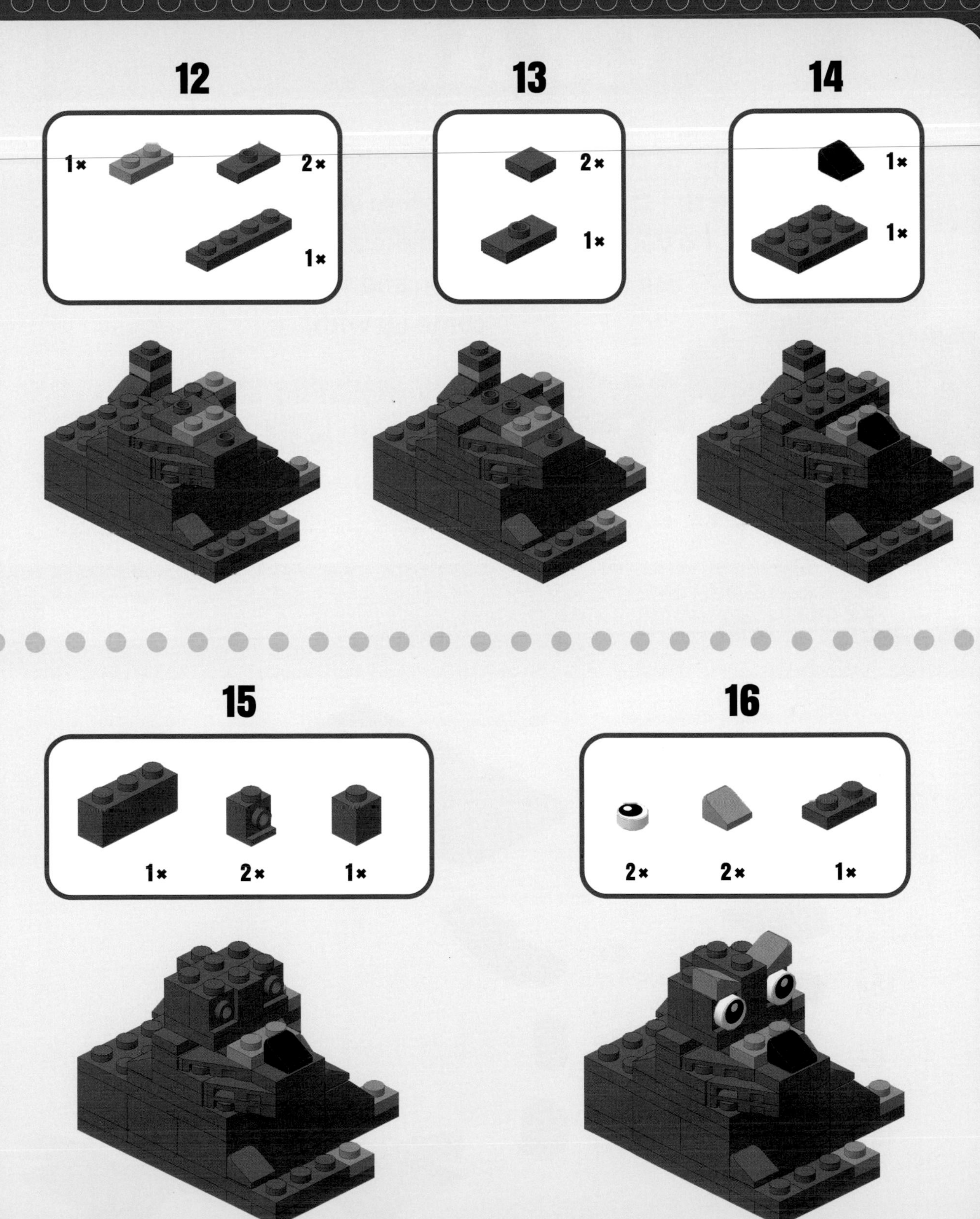
12
1×
2×
1×
13
2×
1×
14
1×
1×
15
1×
2×
1×
16
2×
2×
1×

CRAB

The crab is a type of crustacean—some crabs live by the shore, hiding in the sand, while others live underwater. Do you think you can make a lobster instead? Use your imagination and see what you can come up with!

Try adjusting the position of its legs.

PARTS LIST

DIFFICULTY

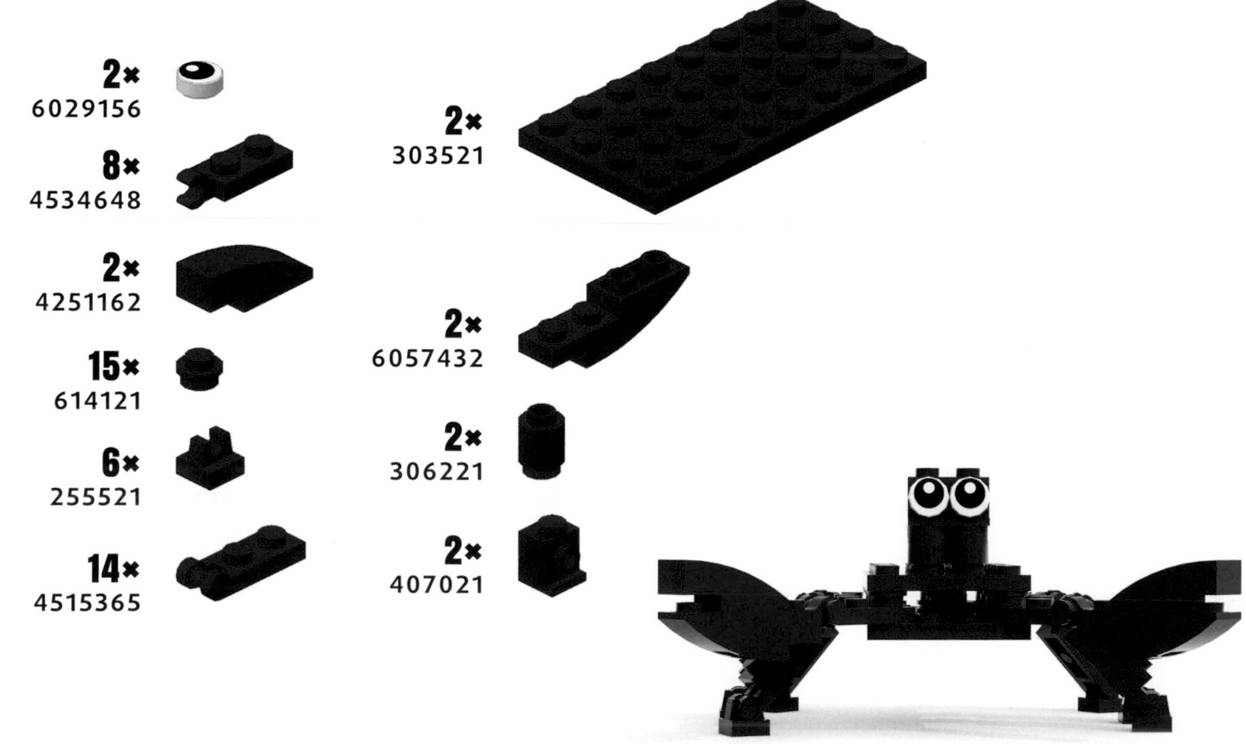

Did you notice that six of its legs are all the same?
1
6×
2
6×
3
6×
1×
4
6×
5
4×
2×
6
2×
3×
7
4×
2×
8
2×
4×
9
1×
10
2×
11
2×
2×

BEAR CUB

This little bear looks just like a stuffed animal! It's just eaten a pot of honey and seems ready for a nap. Look how its paws are slightly askew, which is a technique you haven't seen yet.

Can you build a bear on all fours?

PARTS LIST

DIFFICULTY

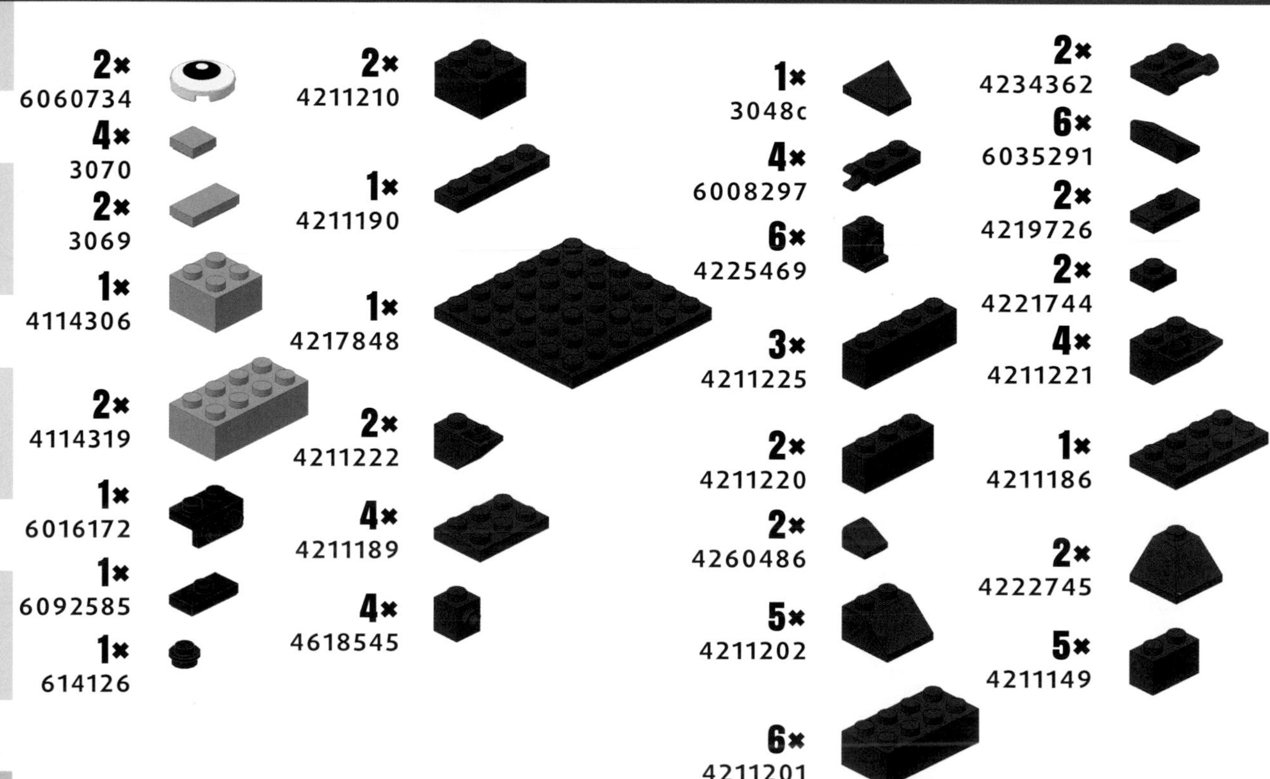

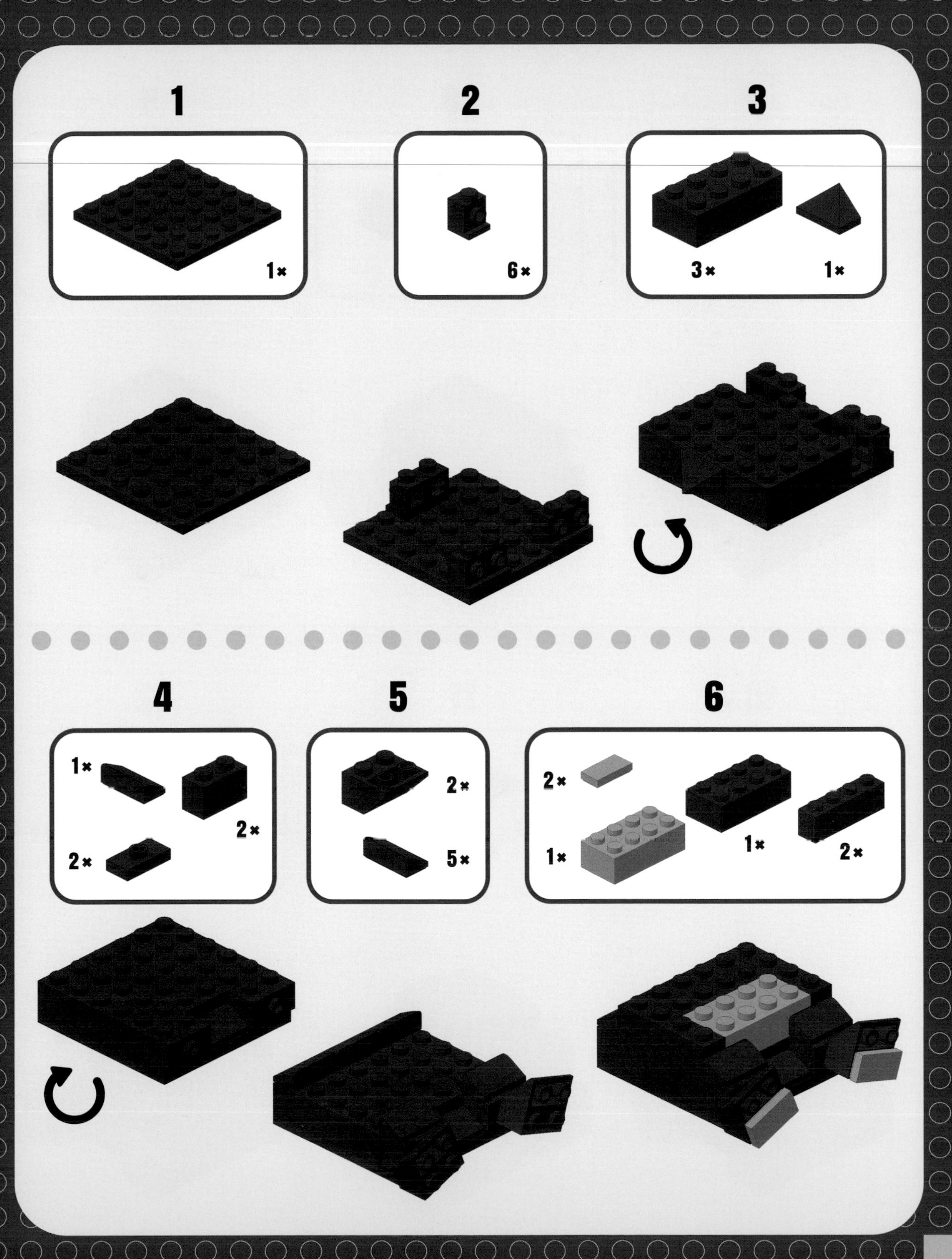

1
1×
2
6×
3
3×
1×
4
1×
2×
2×
5
2×
5×
6
2×
1×
1×
2×

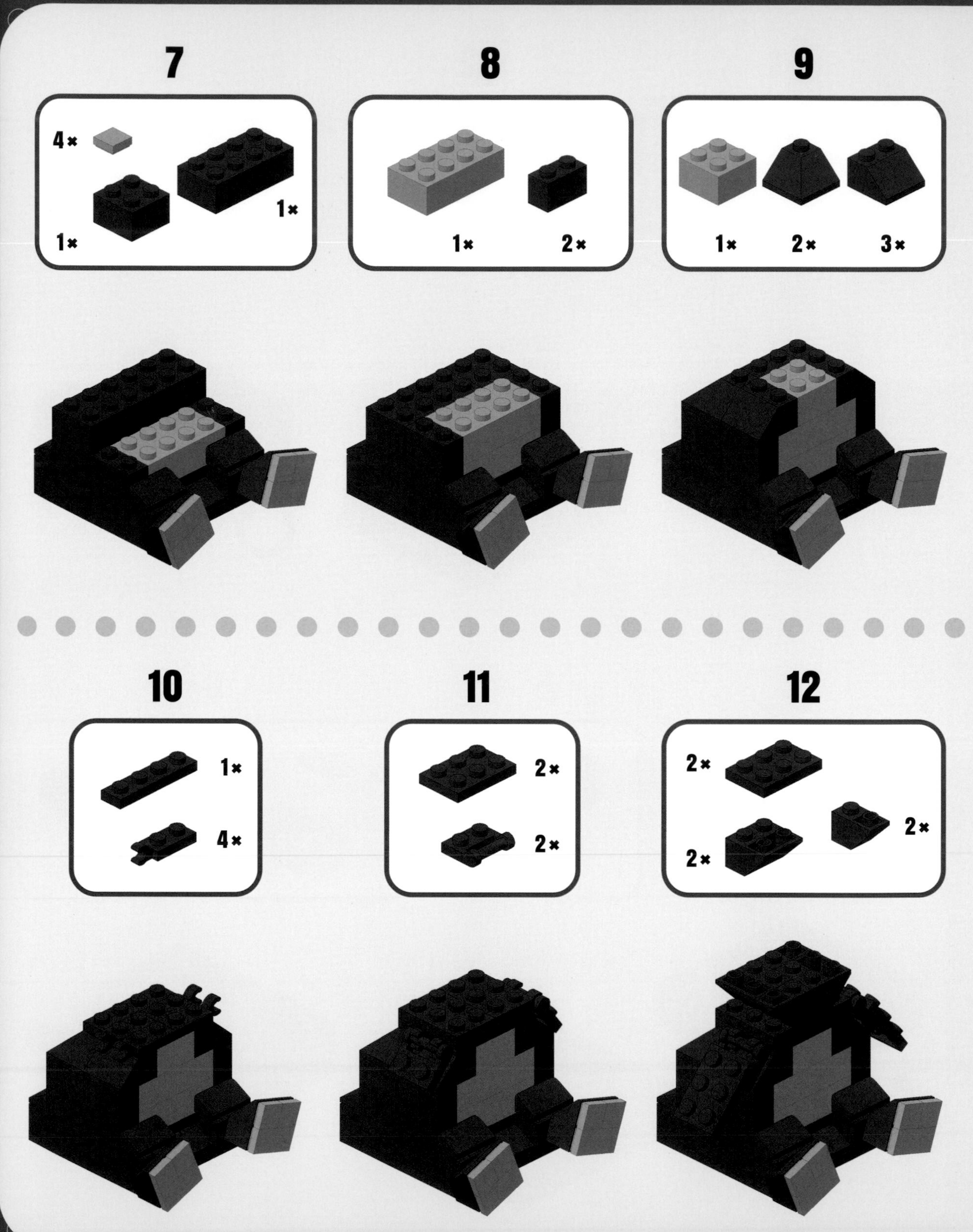

7
4×
1×
1×
8
1×
2×
9
1×
2×
3×
10
1×
4×
11
2×
2×
12
2×
2×
2×

13
1×
1×
2×
14
1×
1×
2×
15
1×
4×
1×
16
1×
2×
1×
17
2×
2×

PARROT

This colorful bird has a peculiar talent: it can imitate people's voices and even learn to speak! Although, to be honest, what they say doesn't make a lot of sense. This one is red, yellow, and blue, but you can change the colors to your liking.

Parrots come in all sorts of colors, so why not build a green one too? Pay attention to how the wings are attached on each side.

PARTS LIST

DIFFICULTY

3× 4558952
2× 6029156
2× 245021
4× 4244371
1× 303921
2× 4185525
1× 4651524
2× 306221
4× 362321
1× 301021
1× 300221
3× 300421
1× 304021
1× 302321
5× 302121
1× 300121
1× 362323
2× 306923
3× 362324
1× 4179094
1× 4179095
1× 4219920
3× 6055069
2× 4188450
1× 4125278

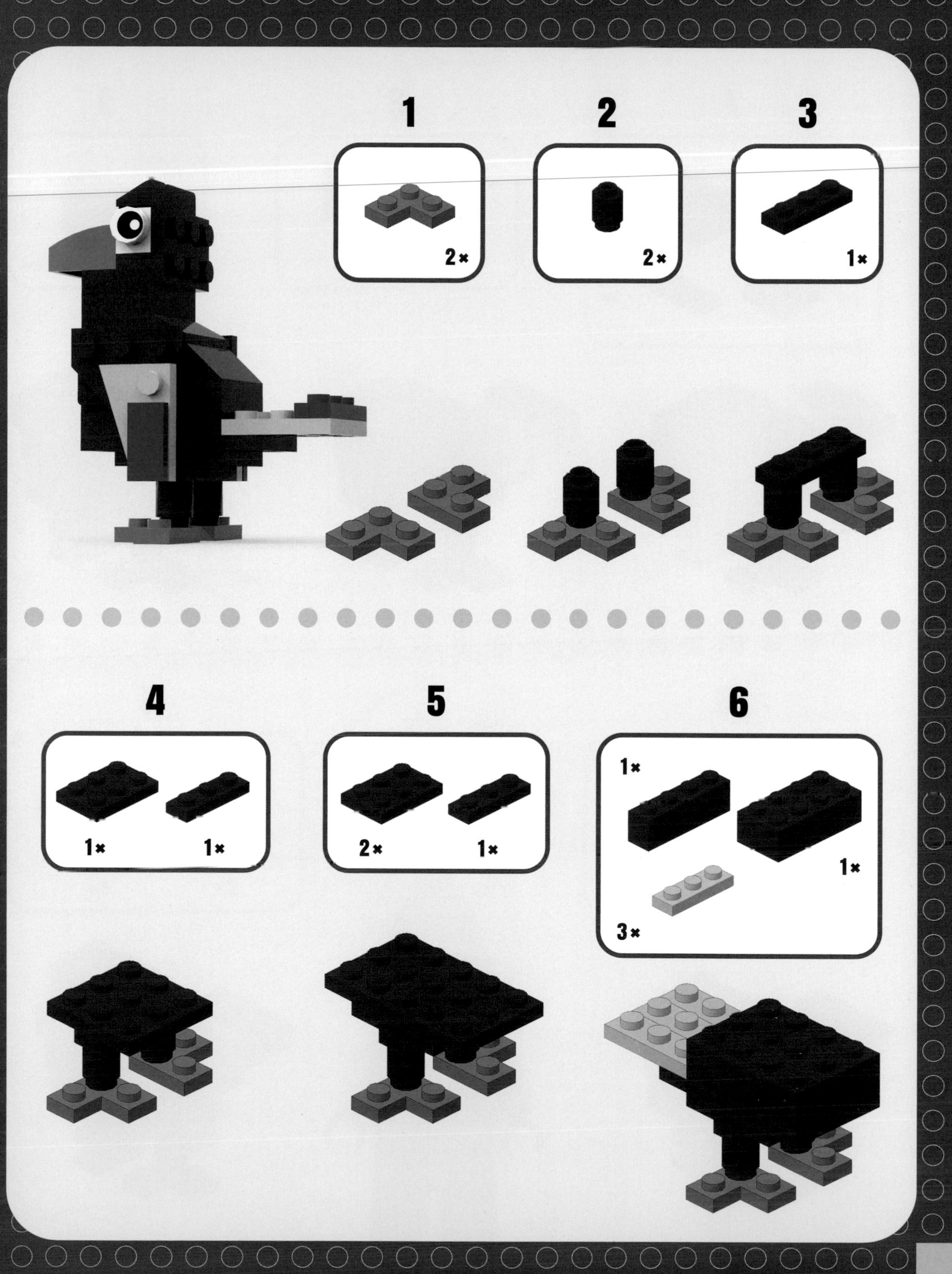
1
2×
2
2×
3
1×
4
1×
1×
5
2×
1×
6
1×
1×
3×

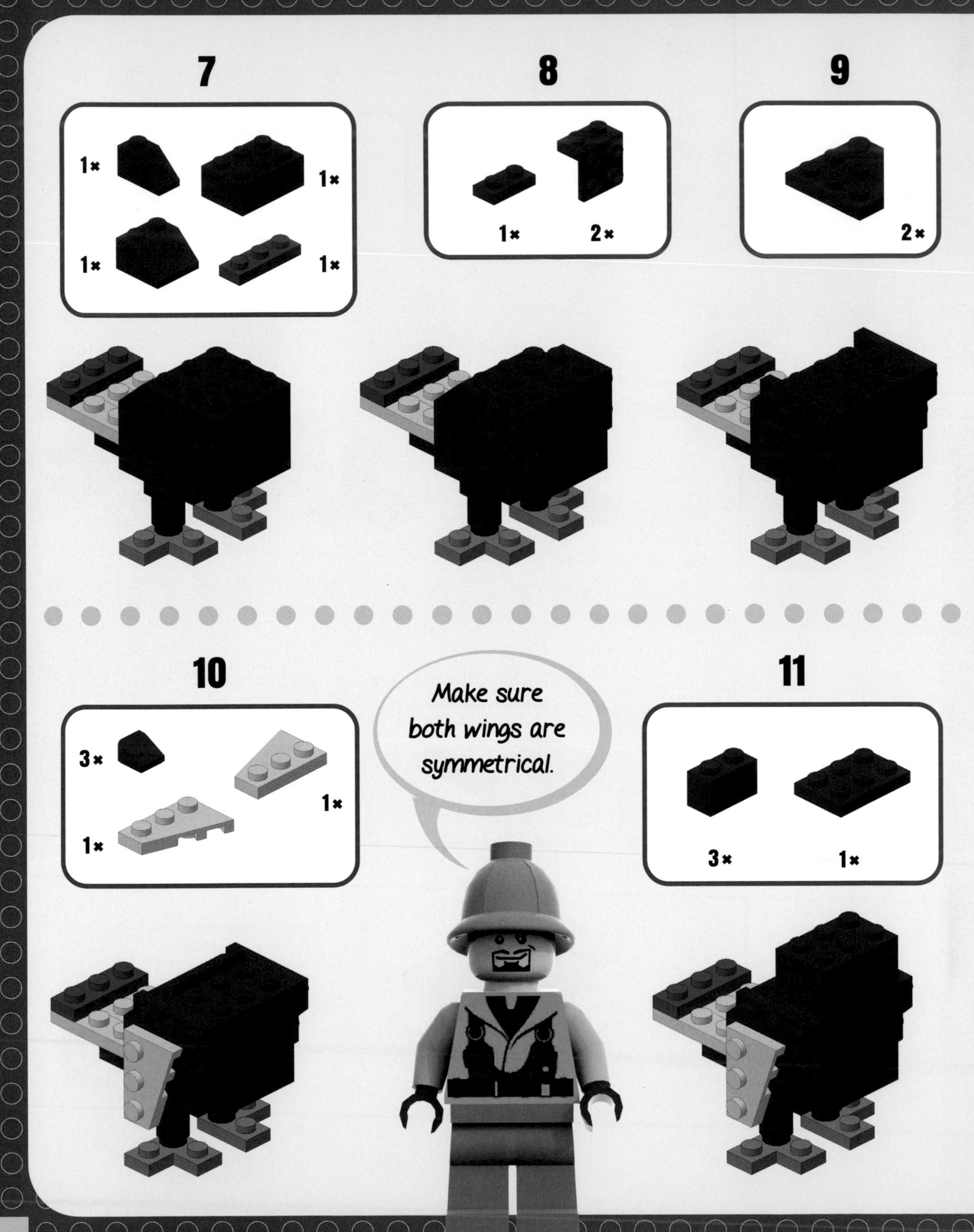
7
1×
1×
1×
1×
8
1×
2×
9
2×
10
3×
1×
1×
Make sure both wings are symmetrical.
11
3×
1×

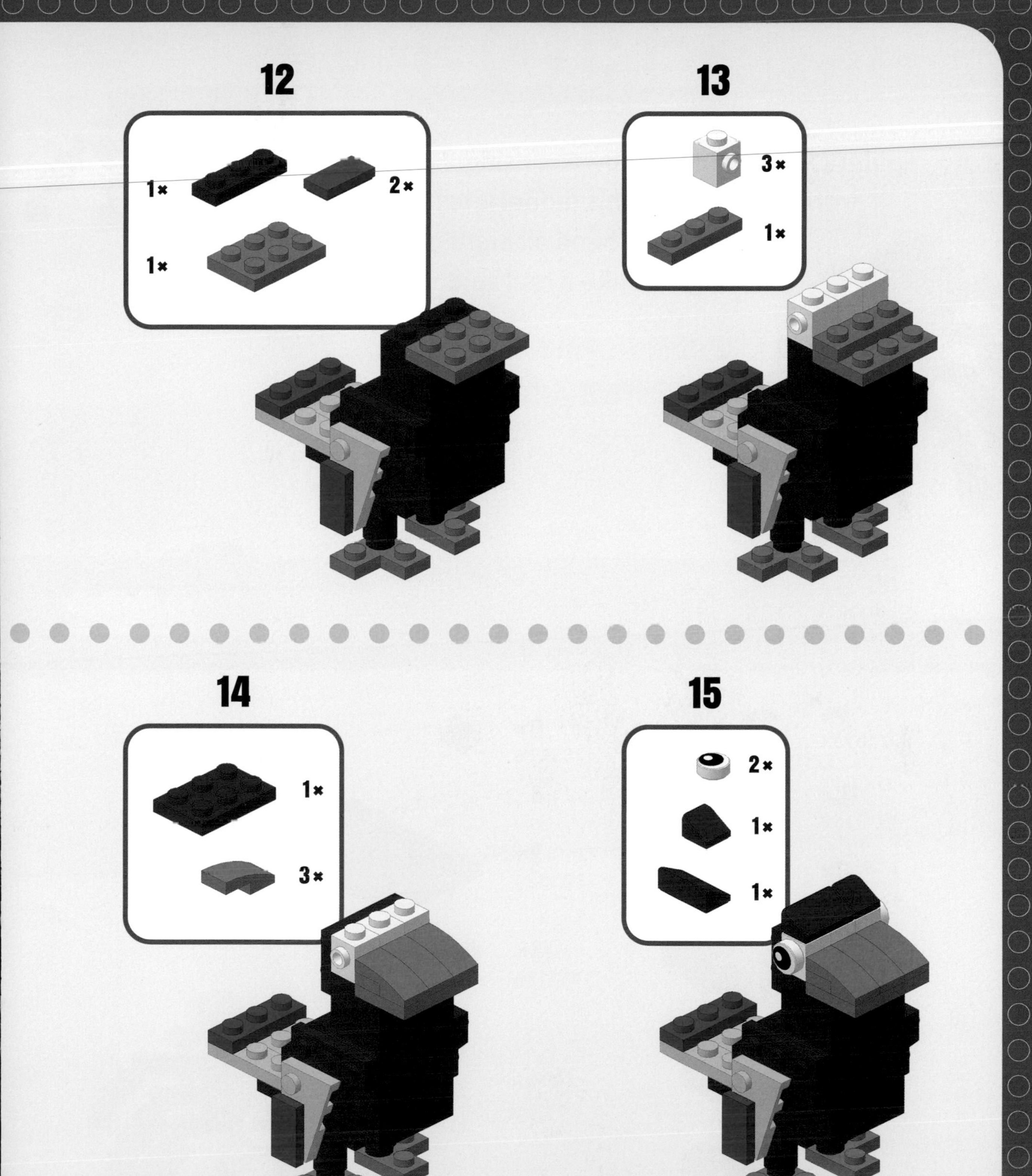

12
1×
2×
1×
13
3×
1×
14
1×
3×
15
2×
1×
1×

SPIDER

Spiders love building cobwebs using intricate designs. This model lets you move and bend all eight of its legs just like a real spider.

Spiders come in all shapes, sizes, and colors. Invent your own!

PARTS LIST

DIFFICULTY

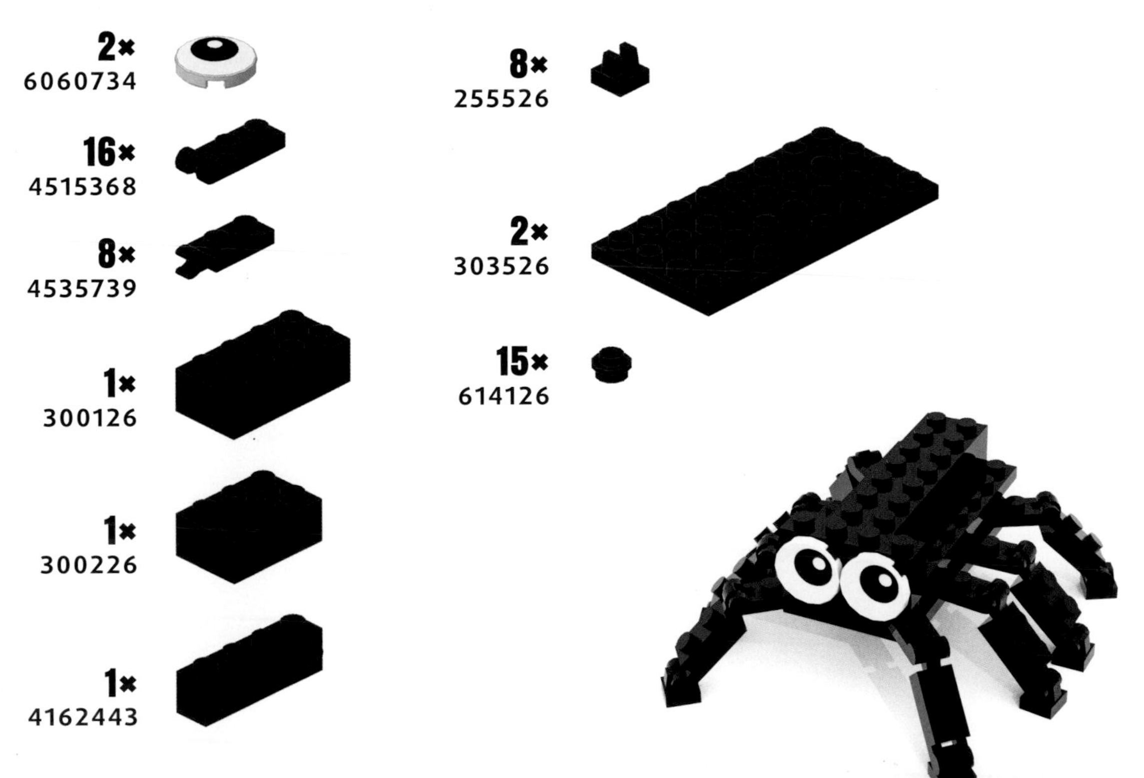

2× 6060734

16× 4515368

8× 4535739

1× 300126

1× 300226

1× 4162443

8× 255526

2× 303526

15× 614126

1
8×
2
8×
Let's build the spider's legs. They're all the same, so make one and then repeat!
3
8×
4
8×

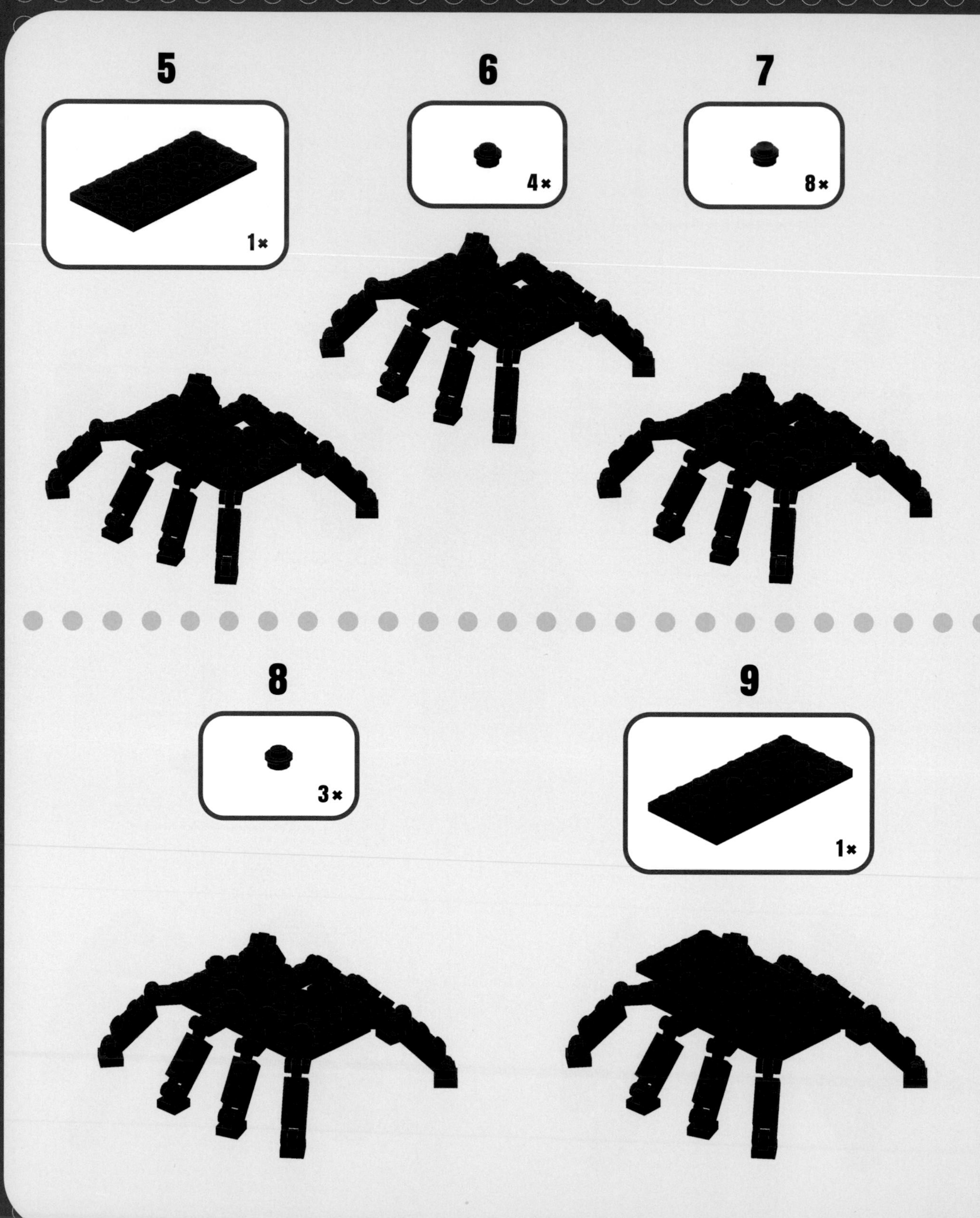
5
1×
6
4×
7
8×
8
3×
9
1×

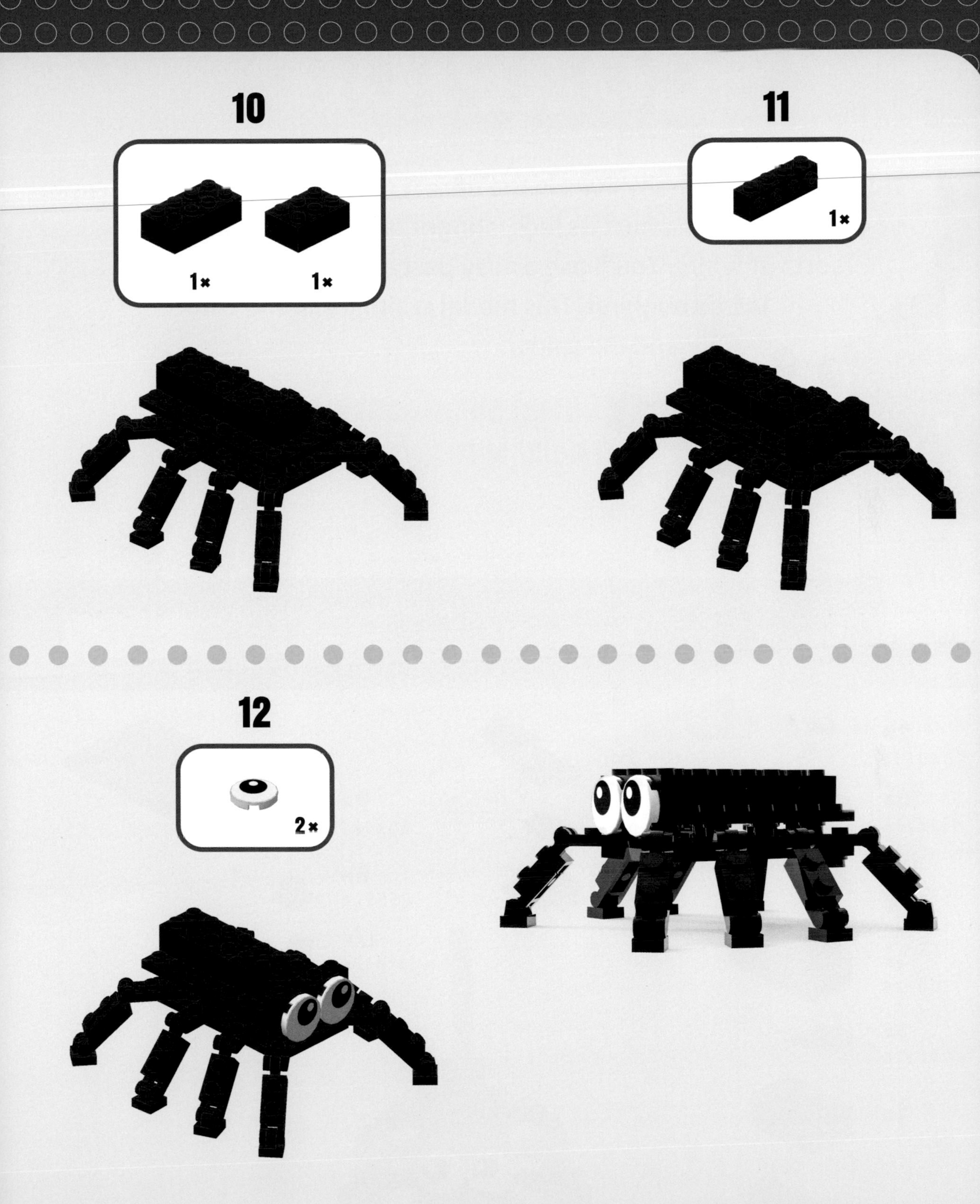
10
1×
1×
11
1×
12
2×

SCORPION

This scorpion normally lives in the desert, but today it's in your zoo! You can adjust its legs, stinger, and claws in all sorts of ways. You'll use a nifty part called plate round 1×1 throughout. This model is similar to the crab and the spider.

What other animals could you build with this technique?

PARTS LIST

DIFFICULTY

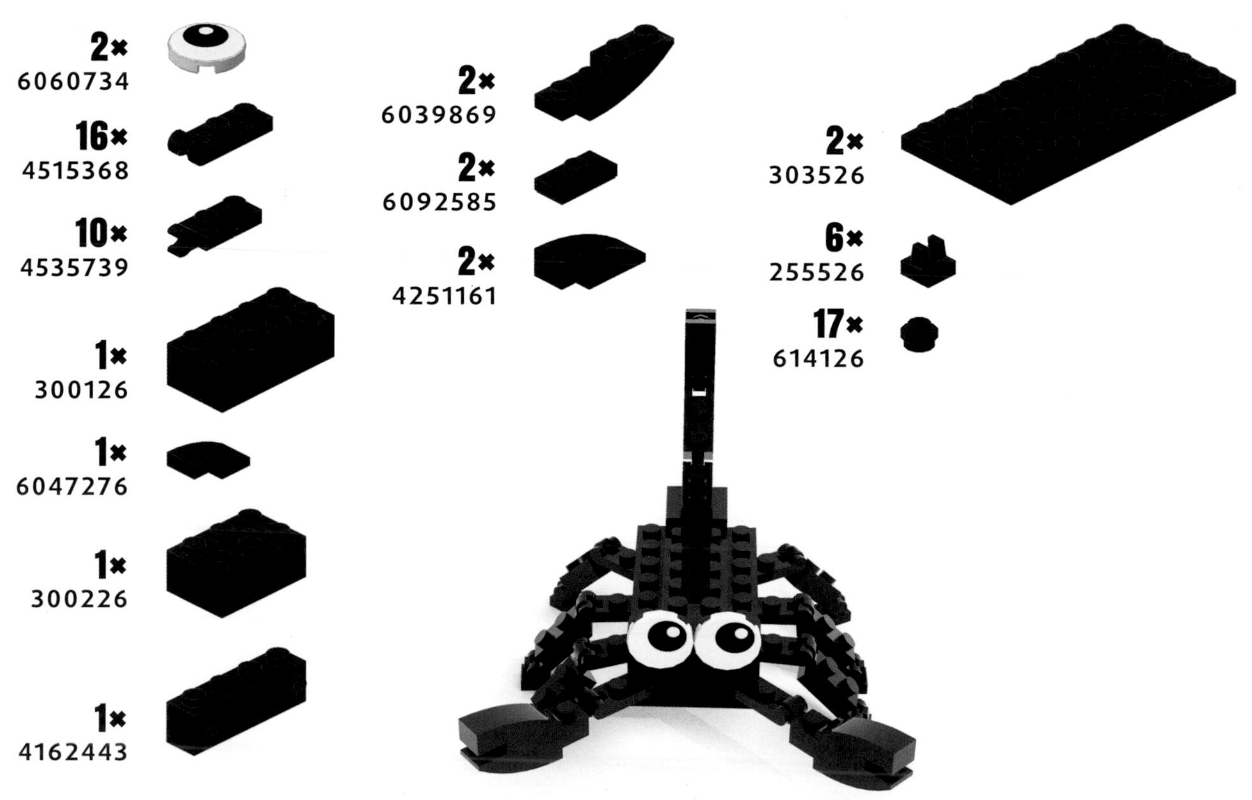

1
1×
2
8×
A
6×
B
6×
C
6×
A
B
C
Since the legs are all the same, make one and repeat the process.
3
2×
1×
4
2×
5
4×

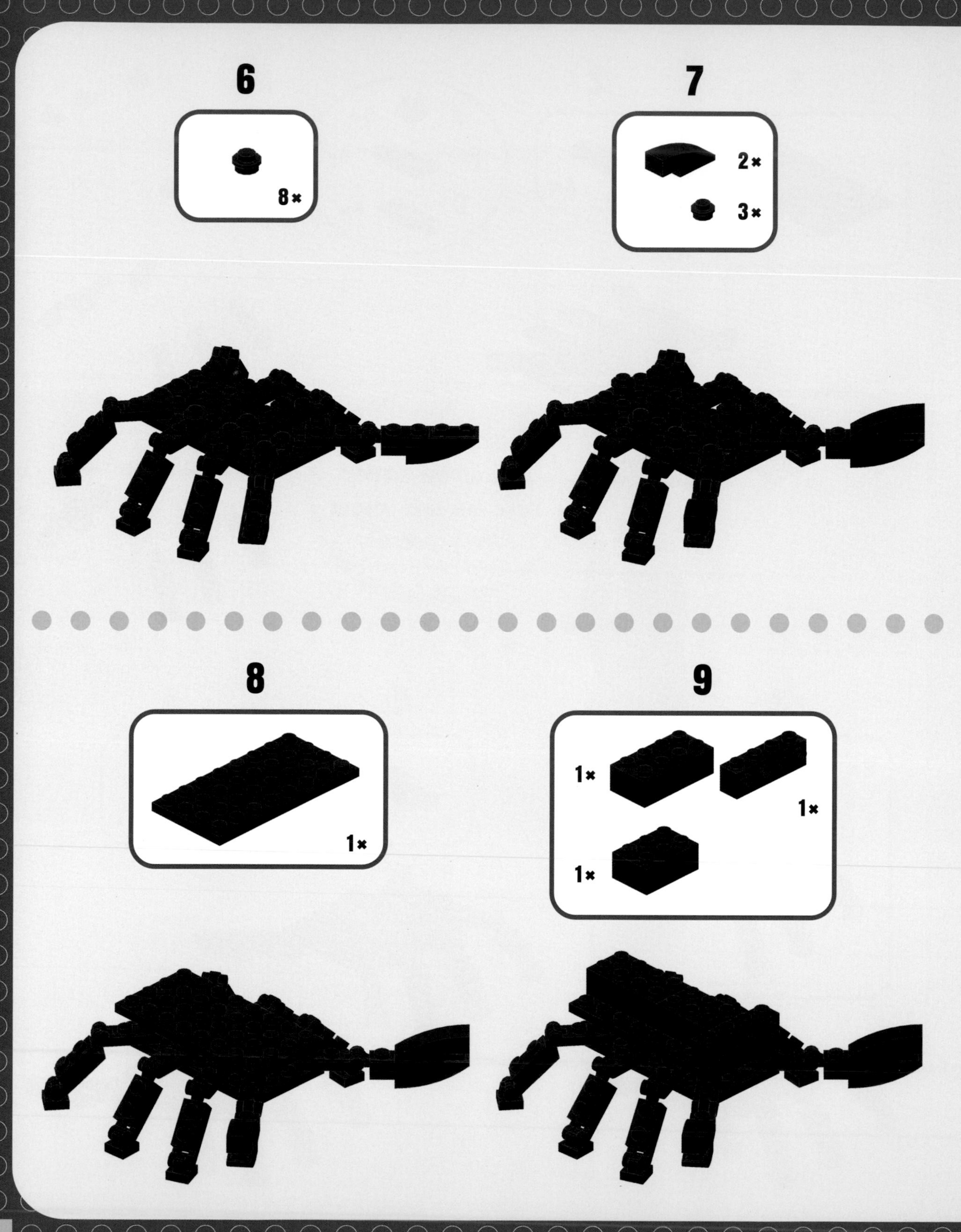

6
8×
7
2×
3×
8
1×
9
1×
1×
1×

10

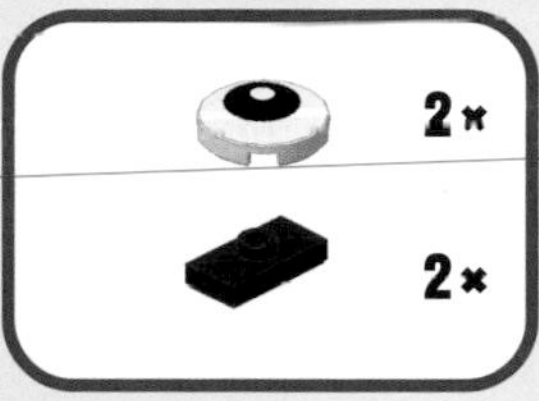

2×

2×

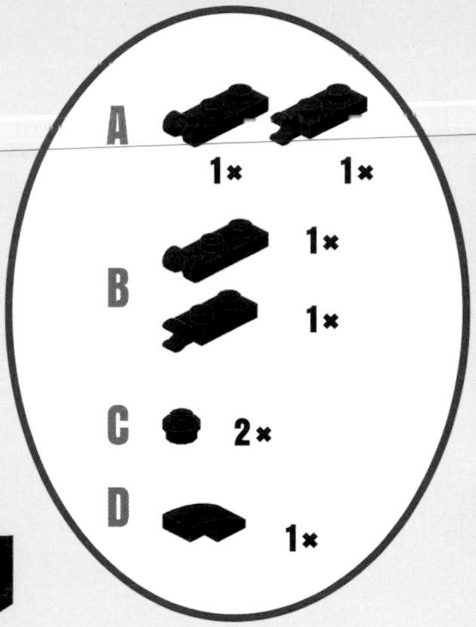

A 1× 1×

B 1× 1×

C 2×

D 1×

A

B

C

D

11

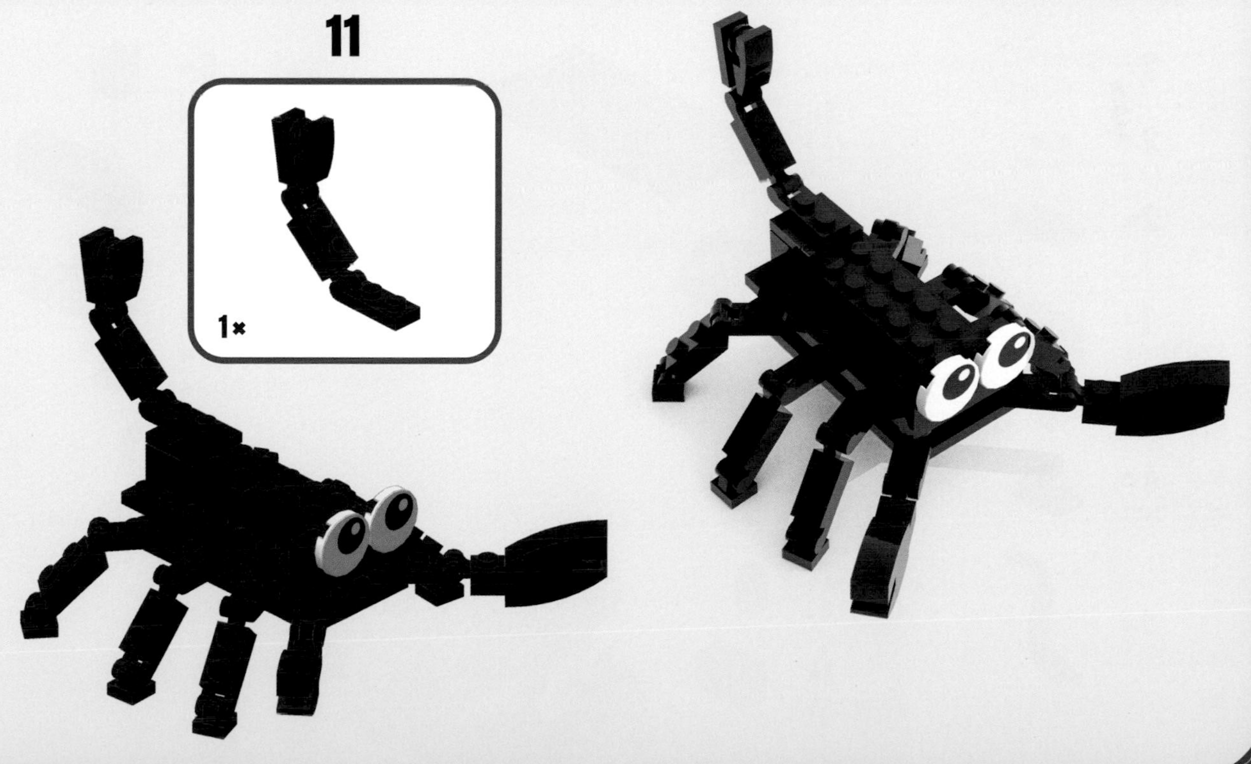

BULL

This normally peaceful bull gets excited when he sees the color red—so watch out! He has a nose ring because he loves jewelry and has long majestic horns.

This one is fun and simple to make, so try it now!

PARTS LIST

DIFFICULTY

2× 6032360 
2× 6060734 
2× 4155708 
1× 4201062 
1× 4143005 
4× 4653087
1× 4626202

1× 4211207
9× 4211202
11× 4211201
2× 4211242 
8× 4211183
1× 4211252

6× 4618545
4× 4211225 
6× 4217916
4× 4260486
2× 4618195 
2× 6071259

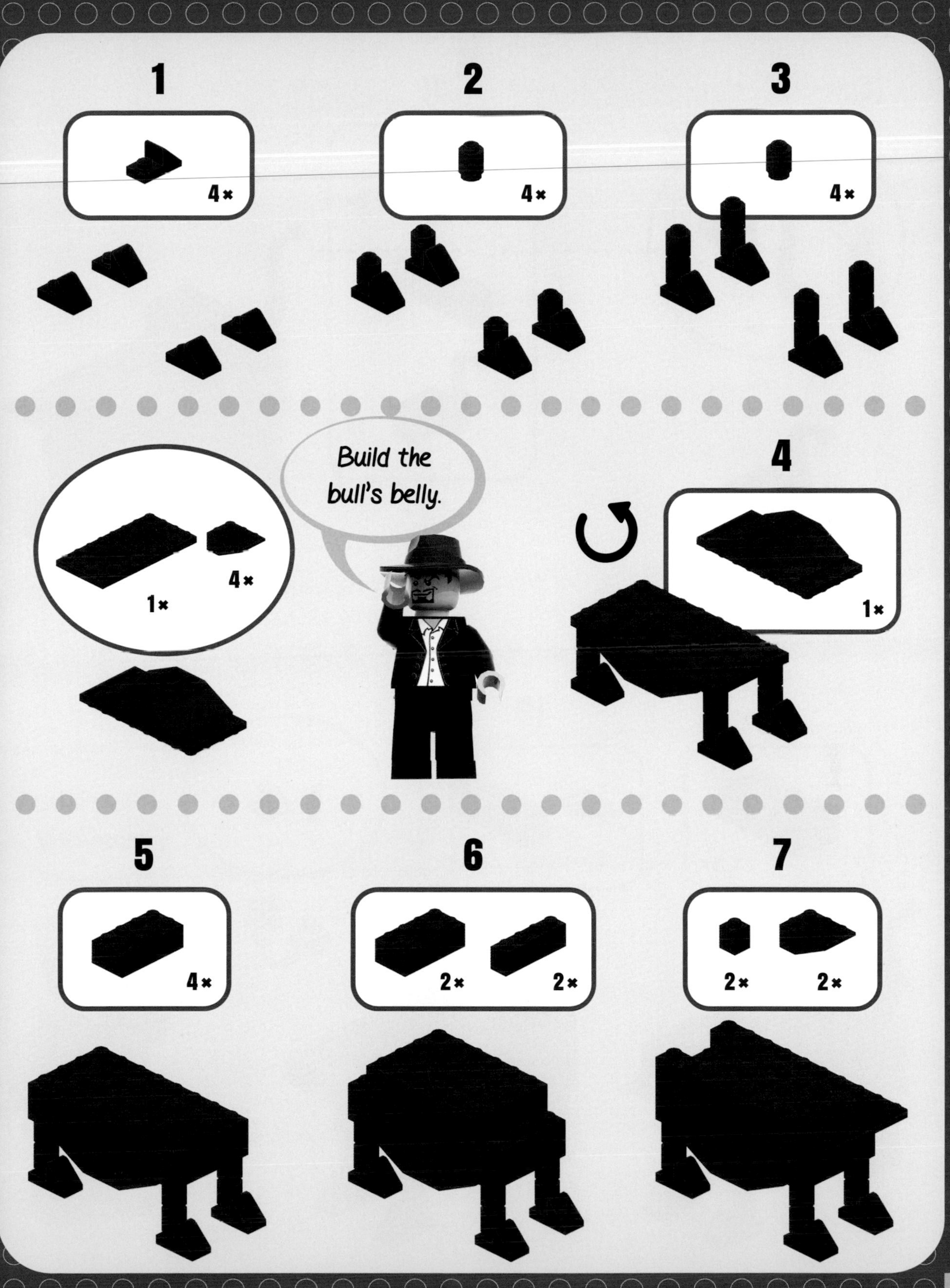
1
4×
2
4×
3
4×
1×
4×
Build the bull's belly.
4
1×
5
4×
6
2×
2×
7
2×
2×

1×
1×
1×
8
2×
1×
1×
9
3×
10
2×
1×
2×
2×
Here's the nose ring!

11
4×
1×
2×
1×
12
2×
4×
13
1×
2×
14
2×
2×
15
2×
2×

HIPPOPOTAMUS

The hippopotamus is a large mammal, and its name comes from the Greek word that means "horse of the river." The hippo doesn't really look like a horse, but it likes to float in the water to rest. Although their big mouths make them look threatening, hippos are peaceful animals when left alone.

Have fun building it!

PARTS LIST

DIFFICULTY

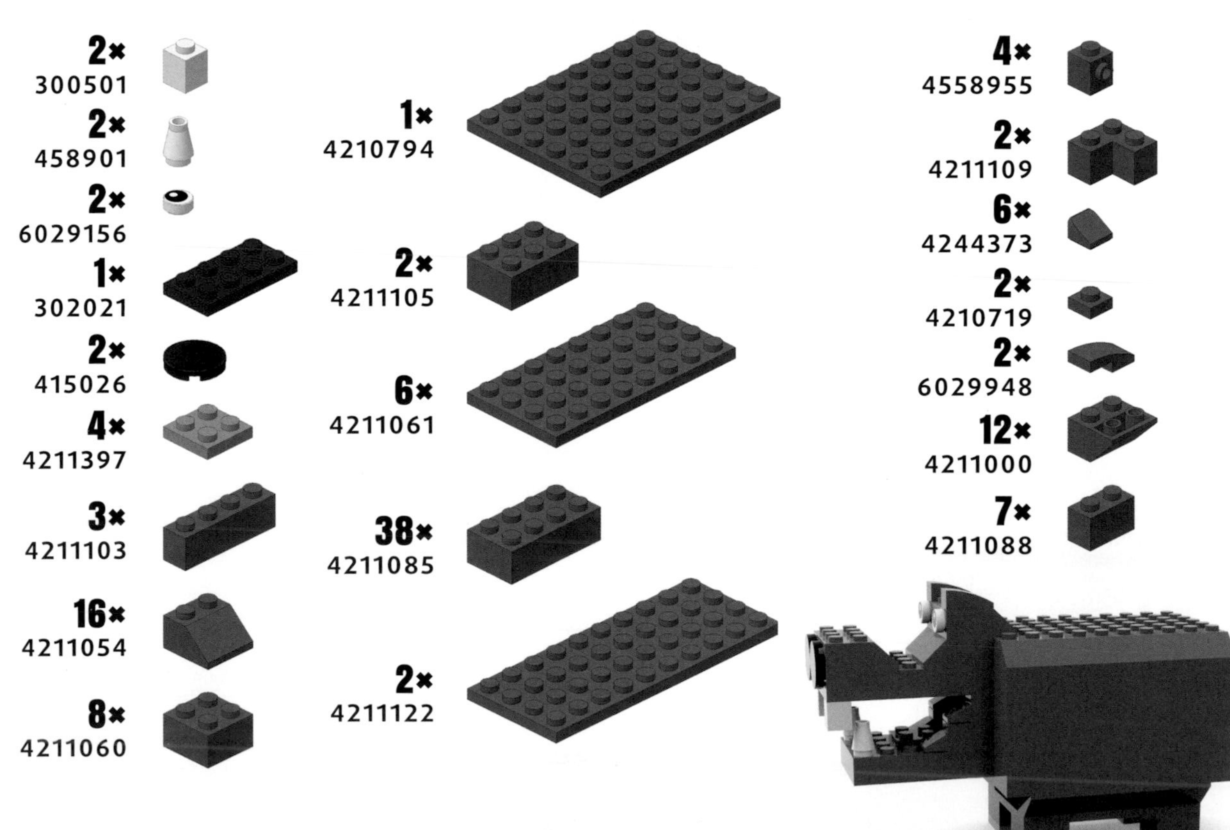

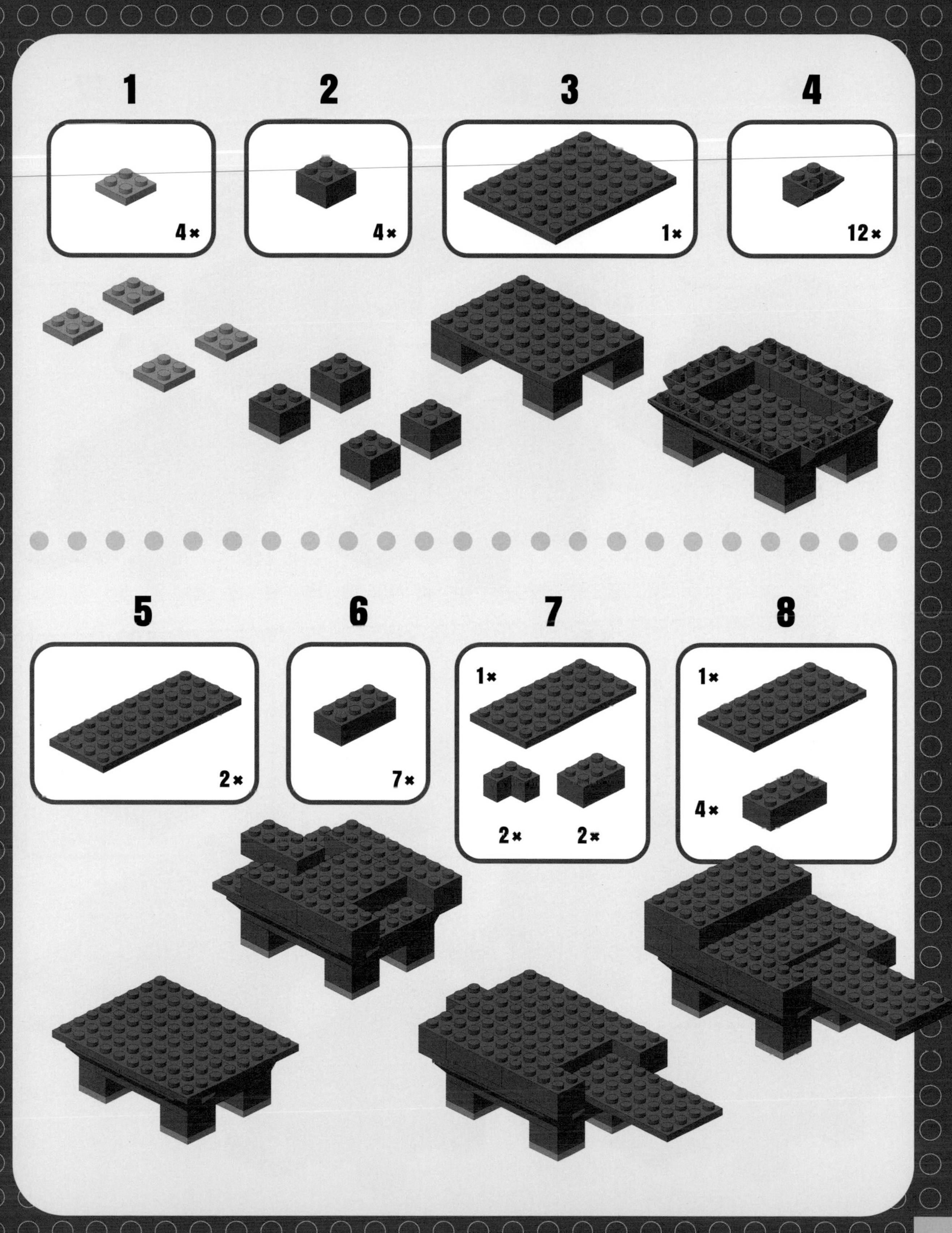
1
4×
2
4×
3
1×
4
12×
5
2×
6
7×
7
1×
2×
2×
8
1×
4×

9
1×
4×
10
2×
2×
1×
2×
2×
11
2×
12
3×
4×
13
1×
2×
4×
14
1×
2×
15
1×
4×
16
2×
4×
1×

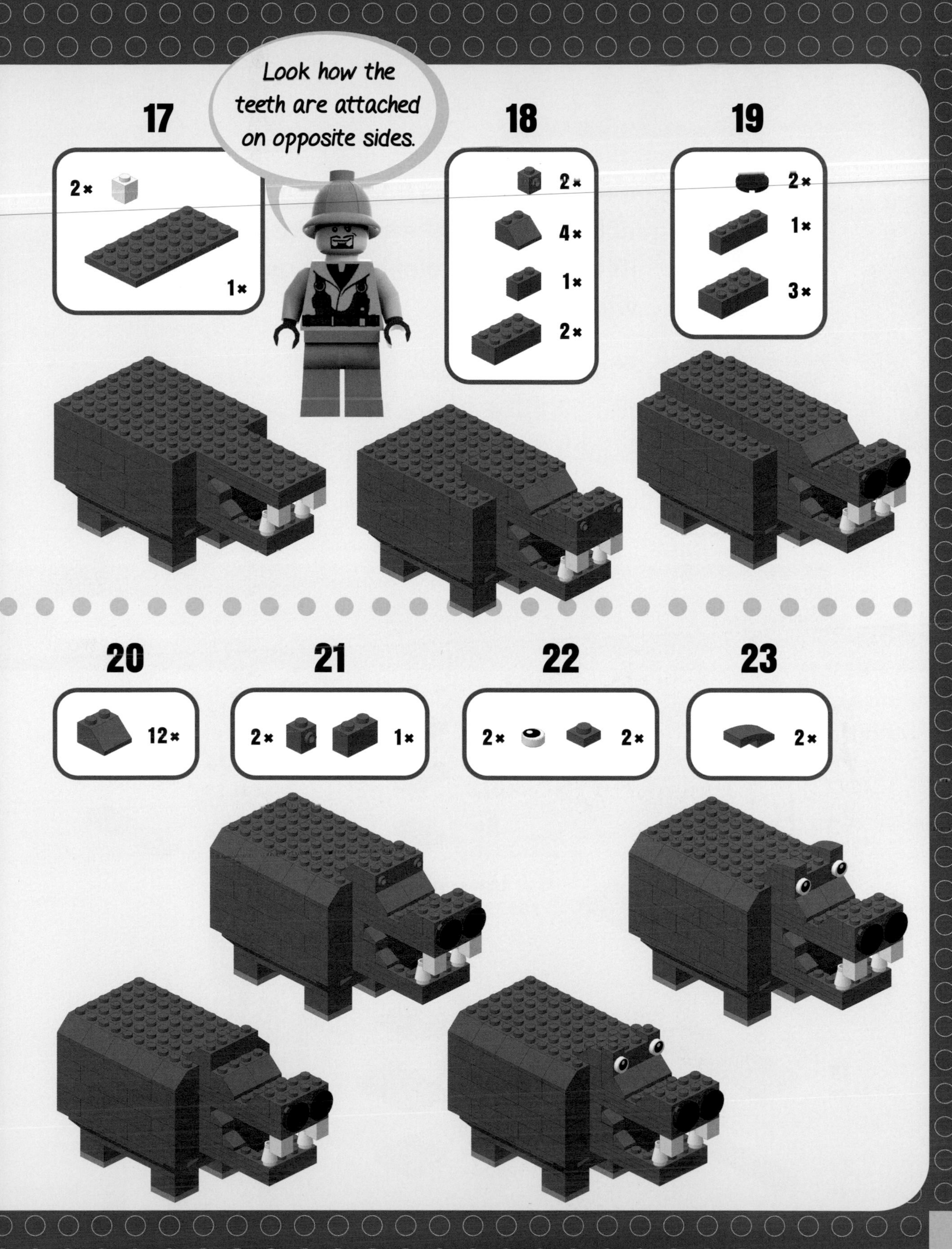

Look how the teeth are attached on opposite sides.
17
2×
1×
18
2×
4×
1×
2×
19
2×
1×
3×
20
12×
21
2×
1×
22
2×
2×
23
2×

PRAYING MANTIS

This insect gets its name from the posture of its front legs, which make it look like it's praying. Its bright green color helps it camouflage with plants.

This model allows you to change the position of the front legs, which attach diagonally to their bases.

PARTS LIST

DIFFICULTY

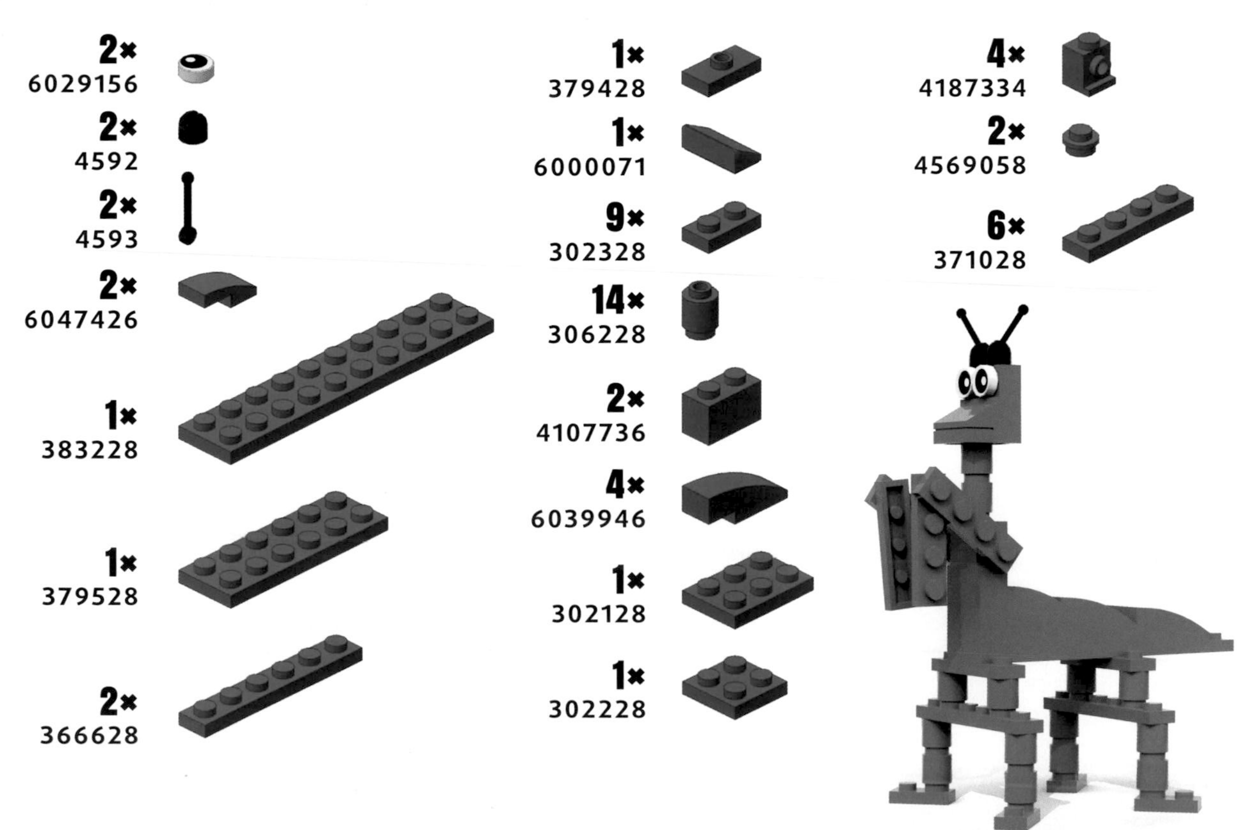

Follow the placement of these parts carefully!
1
4×
2
4×
3
4×
4
2×
5
4×
6
2×

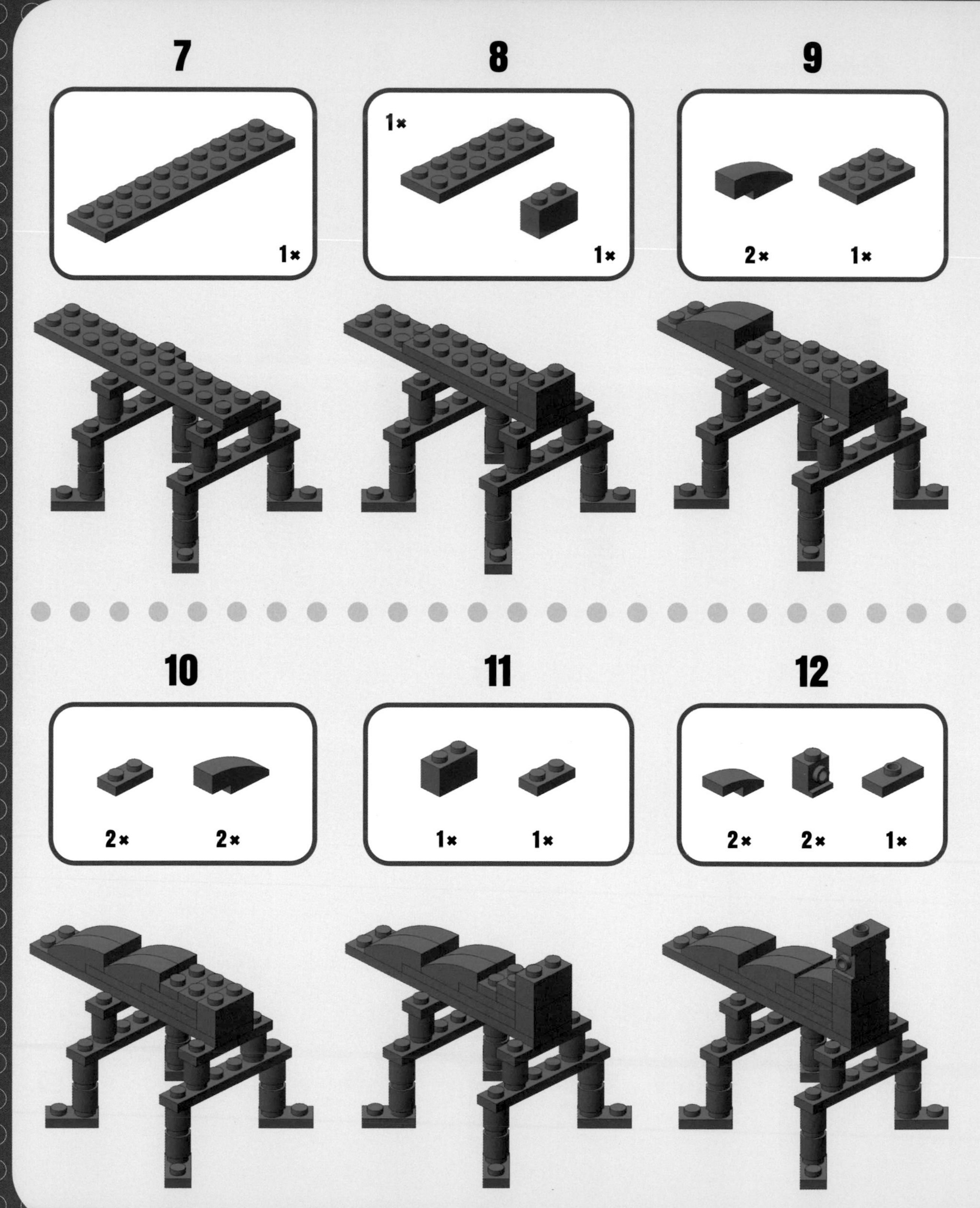
7
1×
8
1×
1×
9
2×
1×
10
2×
2×
11
1×
1×
12
2×
2×
1×

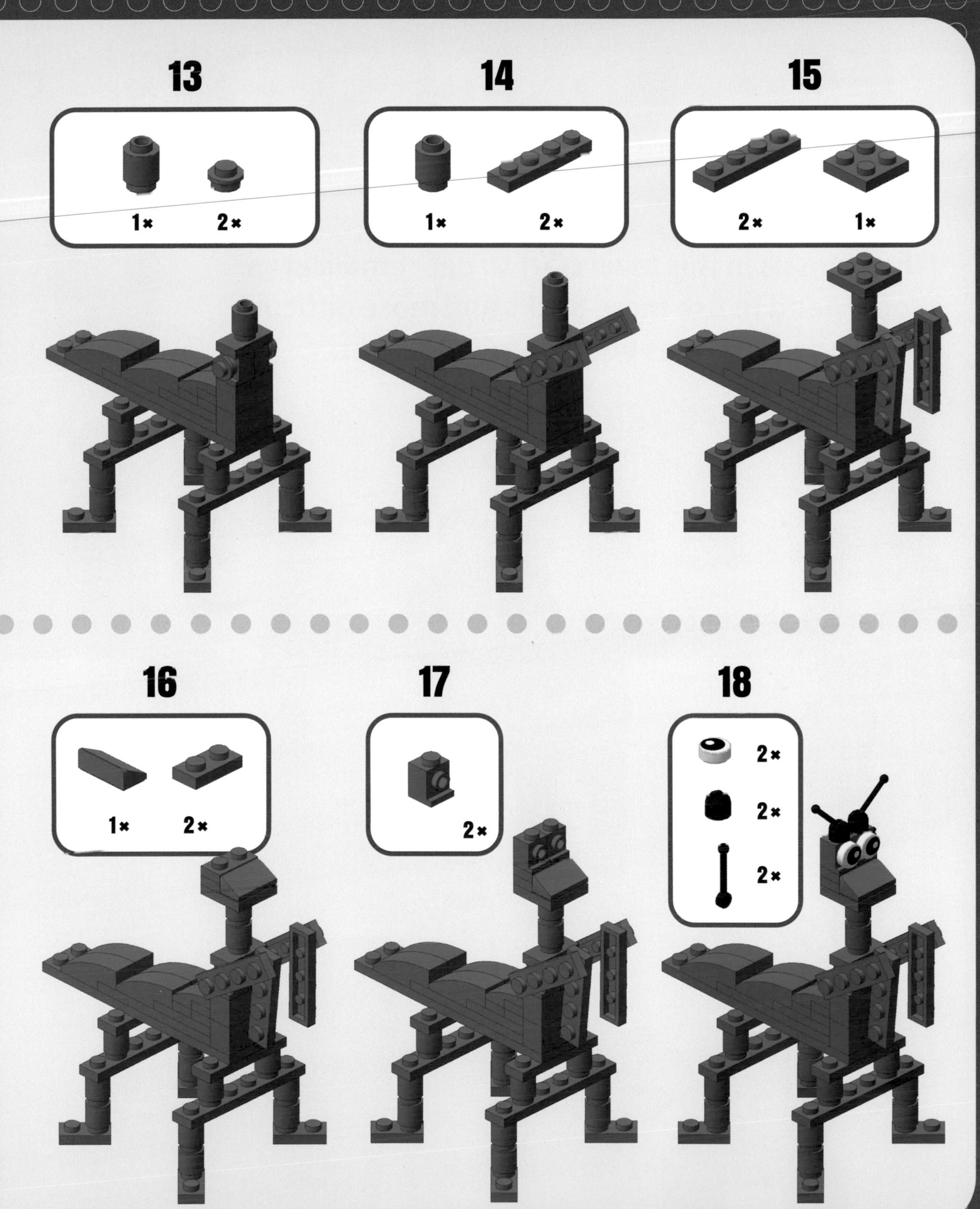
13
1×
2×
14
1×
2×
15
2×
1×
16
1×
2×
17
2×
18
2×
2×
2×

CHAPTER 4

The animals in this level start to get complicated. You'll need to use more bricks and more difficult building techniques you haven't seen yet.

(See page ix for tips on where to find parts!)

KANGAROO

Like the koala, the kangaroo lives in Australia. A kangaroo is a marsupial, which means a female kangaroo has a pouch in her belly that holds her babies until they're old enough to go hopping alone. That's right—the kangaroo gets around by hopping!

Pay attention to the symmetry of arms and ears. You'll do great!

PARTS LIST

DIFFICULTY

2× 6029156
4× 4109995
1× 4118866
1× 302426
1× 614126
4× 4212455
2× 3069
8× 4173805
4× 4121739
1× 4121742
4× 4153827
1× 6224249
1× 4173332
3× 4159007
3× 4158355
2× 4118829
4× 4118828
1× 4542142
4× 4277929
2× 6092599
1× 4648855
4× 4153825
3× 4118782
2× 4125256
2× 4153826
1× 41769
2× 4121741
1× 4177932

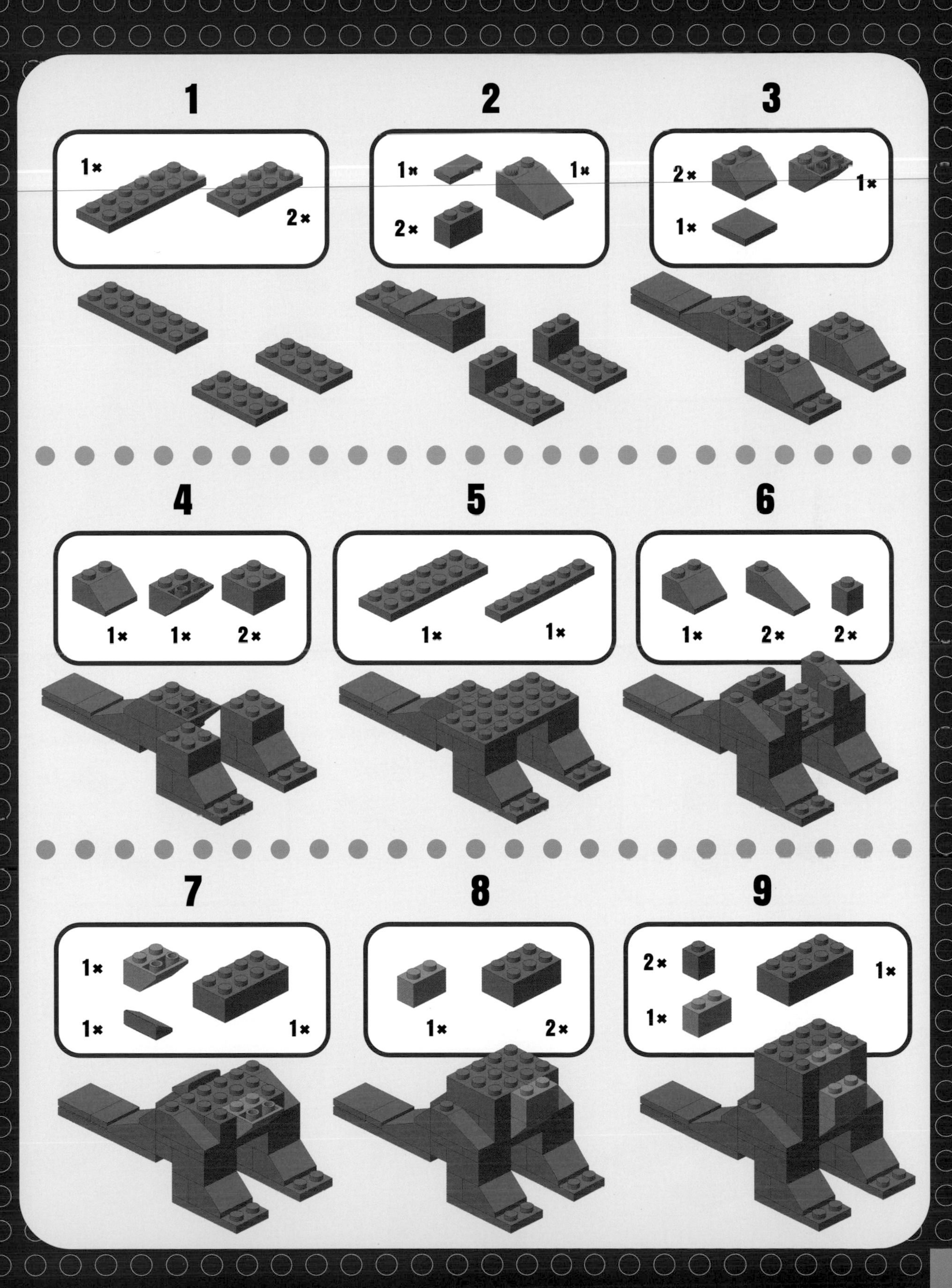
1
1×
2×
2
1×
1×
2×
3
2×
1×
1×
4
1×
1×
2×
5
1×
1×
6
1×
2×
2×
7
1×
1×
1×
8
1×
2×
9
2×
1×
1×

10
1×
1×
1×
2×
11
2×
1×
1×
12
1×
2×
1×
2×
Count the studs on either side to make sure the arms are aligned.
13
1×
1×
3×

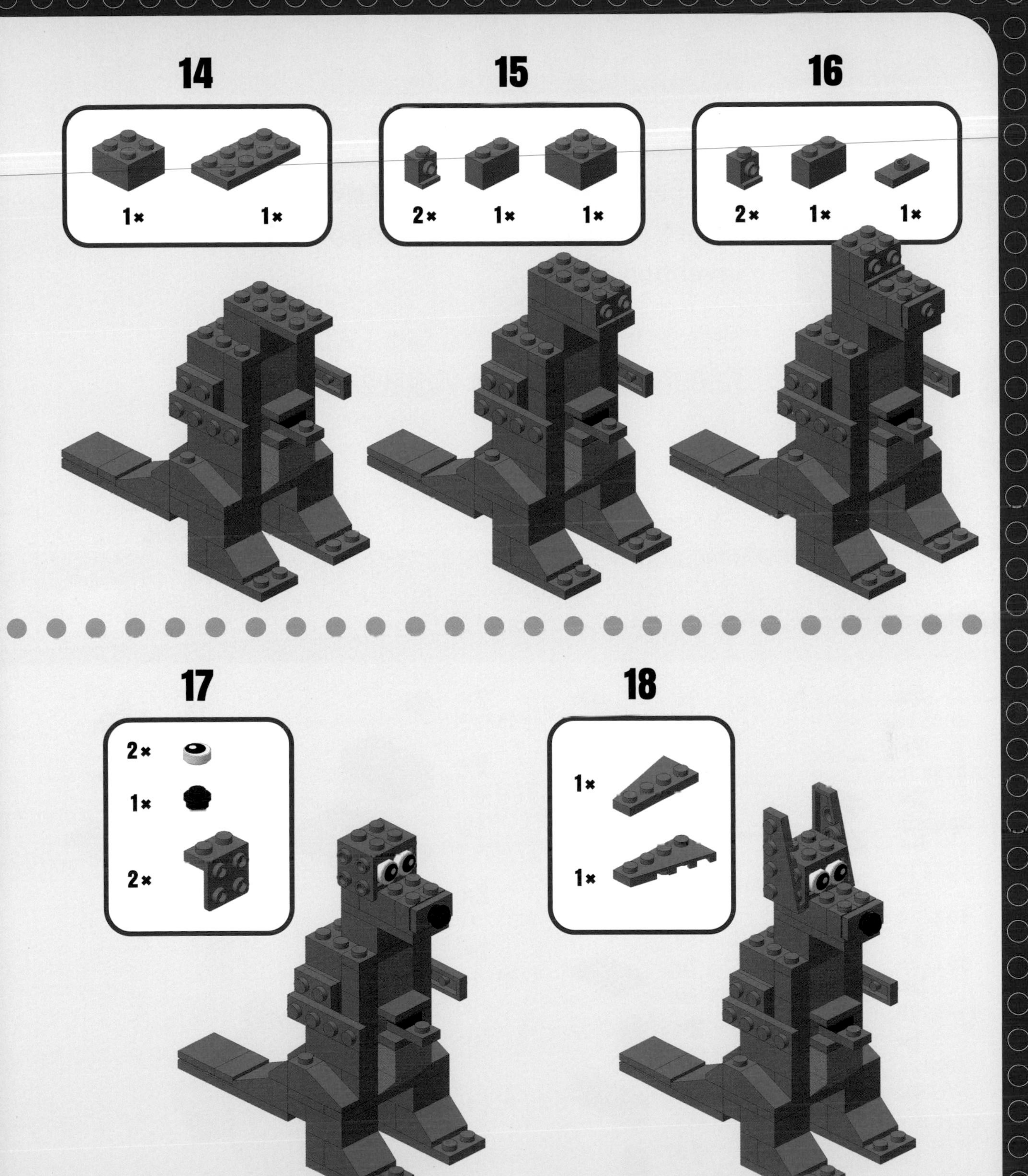
14
1×
1×
15
2×
1×
1×
16
2×
1×
1×
17
2×
1×
2×
18
1×
1×

HORSE

Horses are noble animals that have lived alongside people since the dawn of civilization. In fact, people rode horses long before the invention of cars.

This cute brick horse can't wait for you to build it. What are you waiting for?

PARTS LIST

DIFFICULTY

- 4× 300501
- 2× 6029156
- 3× 306926
- 4× 302426
- 1× 302226
- 2× 302326
- 5× 4548180
- 1× 302126
- 1× 6020193
- 1× 329826
- 2× 301026
- 1× 4211190
- 10× 4211242
- 1× 4211151
- 4× 4211222
- 1× 4211150
- 1× 4211189
- 2× 4618545
- 2× 4211225
- 2× 4225469
- 2× 6075212
- 2× 4260486
- 8× 4211201
- 1× 4271874
- 3× 6035291
- 2× 4221744
- 1× 4216695
- 2× 4211221
- 1× 4211186
- 2× 4211149

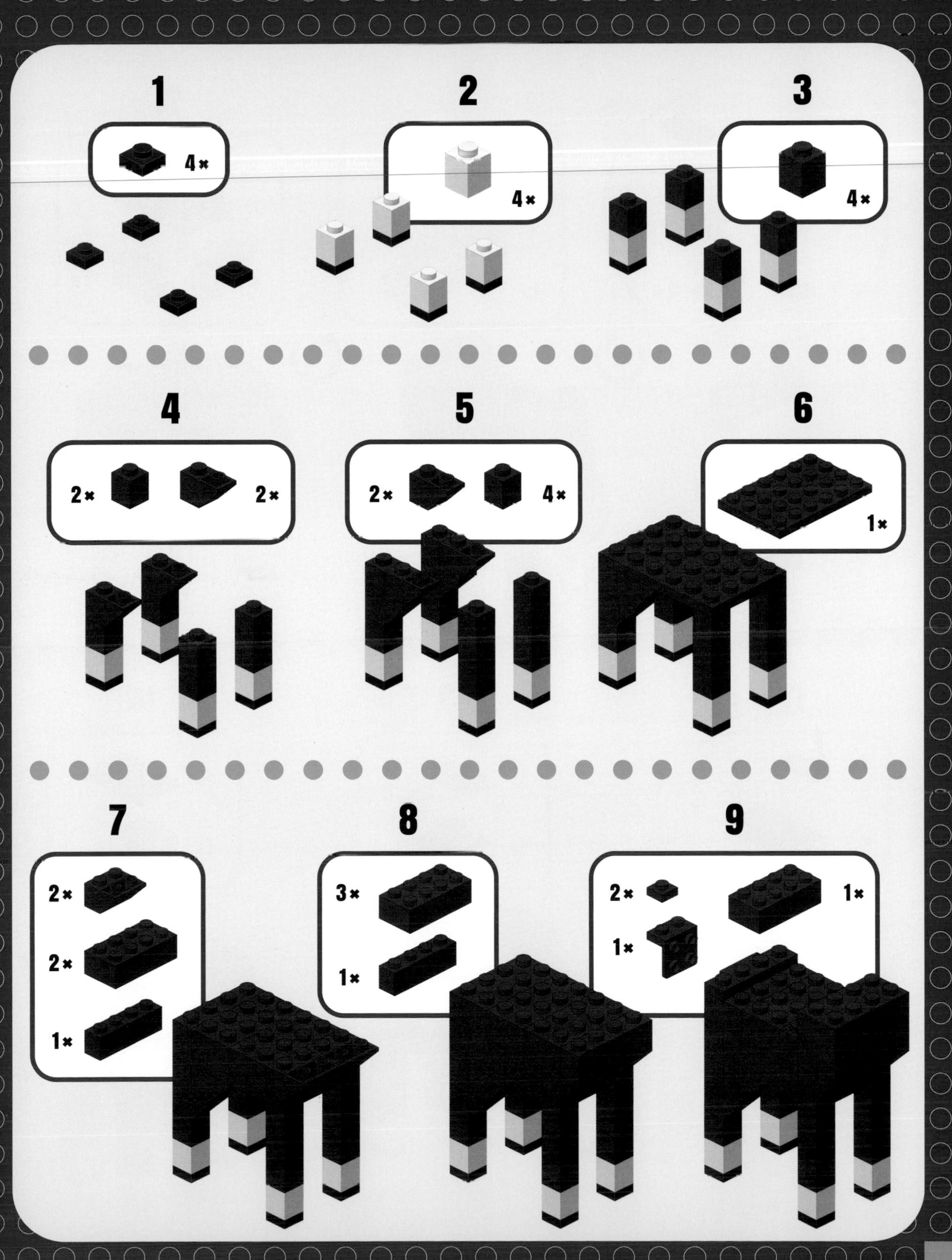
1
4×
2
4×
3
4×
4
2×
2×
5
2×
4×
6
1×
7
2×
2×
1×
8
3×
1×
9
2×
1×
1×

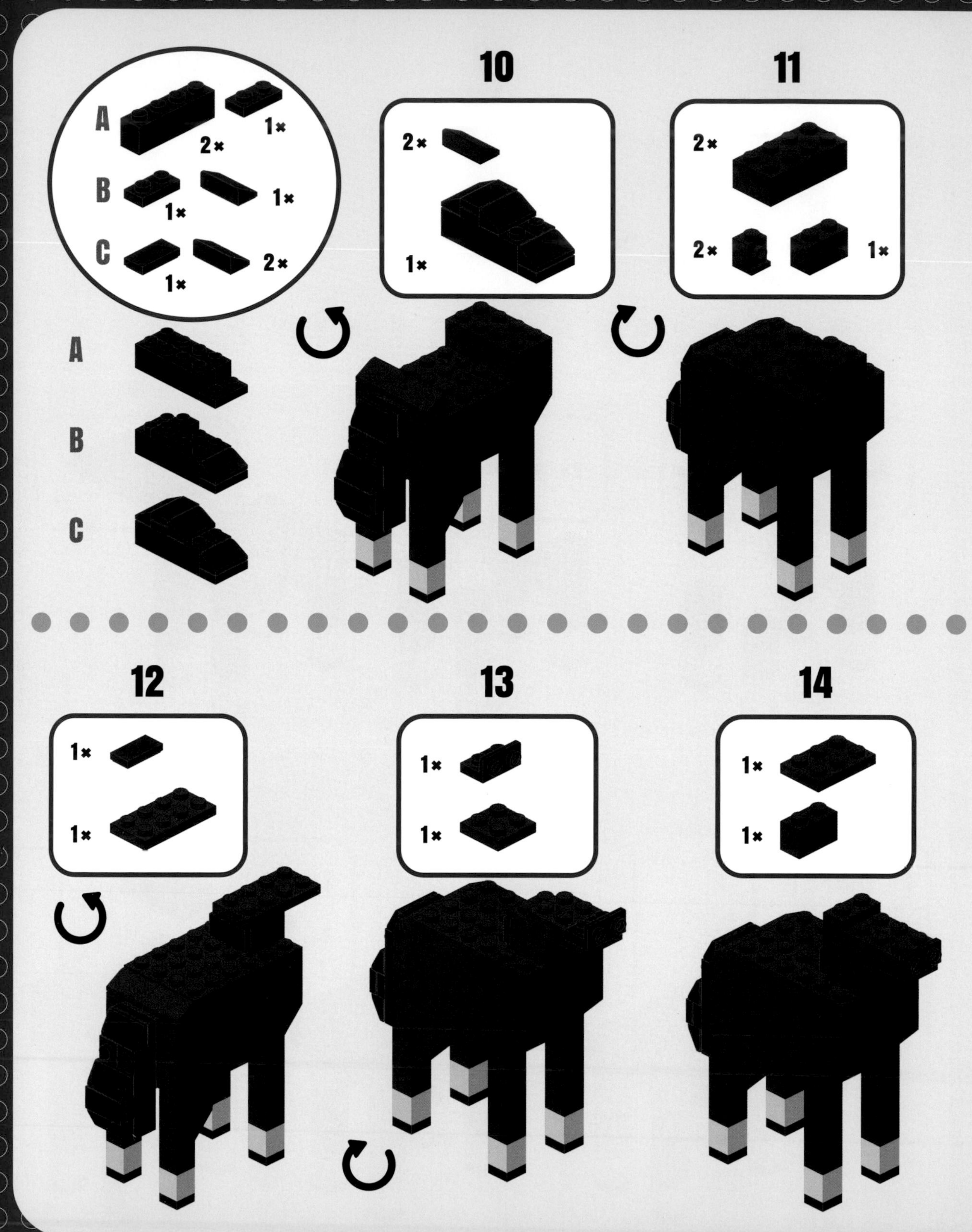
A
2×
1×
B
1×
1×
C
1×
2×
A
B
C
10
2×
1×
11
2×
2×
1×
12
1×
1×
13
1×
1×
14
1×
1×

15
1×
1×
2×
1×
16
1×
1×
1×
1×
Attach the mane to your horse.
17
2×
1×
18
2×
1×
19
1×
2×

DEER

The deer is the prince of the forest. Because of their long, dignified antlers, deer have long represented majesty and royalty. In fact, in the Middle Ages, they were protected animals. This brick version has antlers and spots just like a real deer.

Try making different types of deer with the same bricks!

PARTS LIST

DIFFICULTY

Qty	Part
5×	302301
2×	4515364
2×	255501
2×	300501
2×	302401
2×	6029156
5×	4125253
1×	4113993
1×	4113917
3×	4114306
1×	4155708
7×	4159553
1×	614126
2×	4212455
12×	4173805
2×	4121739
3×	4153827
1×	4295308
3×	4173332
5×	4524929
2×	4219920
2×	4248195
2×	4648855
1×	4153825
2×	4121740
10×	4177932
1×	4125278
4×	4221744

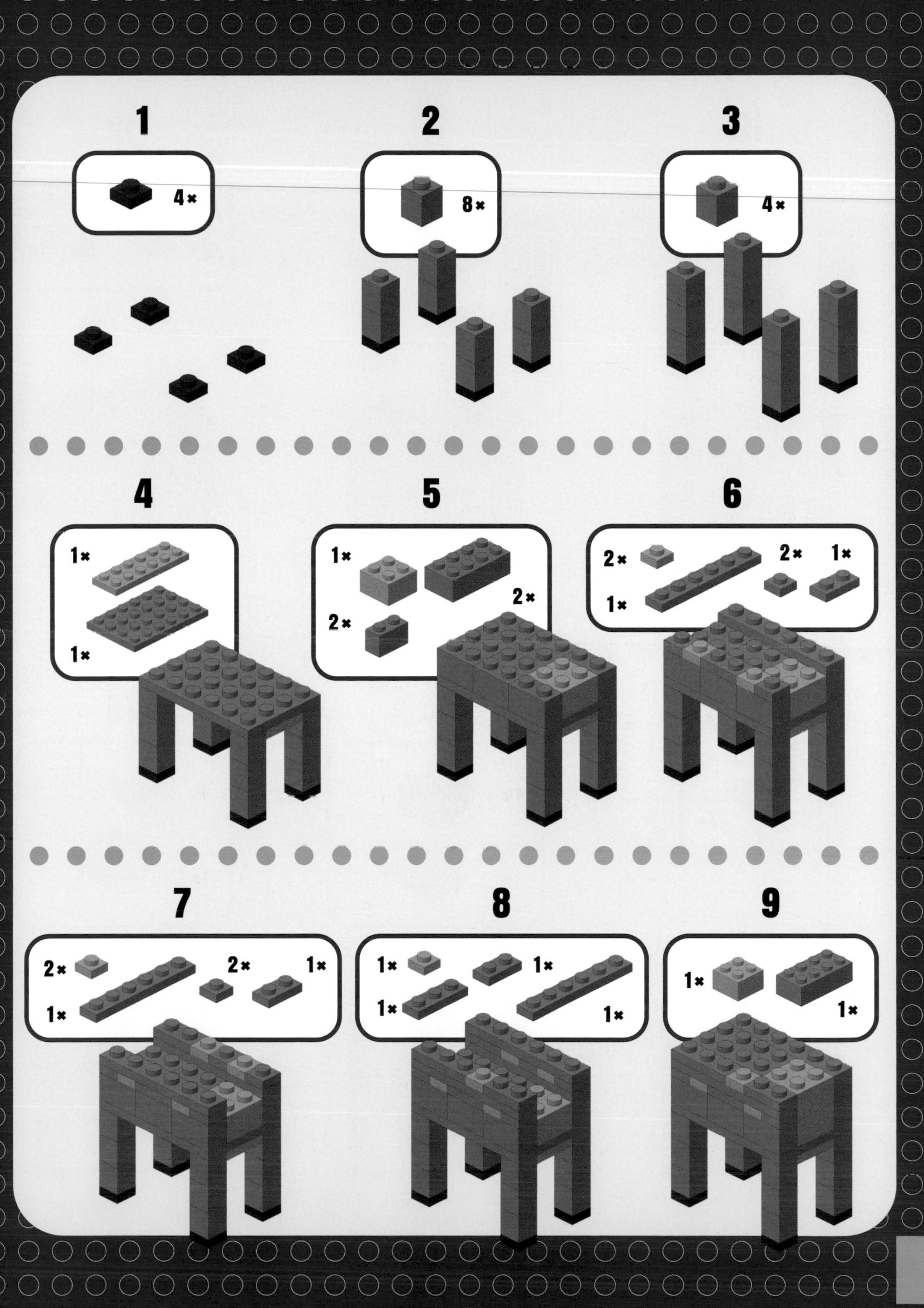

1
4×
2
8×
3
4×
4
1×
1×
5
1×
2×
2×
6
2×
2×
1×
1×
7
2×
2×
1×
1×
8
1×
1×
1×
1×
1×
9
1×
1×

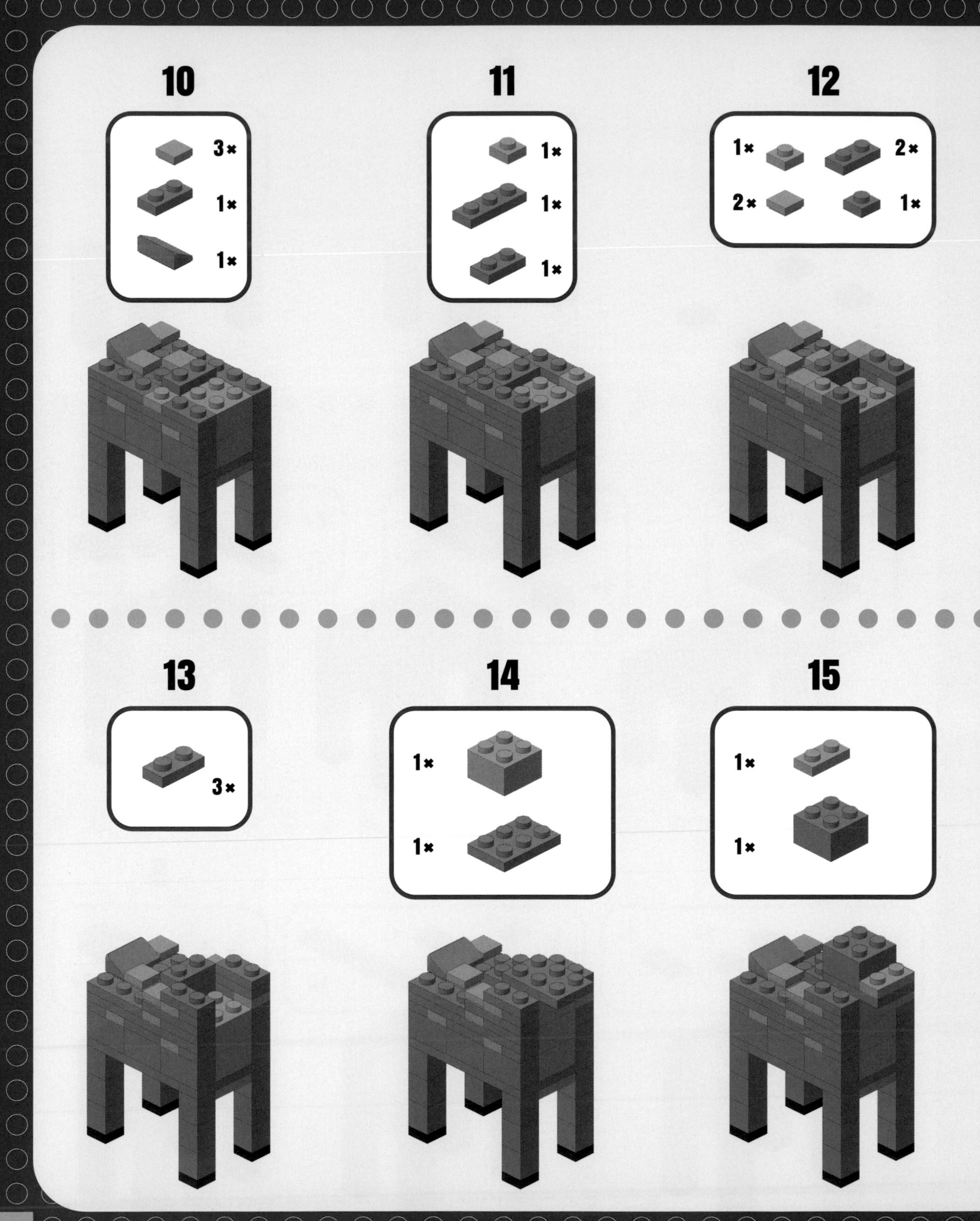
10
3×
1×
1×
11
1×
1×
1×
12
1×
2×
2×
1×
13
3×
14
1×
1×
15
1×
1×

16
1×
2×
2×
17
1×
2×
1×
18
2×
2×
1×
19
2×
20
4×
You can change the angle of the horns!
21
2×
2×

RABBIT

Rabbits are always hungry for carrots. This brick bunny has ears that stick out at different angles.

You'll use two headlight pieces normally used to create the headlights of cars! Can you tell what they're used for in this model?

PARTS LIST

DIFFICULTY

2× 307001
2× 300201
1× 303101
2× 4547489
3× 302301
1× 300401
1× 4203147
2× 4244370
2× 6047220
1× 4124120
2× 306901
4× 300101
1× 366601
1× 379401
1× 302201
1× 6018774
2× 366001
2× 6029156
1× 301001
1× 307021
1× 300426
4× 4567887
2× 4210635
4× 6029948
8× 4211063
2× 4211043
4× 4210797
2× 4211044
7× 4211052
2× 4211060
2× 6071261
1× 4210997
1× 4211056
2× 4211094
2× 4211065

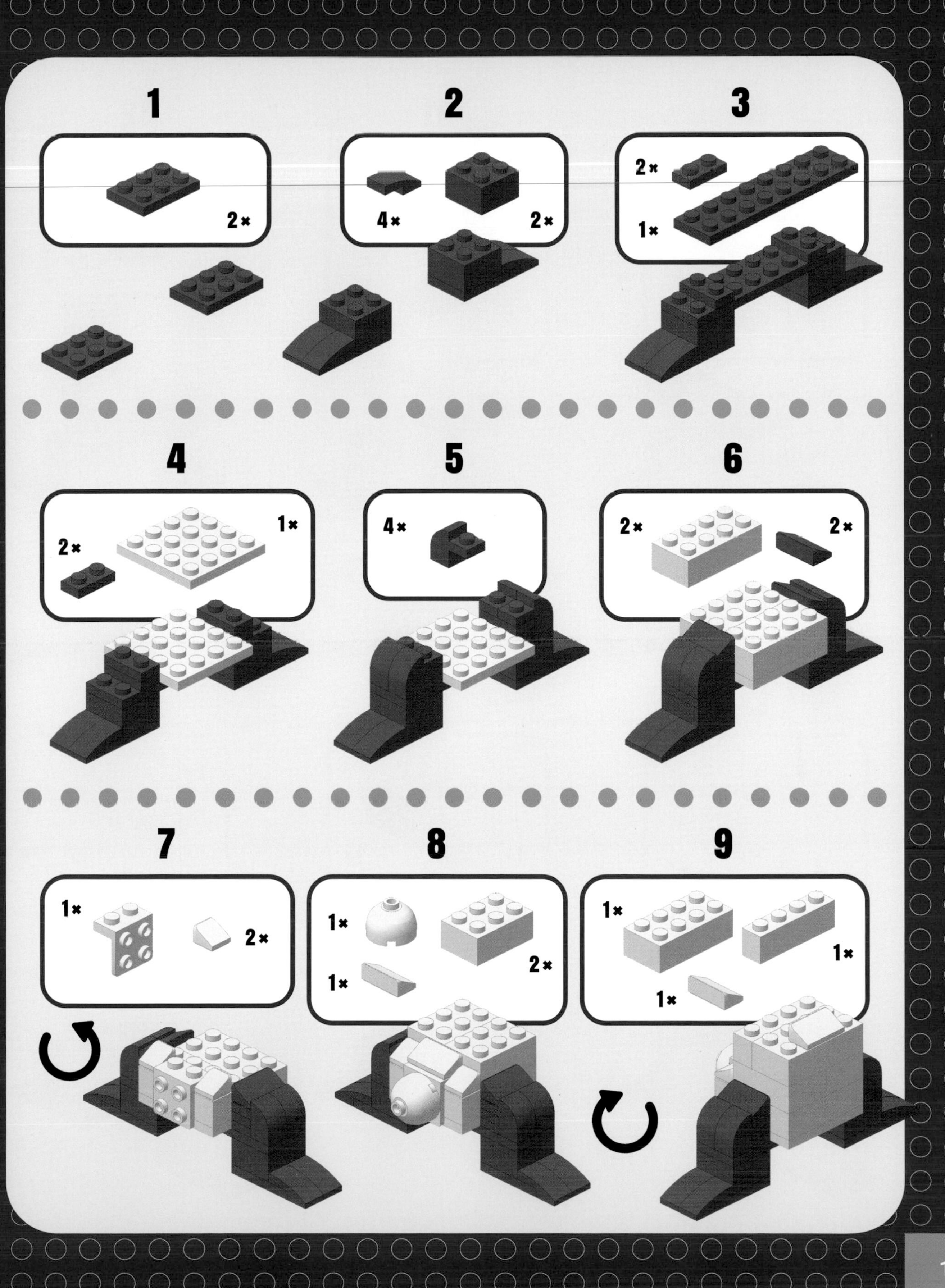
1
2×
2
4×
2×
3
2×
1×
4
1×
2×
5
4×
6
2×
2×
7
1×
2×
8
1×
2×
1×
9
1×
1×
1×

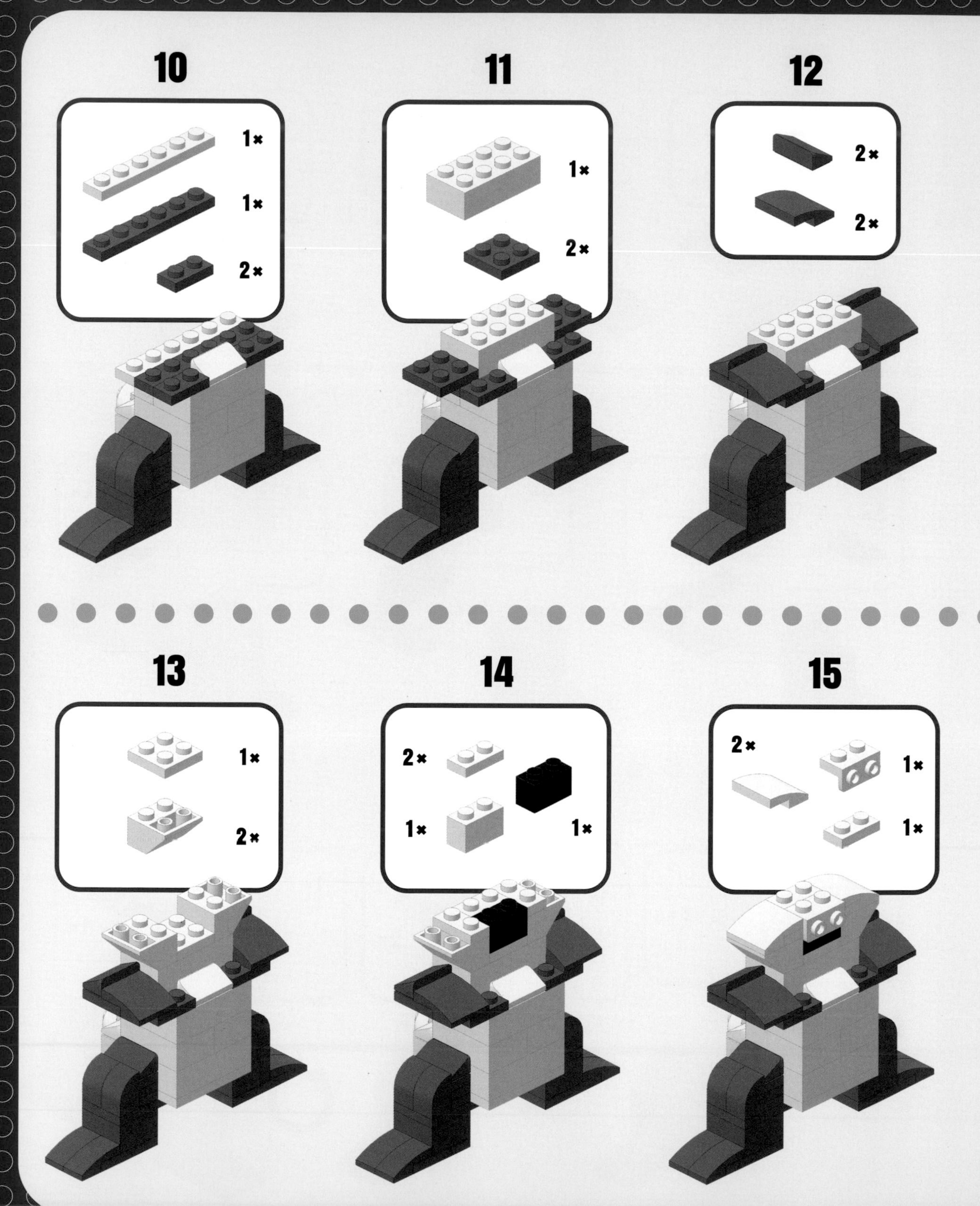
10
1×
1×
2×
11
1×
2×
12
2×
2×
13
1×
2×
14
2×
1×
1×
15
2×
1×
1×

16
2×
1×
17
1×
1×
1×
18
2×
2×
19
2×
1×
2×
20
2×
6×
This is how we build the bunny's ears!

FLAMINGO

The flamingo is a colorful and bizarre animal with bright pink feathers. You may have seen it in *Alice in Wonderland*. This model stands in a flamingo's typical pose with intertwined legs you can adjust.

You might have to place it on a baseplate for stability, but in reality flamingos don't need any support—they can stand like this for hours!

PARTS LIST

DIFFICULTY

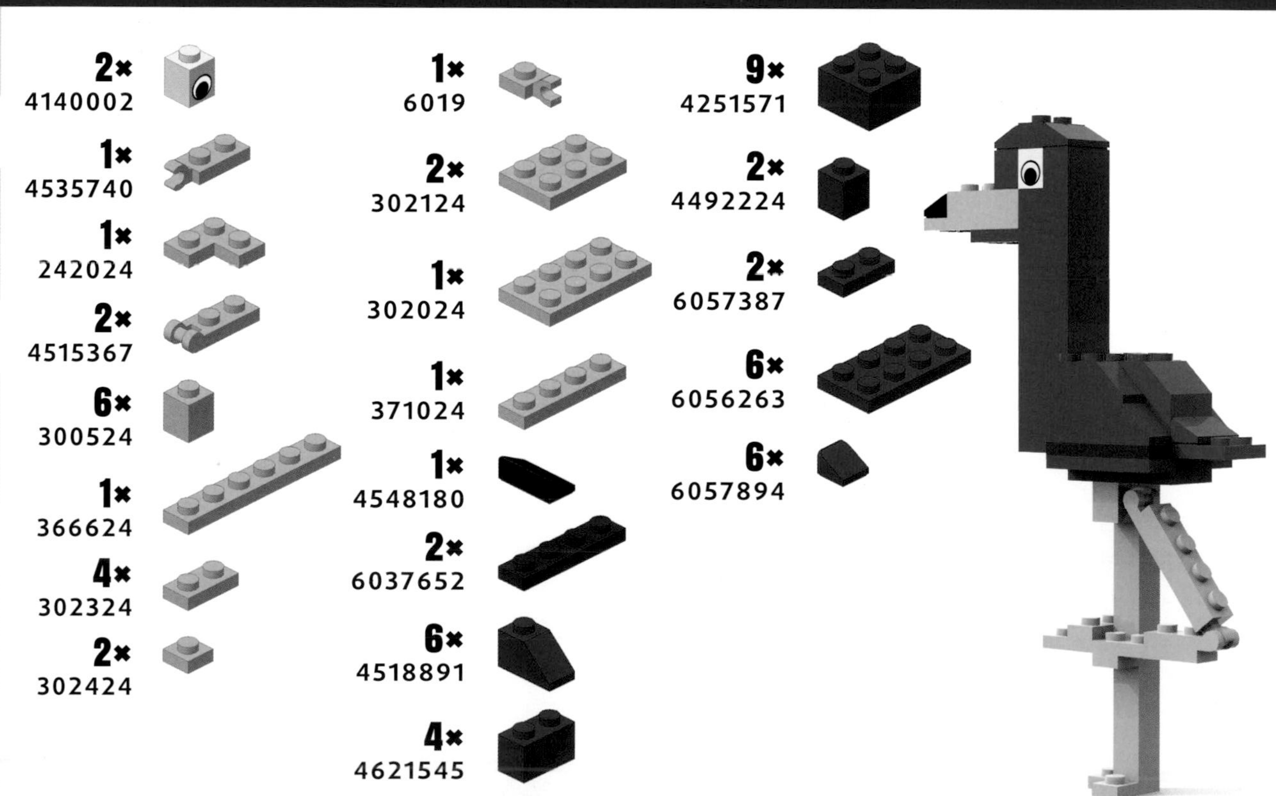

1
1×
3×
2
2×
1×
3
1×
1×
1×
A
1×
1×
1×
B
1×
1×
1×
C
1×
1×
1×
4
1×
5
1×
This baseplate helps support the flamingo's body.

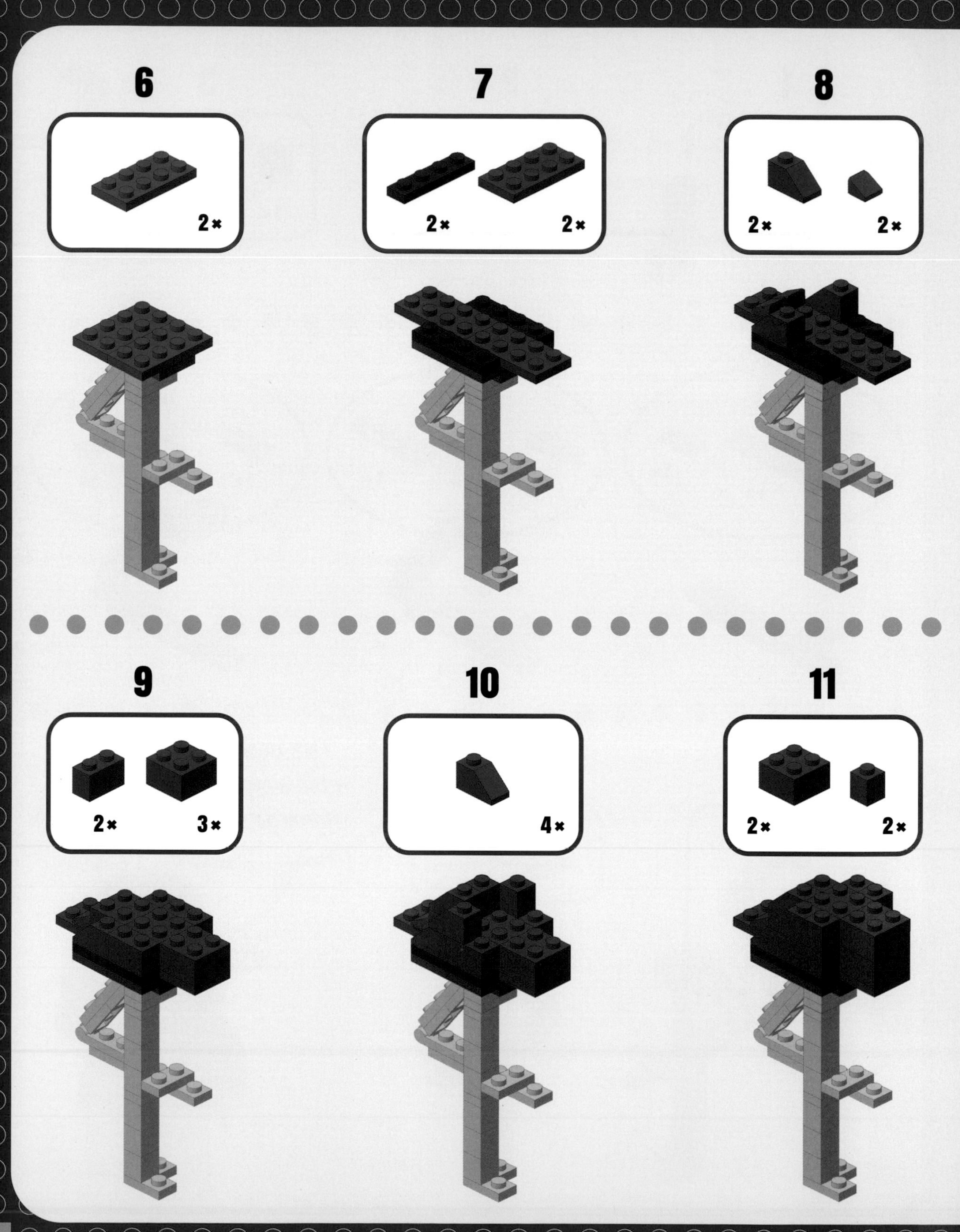
6
2×
7
2×
2×
8
2×
2×
9
2×
3×
10
4×
11
2×
2×

12

3×

13

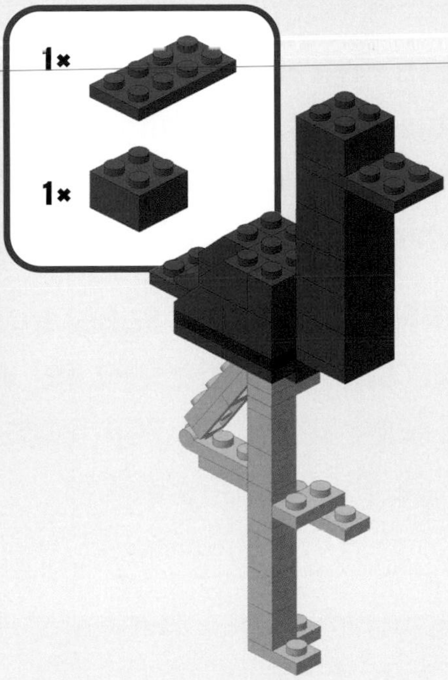

1×

1×

14

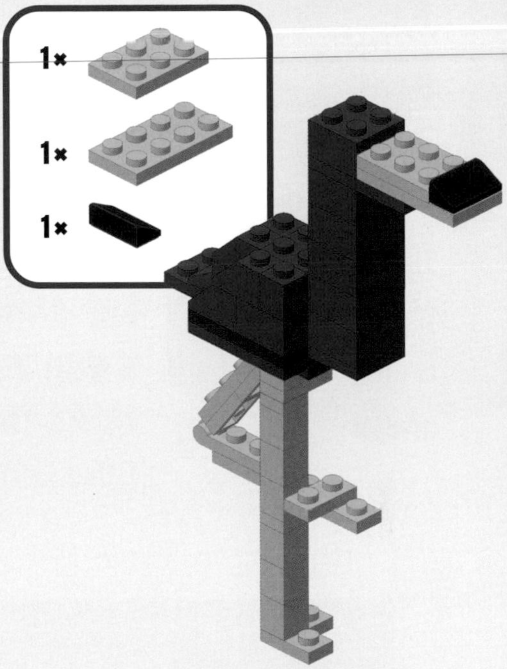

1×

1×

1×

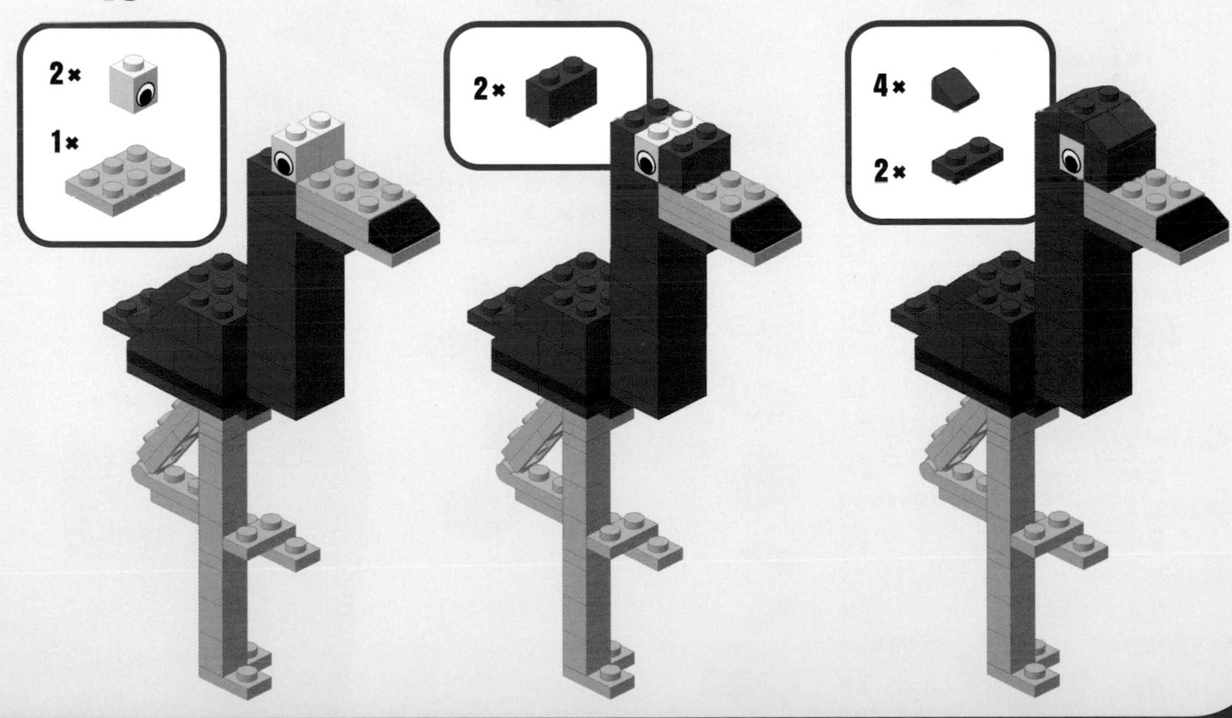

KOALA

This iconic Australian animal loves munching on eucalyptus leaves. Like kangaroos, female koalas carry their young with them wherever they go, which you can see in this model!

For stability, place your koala on a base. If you have other brown bricks, you can make the tree as tall as you want—the only limit is your imagination!

PARTS LIST

DIFFICULTY

2× 302401
1× 306926
4× 302426
1× 4558170
4× 4211190
24× 4211201
1× 4211451
4× 6028813
2× 4211353
2× 4558953
4× 4211385

1× 4211407
2× 4211349
6× 4211399
1× 4211397
2× 4211436
1× 4211395
2× 4211054
1× 4211119
2× 4567887
1× 4211105

1× 4211061
1× 4211089
4× 6029948
5× 4211063
3× 4211043
2× 4211044
2× 4211060

8× 4210997
31× 4211085
6× 4210719
4× 4211000

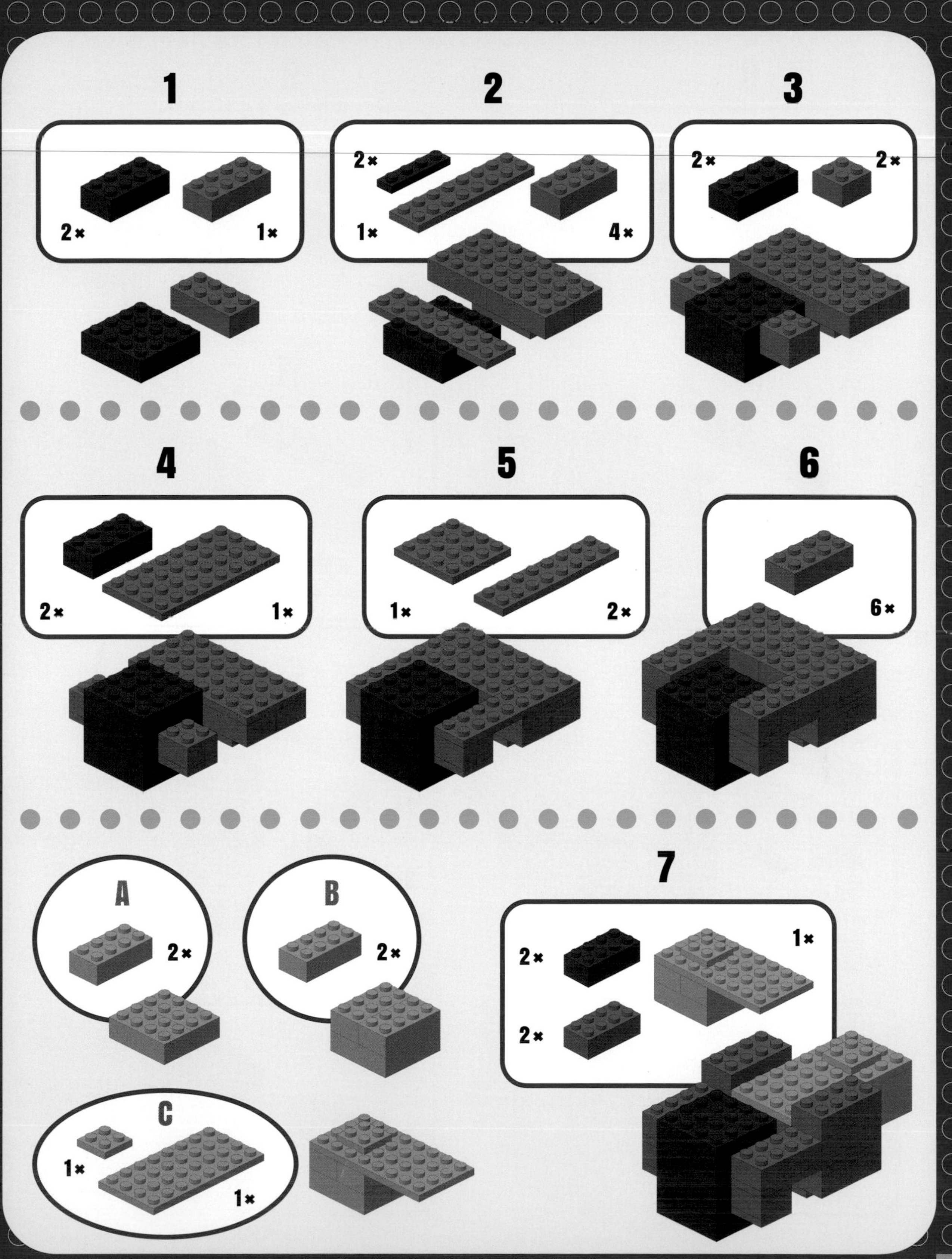
1
2×
1×
2
2×
1×
4×
3
2×
2×
4
2×
1×
5
1×
2×
6
6×
A
2×
B
2×
C
1×
1×
7
2×
1×
2×

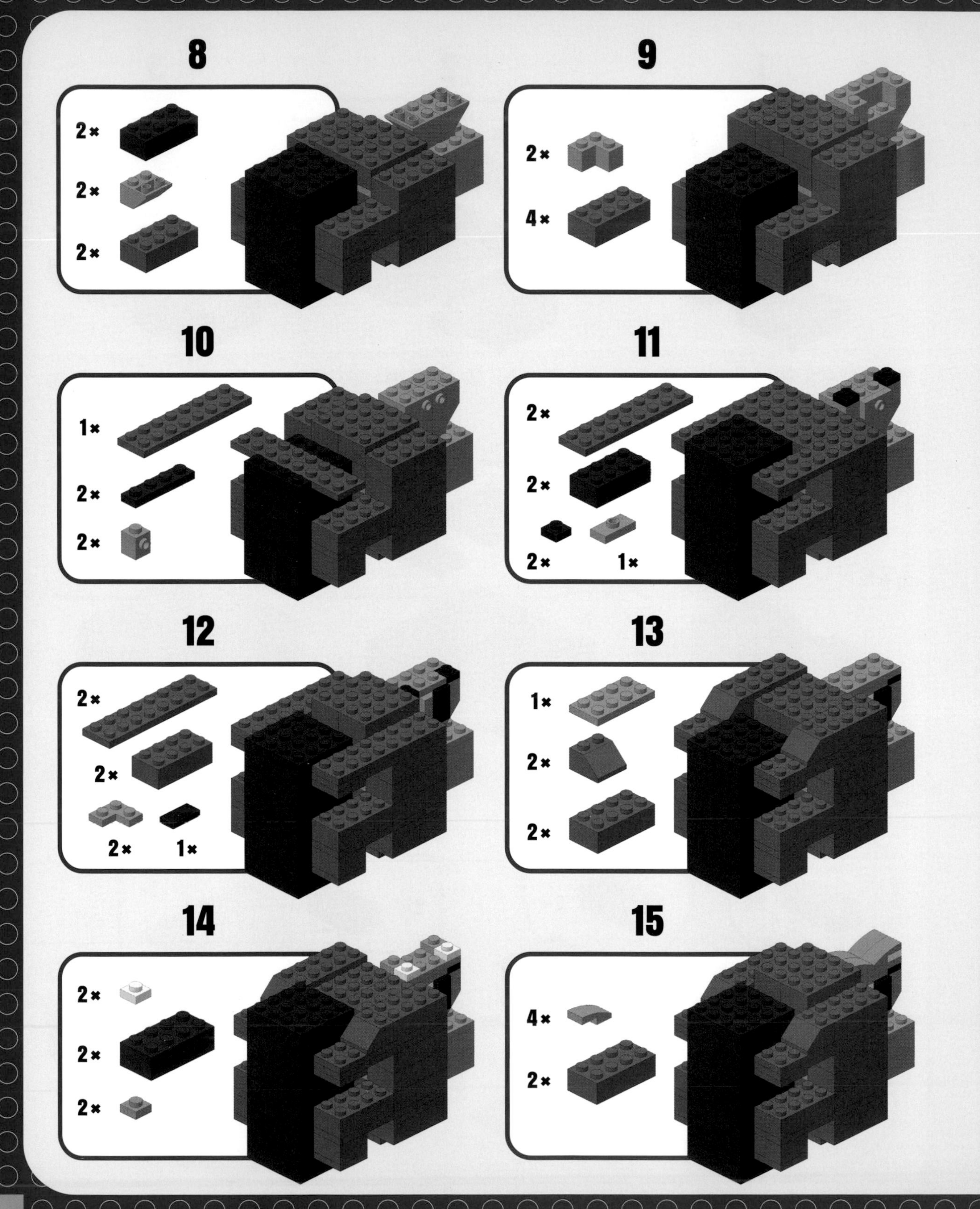
8
2×
2×
2×
9
2×
4×
10
1×
2×
2×
11
2×
2×
2×
1×
12
2×
2×
2×
1×
13
1×
2×
2×
14
2×
2×
2×
15
4×
2×

Count the studs on either side to make sure the arms are aligned.
16
2×
4×
1×
17
2×
1×
2×
2×
18
2×
2×
1×
1×
3×
19
1×
2×
3×
20
2×
2×
4×
21
2×
2×
2×
22
2×
4×
2×

COW

Moooo says the cow! To build this animal, you'll attach the tiles laterally, on top, and also on each side of its head. We use this technique to distinguish one part of the cow from another.

Change the positions of the tiles to create different spots for your cow!

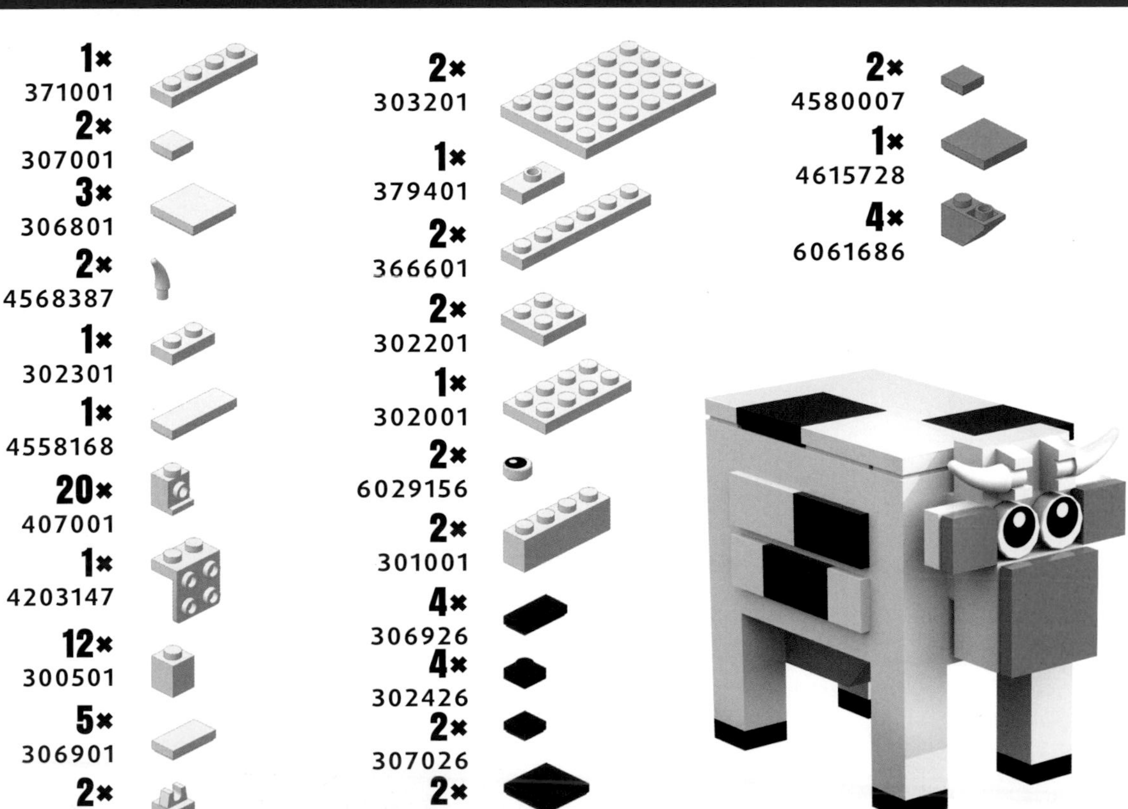

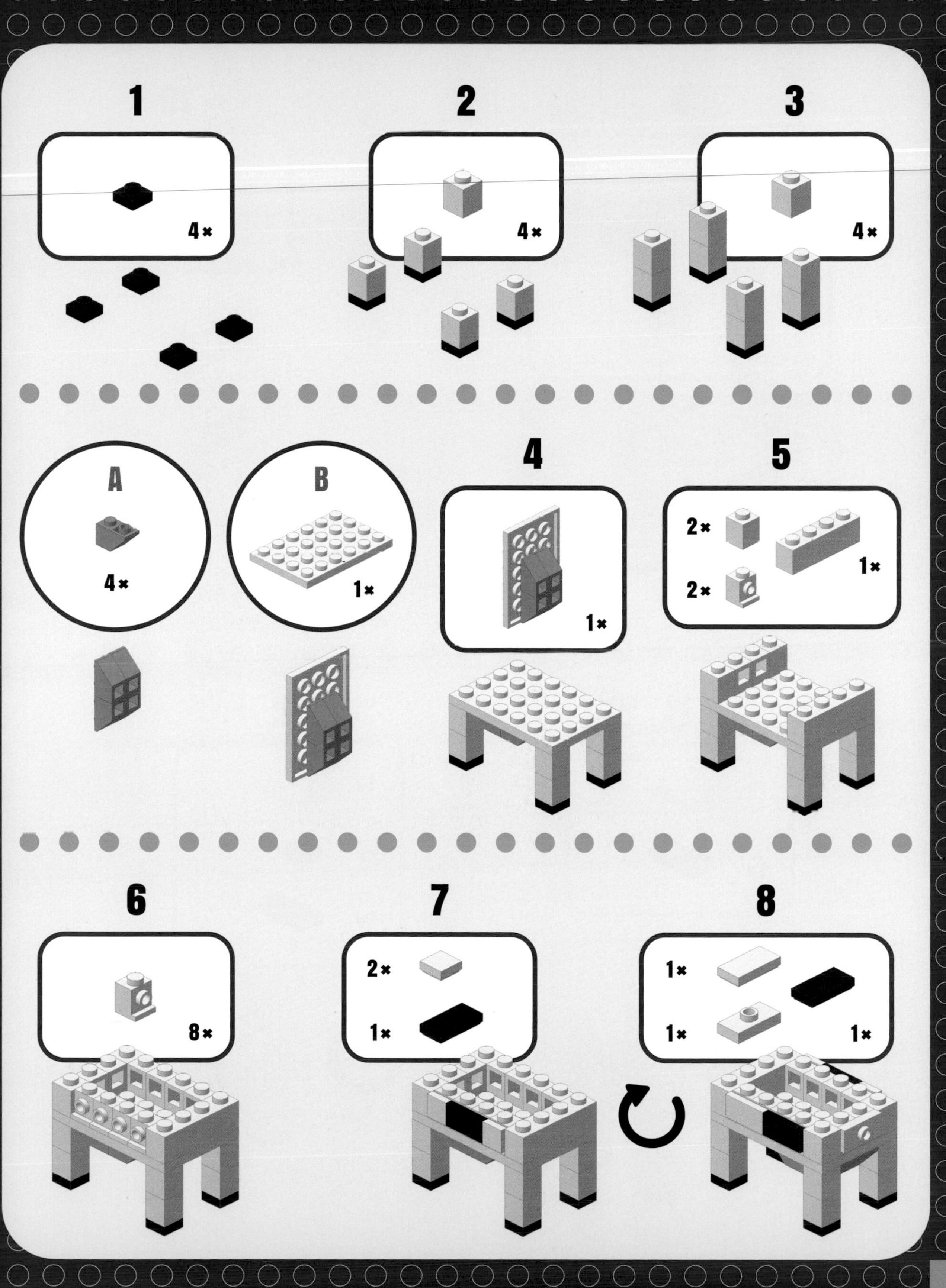
1
4×
2
4×
3
4×
A
4×
B
1×
4
1×
5
2×
1×
2×
6
8×
7
2×
1×
8
1×
1×
1×
1×

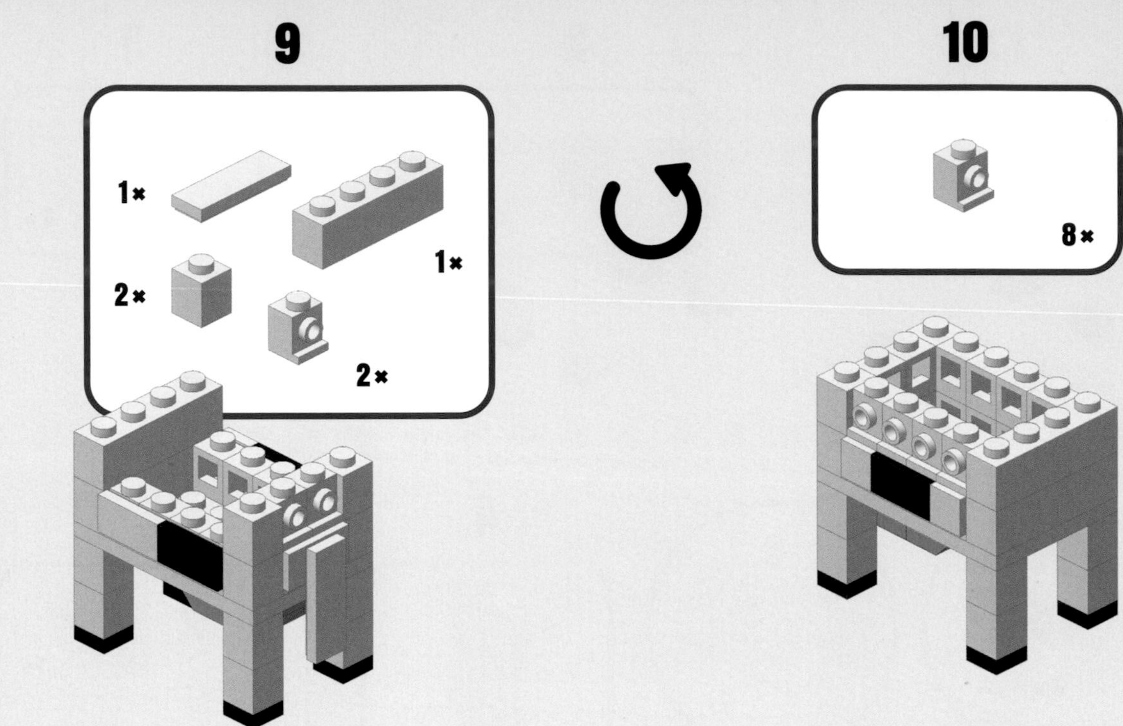
9
1×
1×
2×
2×
10
8×

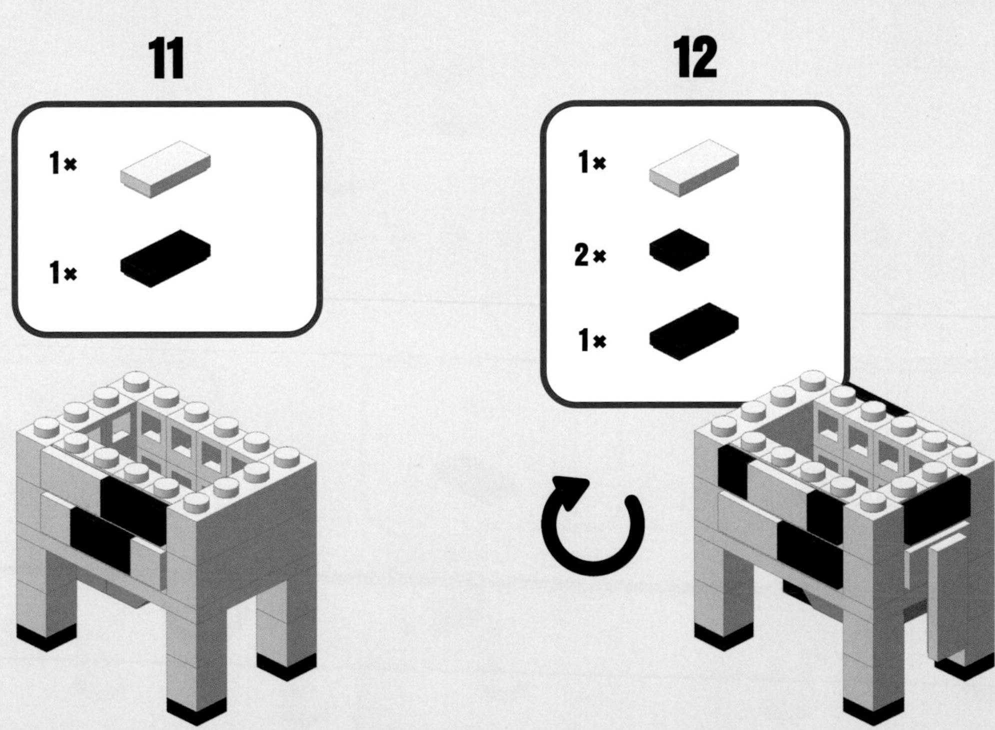
11
1×
1×
12
1×
2×
1×

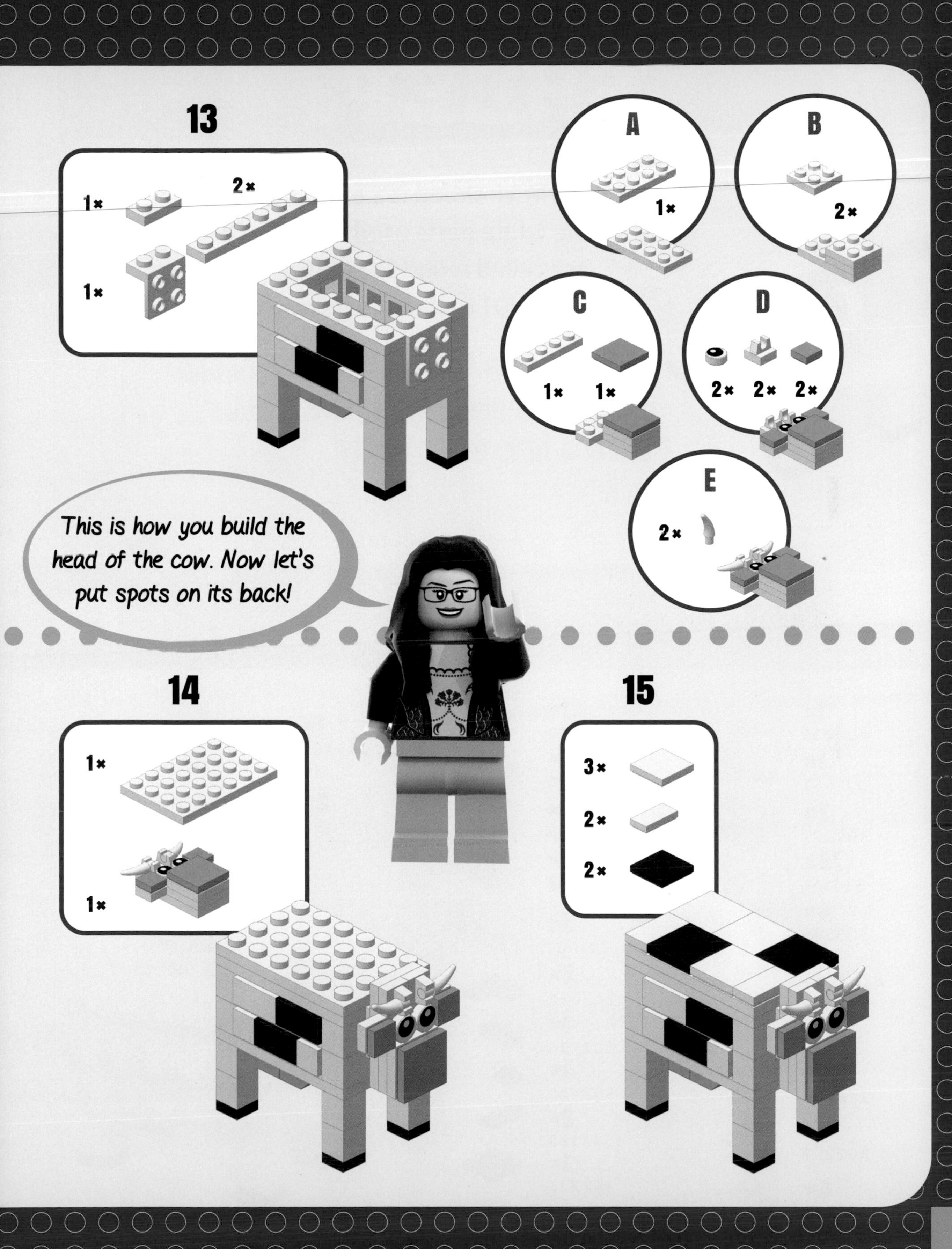
13
1×
2×
1×
A
1×
B
2×
C
1×
1×
D
2×
2×
2×
E
2×
This is how you build the head of the cow. Now let's put spots on its back!
14
1×
1×
15
3×
2×
2×

SHEEP

This brick sheep is a bit more complex. The white parts used to make its wool are called round 1×1 plates. You'll use the SNOT technique throughout.

See how the stud of each round plate fits perfectly in the middle between four other studs.

PARTS LIST

DIFFICULTY

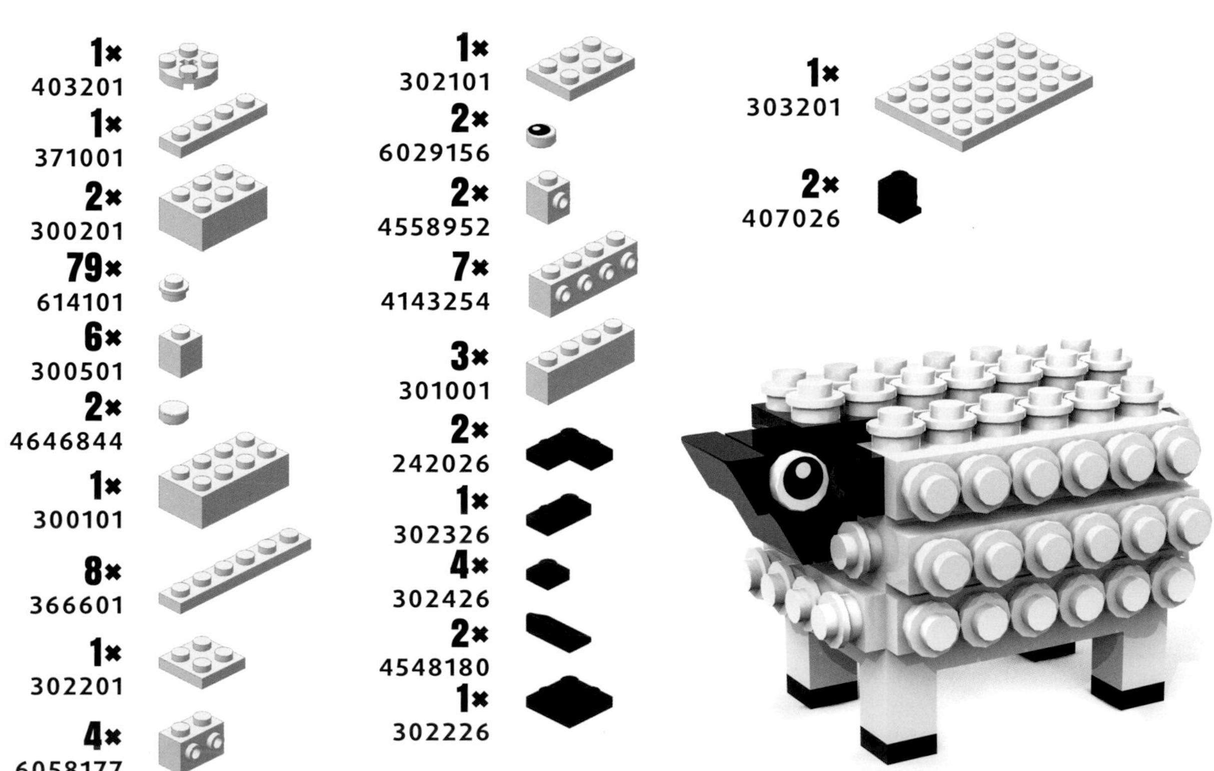

1
4×
2
4×
3
1×
4
1×
3×
Make sure each side looks like the other!
5
1×
1×
1×
6
2×
7
8×
8
12×

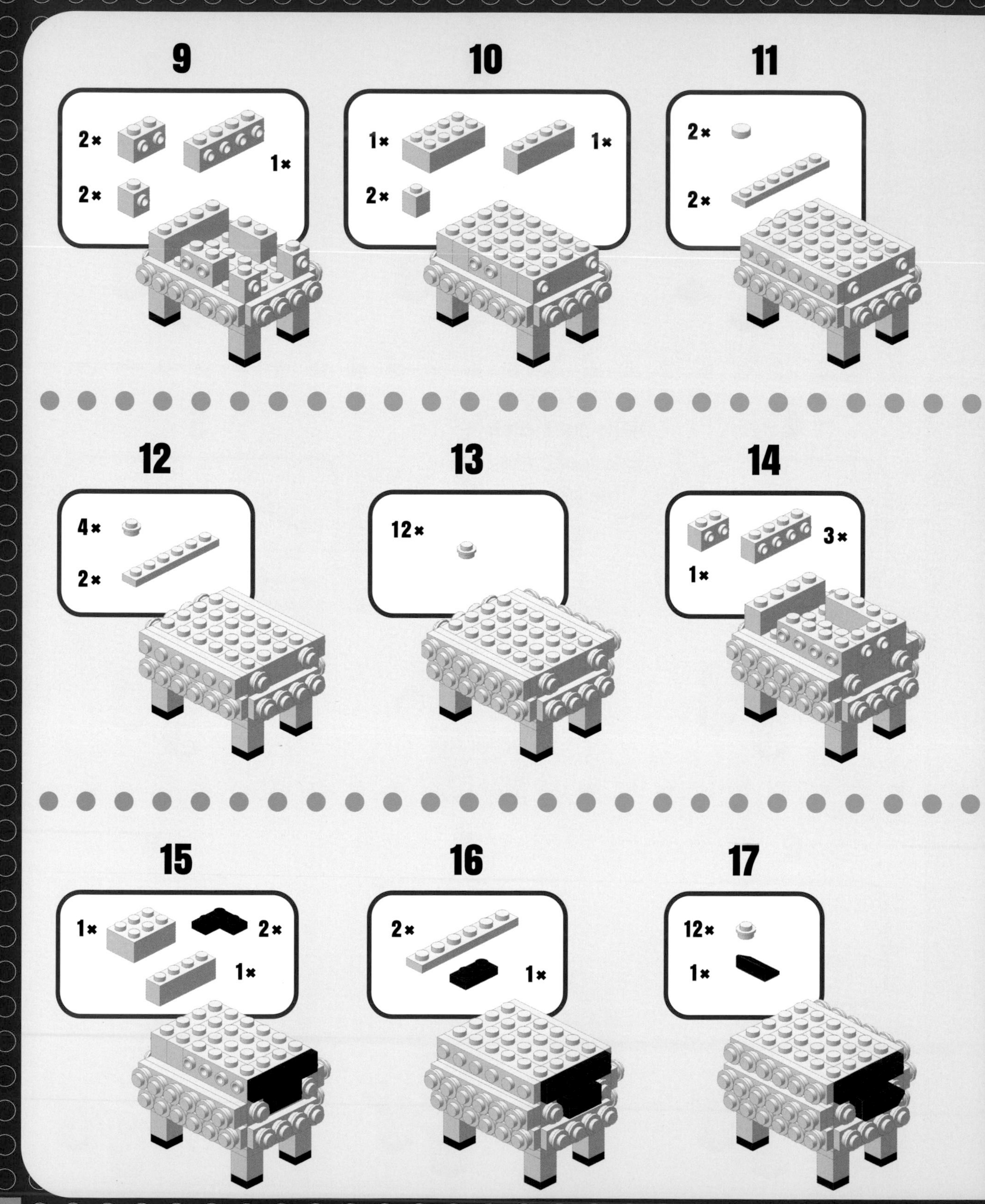

9
2×
1×
2×
10
1×
1×
2×
11
2×
2×
12
4×
2×
13
12×
14
3×
1×
15
1×
2×
1×
16
2×
1×
17
12×
1×

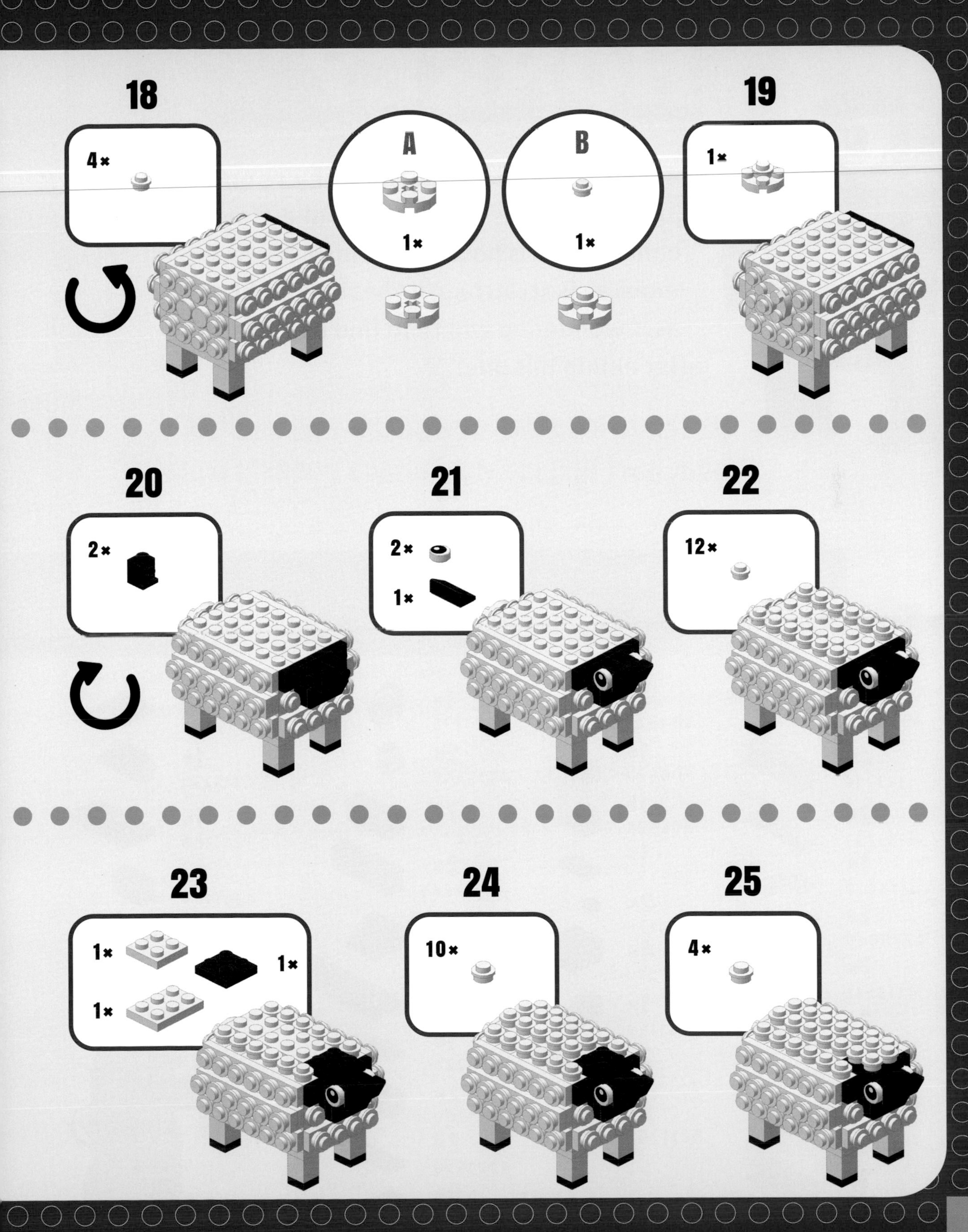
18
4×
A
1×
B
1×
19
1×
20
2×
21
2×
1×
22
12×
23
1×
1×
1×
24
10×
25
4×

MONKEY

Monkeys are very intelligent—they're primates, just like us! This cute little monkey loves bananas and is holding one in its hand. The monkey is scratching its head thoughtfully, as if wondering where to find another one after eating this one!

Its tail is long and curled up—can you tell what part this is? It's Indiana Jones's whip!

PARTS LIST

DIFFICULTY

Qty	Part
2×	6060734
4×	4113916
3×	4113233
4×	4114077
2×	4278069
7×	4113917
2×	4124067
2×	4159553
1×	4114084
1×	4201062
1×	304024
1×	300524
1×	366524
1×	302326
2×	614126
4×	4211210
1×	4211199
2×	4211190
2×	4211242
1×	4521275
2×	4225469
7×	4211220
2×	4211225
3×	4211202
1×	4211211
1×	4219726
2×	4211200
2×	4221590
6×	4221744
1×	4216695
1×	4211221
1×	4211186
4×	4211149

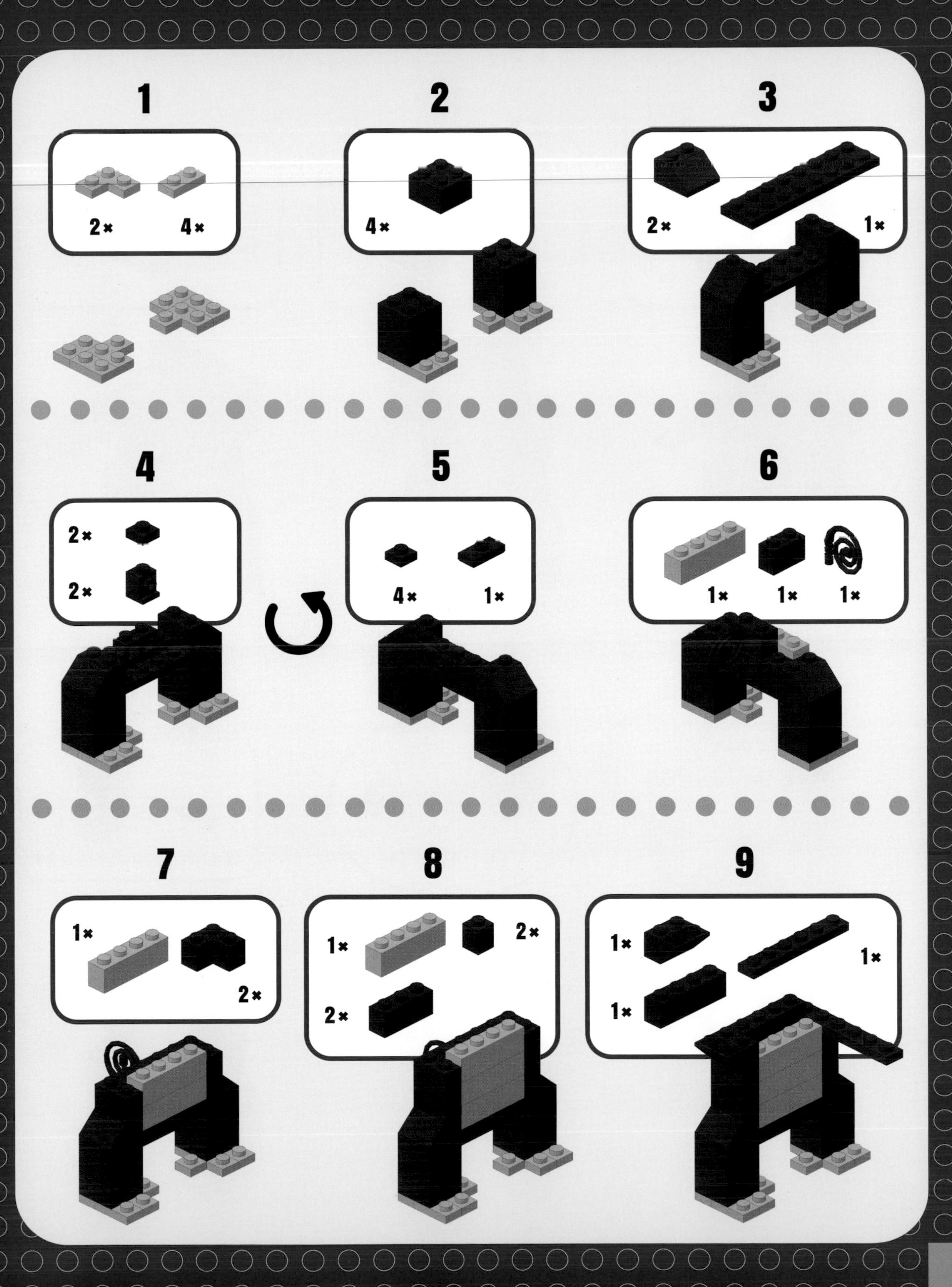
1
2×
4×
2
4×
3
2×
1×
4
2×
2×
5
4×
1×
6
1×
1×
1×
7
1×
2×
8
1×
2×
2×
9
1×
1×
1×

10
1×
1×
1×
2×
1×
11
1×
1×
1×
1×
12
2×
1×
1×
1×
Here's how you make the banana!
1×
1×
1×
13
1×
1×

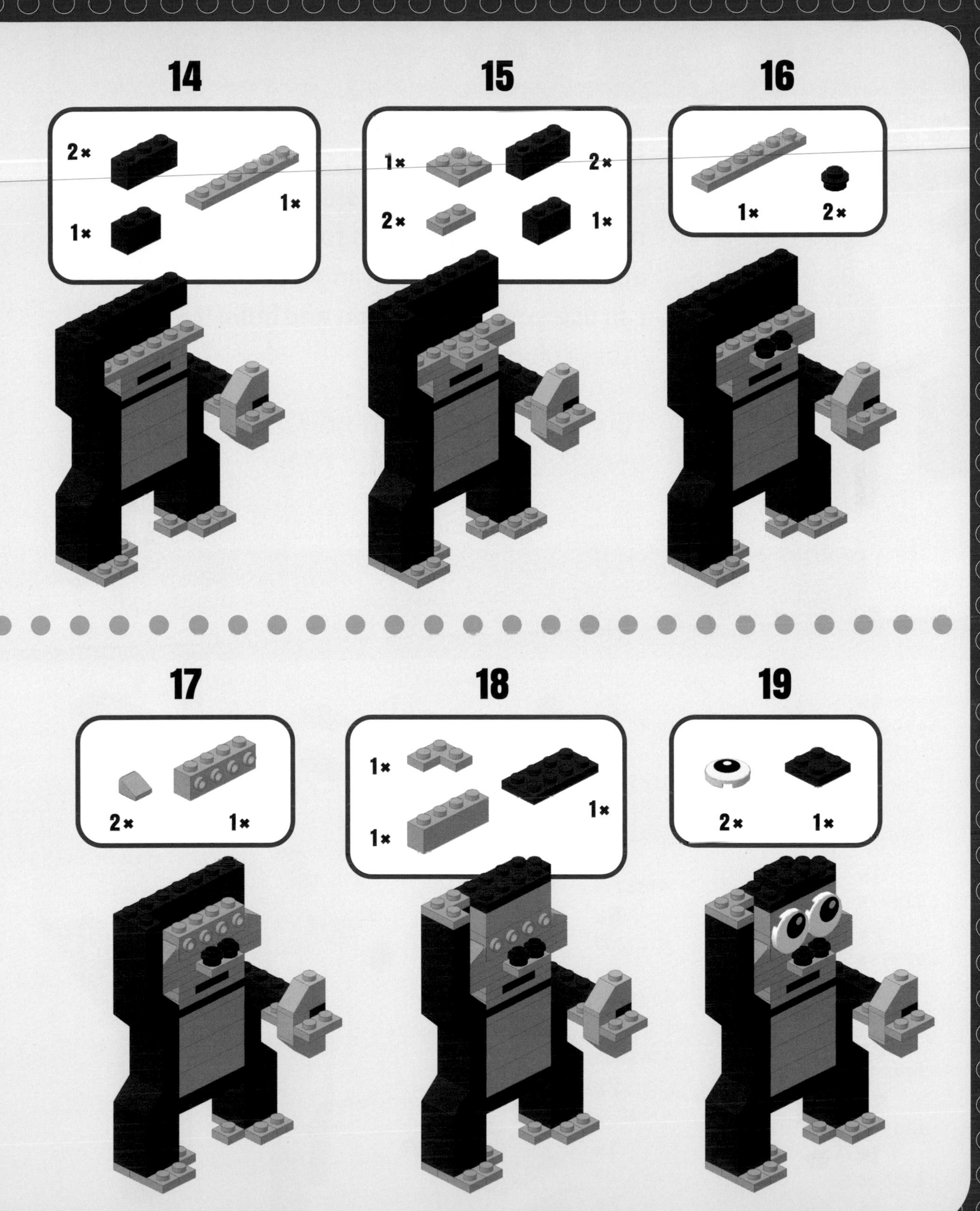

14
2×
1×
1×
15
1×
2×
2×
1×
16
1×
2×
17
2×
1×
18
1×
1×
1×
19
2×
1×

FOX

Foxes are said to be very clever animals. They live in the countryside, so they're not so easy to spot! This fox has an adjustable tail and is orange, but you can use your imagination and build it in other colors.

This cute animal will make a great addition to your zoo!

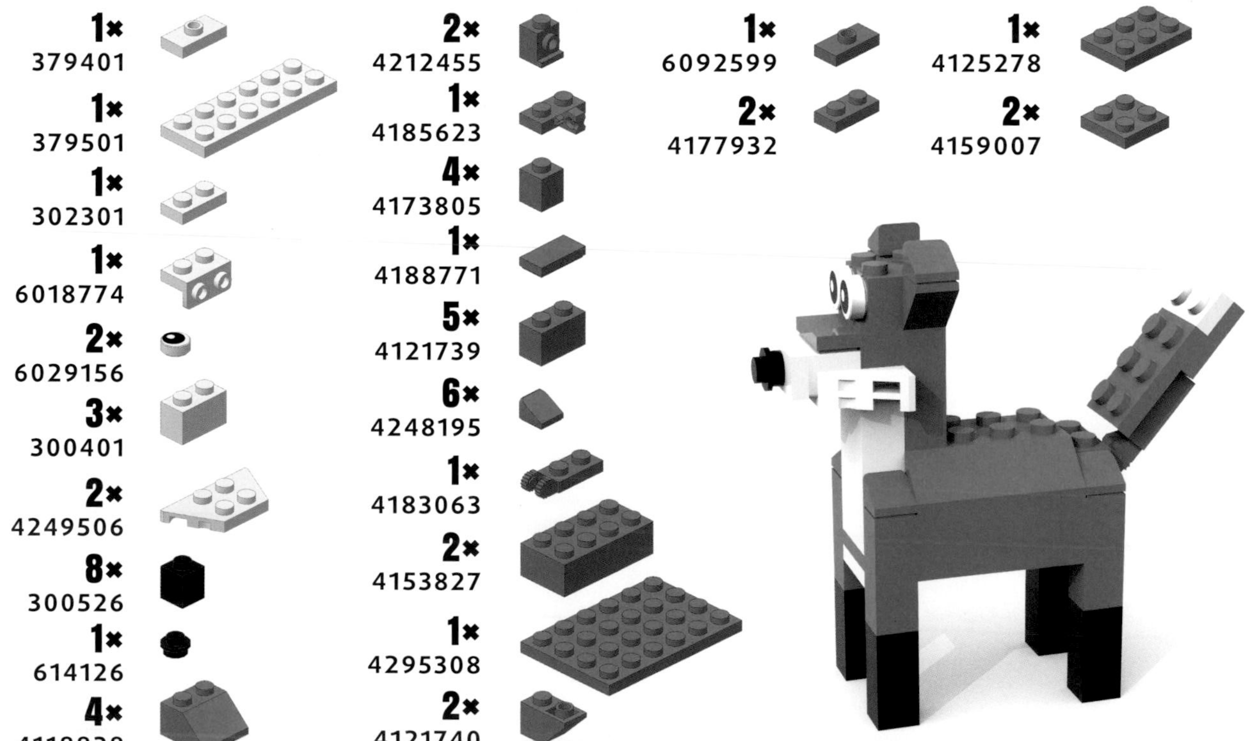

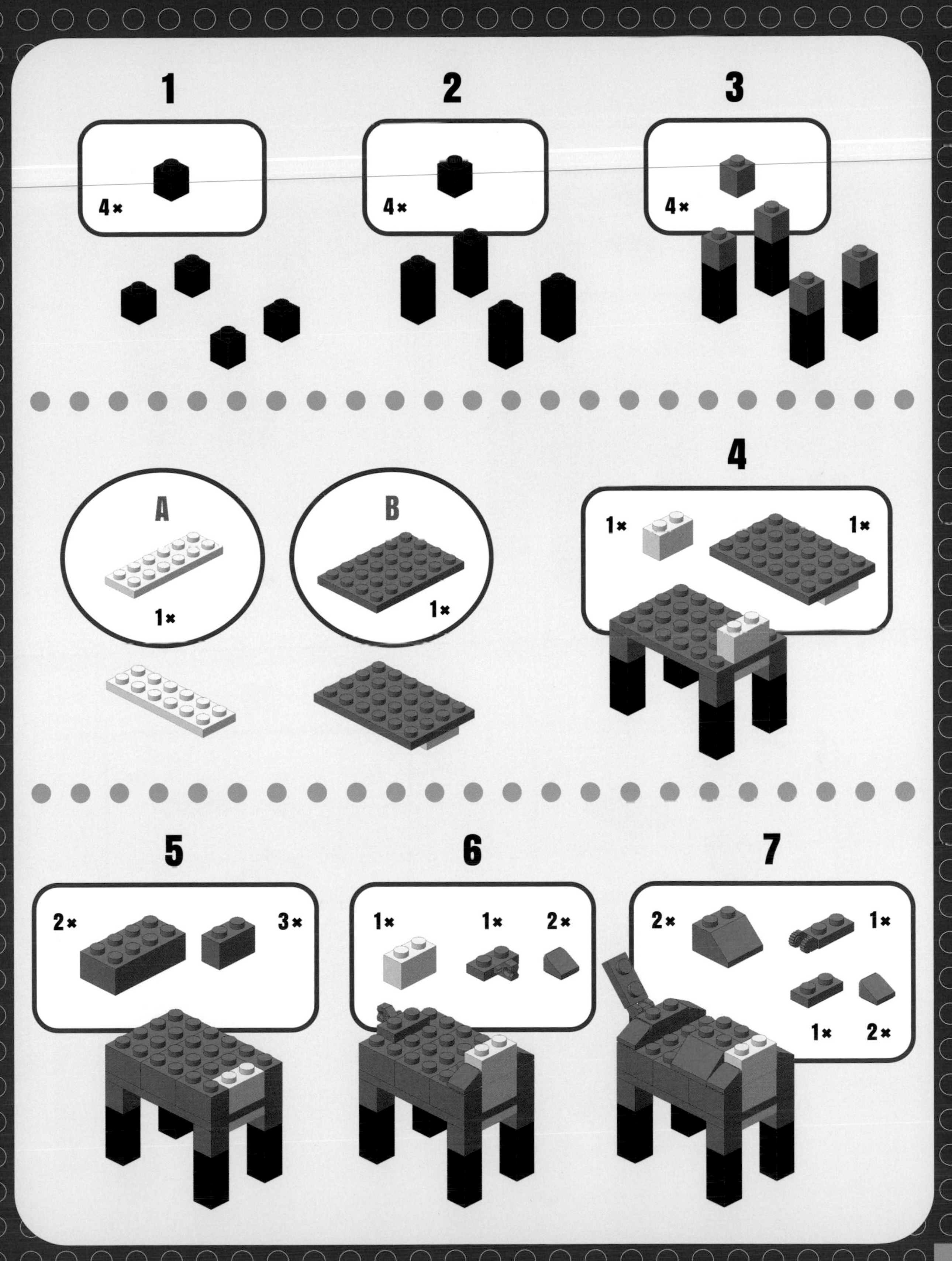
1
4×
2
4×
3
4×
A
1×
B
1×
4
1×
1×
5
2×
3×
6
1×
1×
2×
7
2×
1×
1×
2×

8

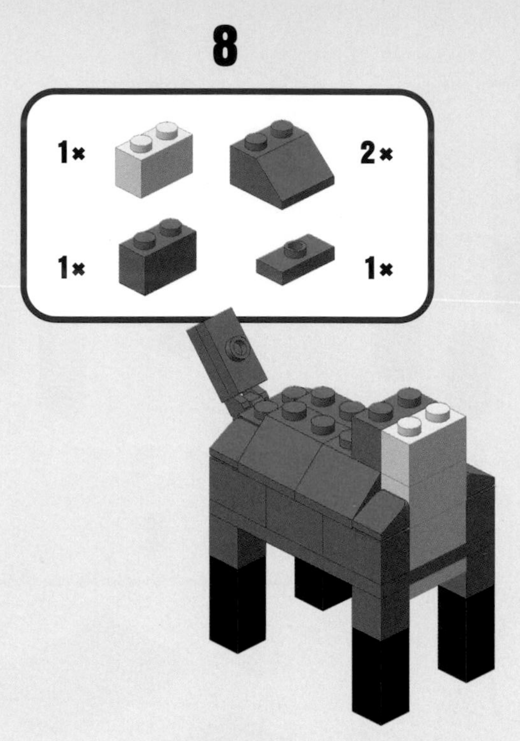

9

10

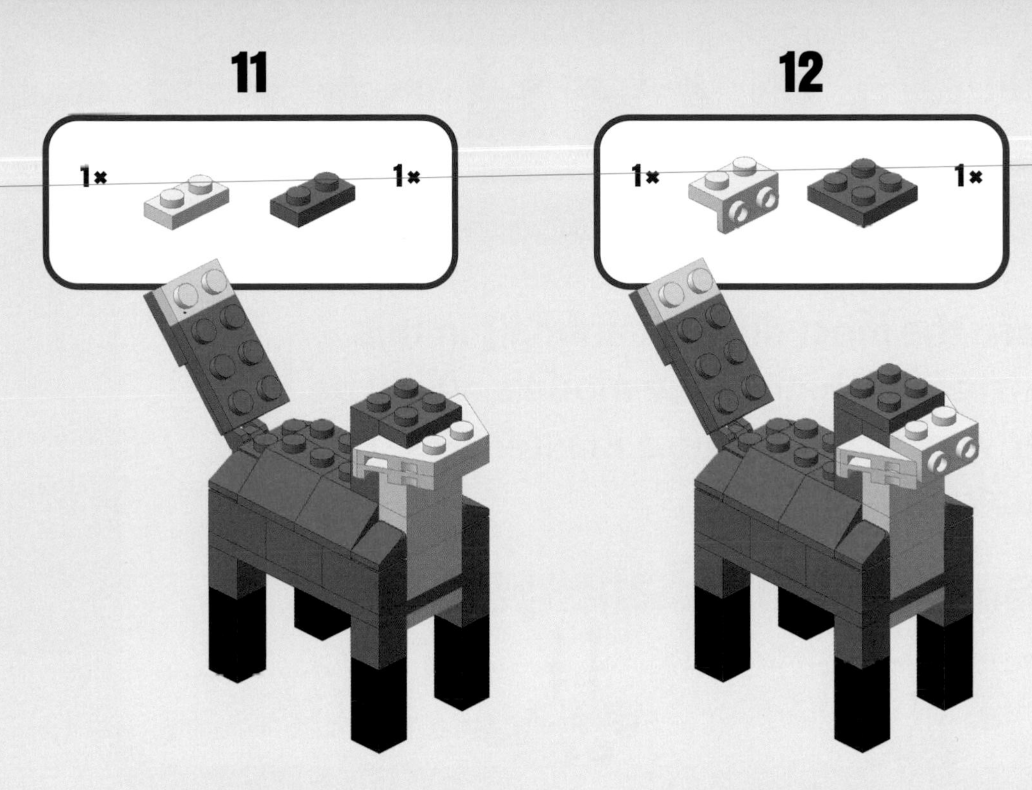
11
1×
1×
12
1×
1×

13
1×
2×
1×
2×

14
2×
1×
2×

CHAPTER 5

These are the most difficult animals in this book. After finishing these models, you'll be on your way to becoming a master LEGO builder (and zookeeper)!

Are you up for the challenge?

(See page ix for tips on where to find parts!)

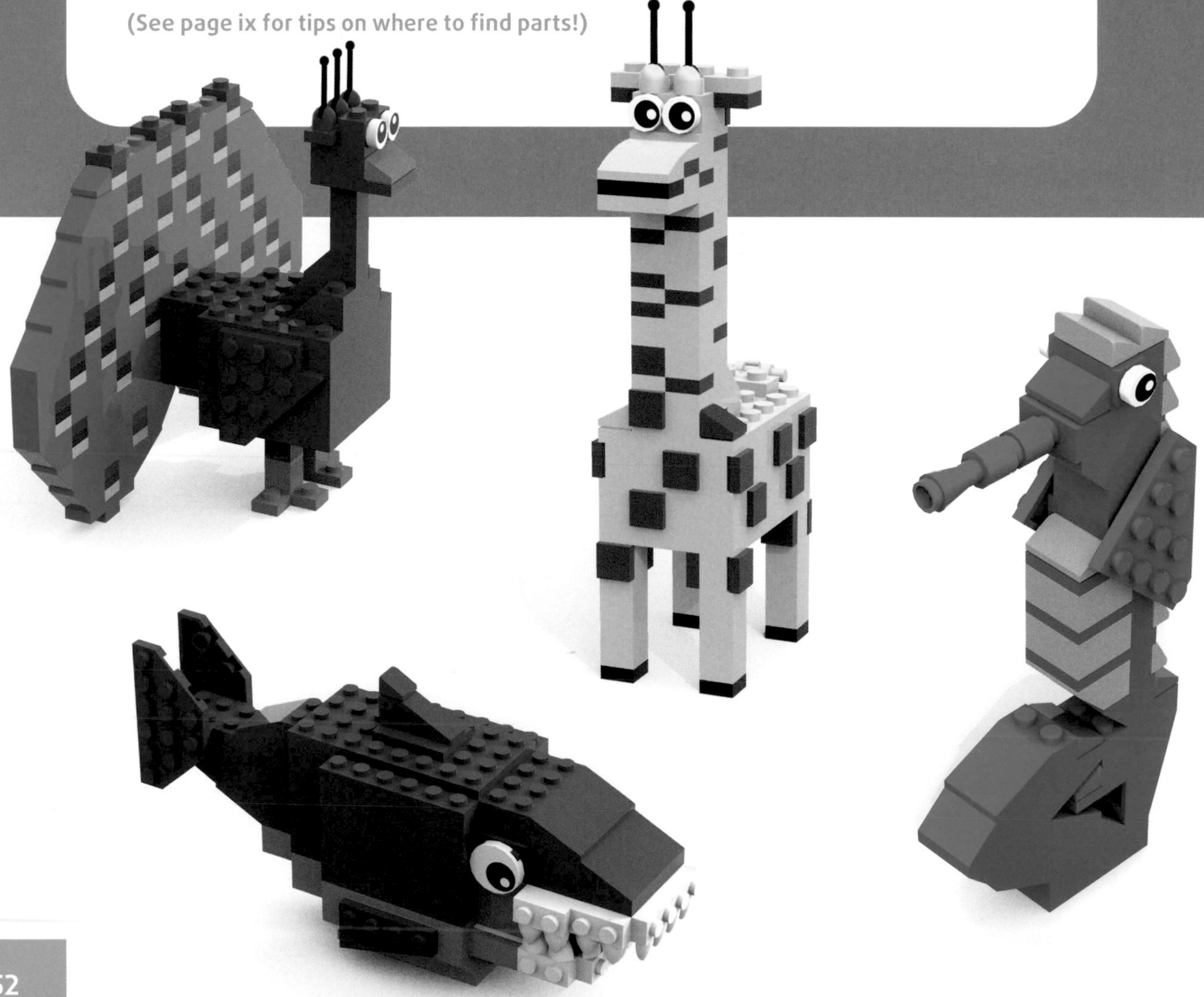

BUTTERFLY

Butterflies are gorgeous insects that come in many different colors and shapes. The wings of this model are totally adjustable—try building butterflies in other colors.

The only limit is your imagination!

PARTS LIST

DIFFICULTY

2× 6029156
4× 4515368
4× 601926
2× 4593
2× 4592
2× 4210215
2× 4586276
1× 4164034
2× 4537922
2× 4537937
4× 4537936

1× 4164033
2× 4210210
2× 4586277
2× 4504705
18× 4657974
1× 6133921
1× 4566607
1× 6107200
2× 6063897
1× 4225125
1× 4223712

2× 4164032
18× 4654127
1× 6054404
1× 4224862
1× 4235123

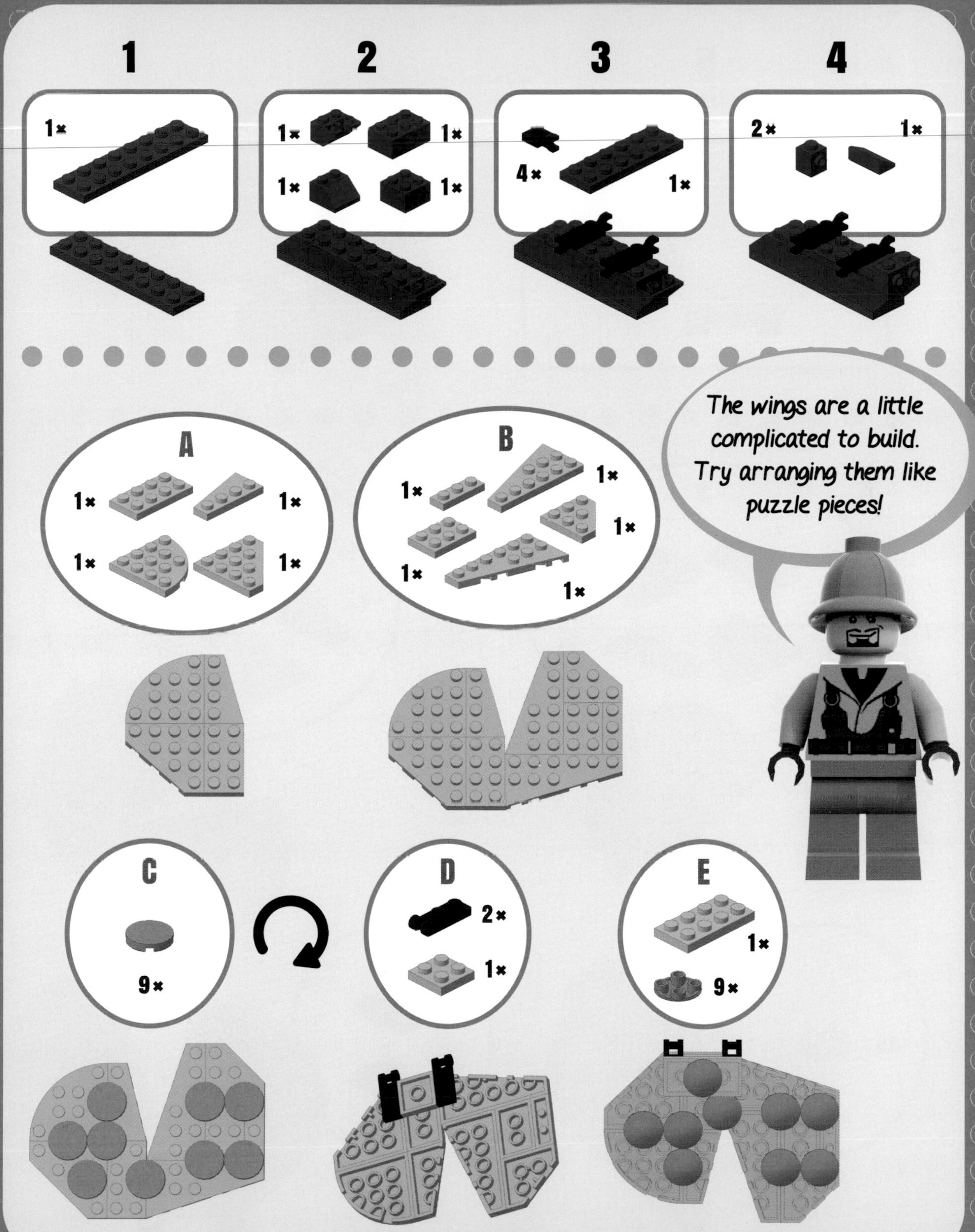
1
2
3
4
1×
1×
1×
1×
1×
2×
1×
4×
1×
A
1×
1×
1×
1×
B
1×
1×
1×
1×
1×
1×
The wings are a little complicated to build. Try arranging them like puzzle pieces!
C
9×
D
2×
1×
E
1×
9×

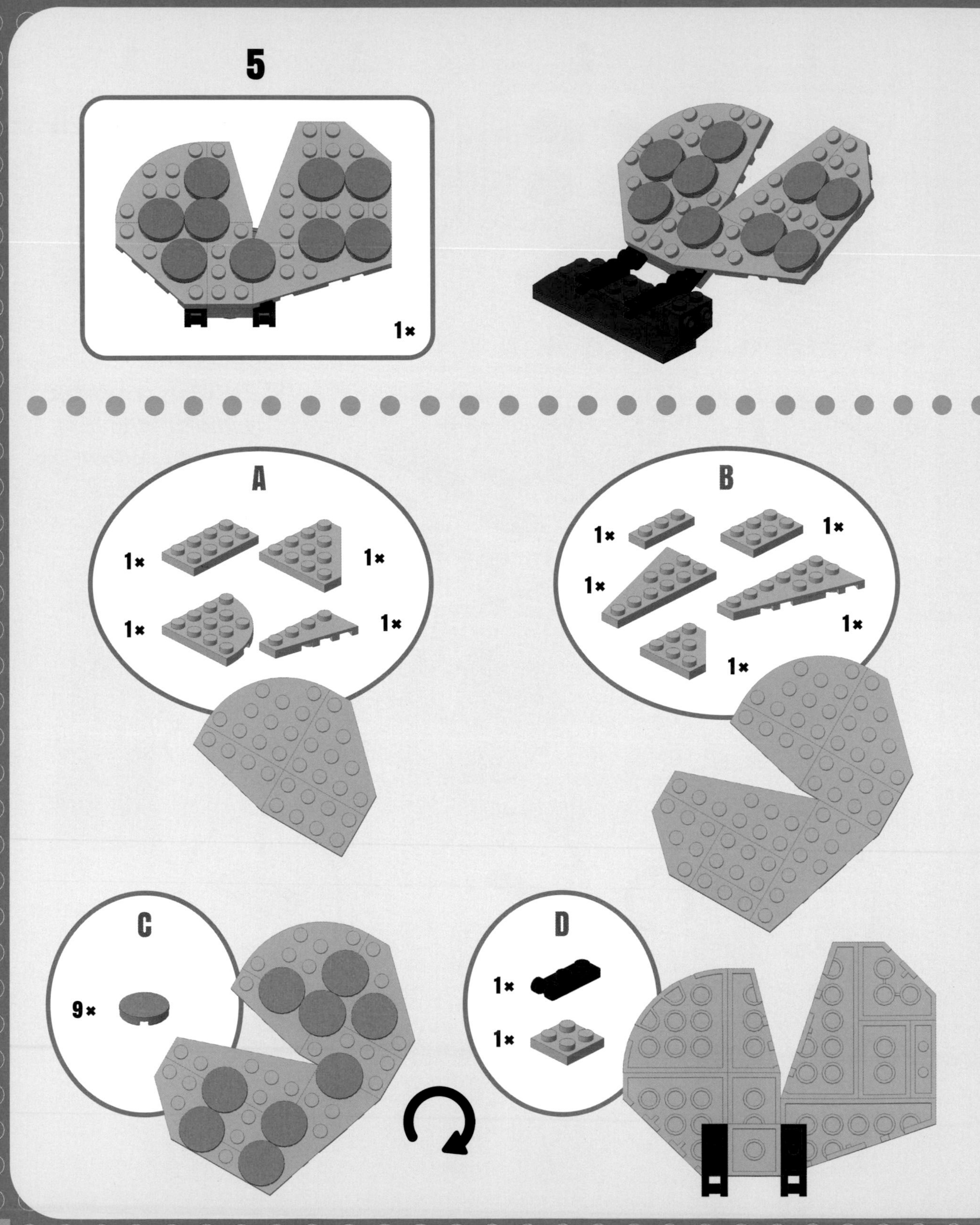
5
1×
A
1×
1×
1×
1×
B
1×
1×
1×
1×
1×
C
9×
D
1×
1×

E

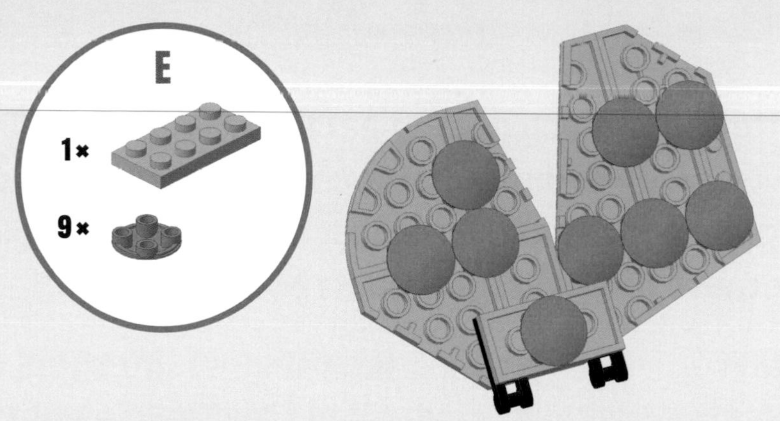

6

7

GIRAFFE

A giraffe uses its long neck to eat the leaves of the tallest trees, even those that seem unreachable. This brick giraffe is one of the hardest models in the book because of all the spots on its body.

Have fun changing the positions of the spots as you build. These instructions are only a guide—in the end, you get to decide what your giraffe will look like!

PARTS LIST

DIFFICULTY

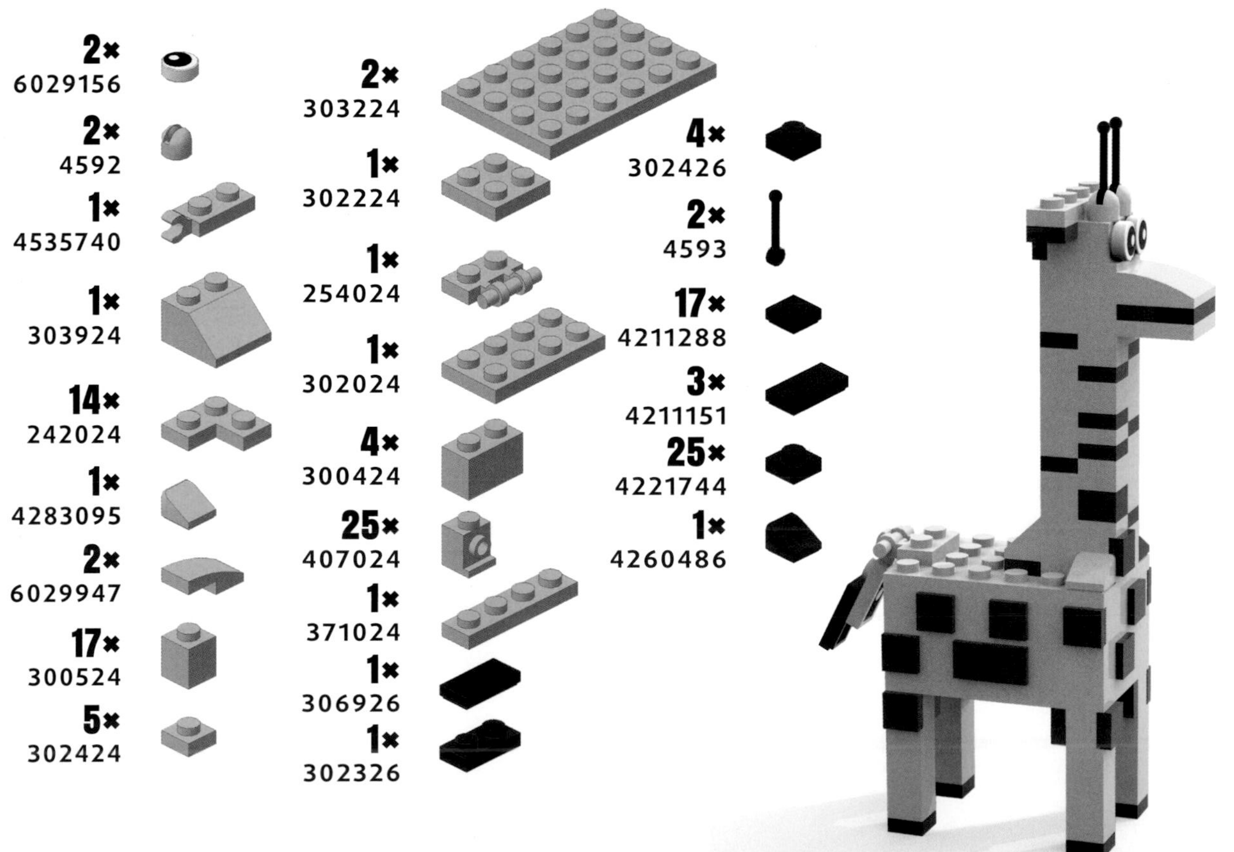

1
4×
2
4×
3
4×
4
4×
5
4×
4×
6
1×
7
4×
2×
1×
8
3×
1×
2×
Rotate the giraffe to make sure you don't miss anything.
9
2×
1×

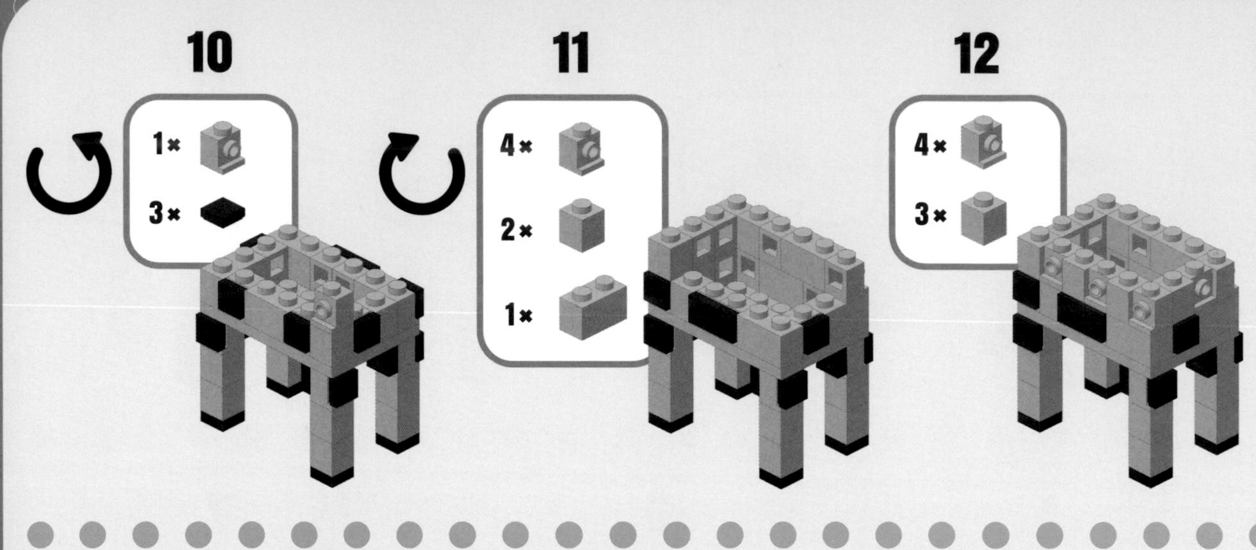
10
1×
3×
11
4×
2×
1×
12
4×
3×

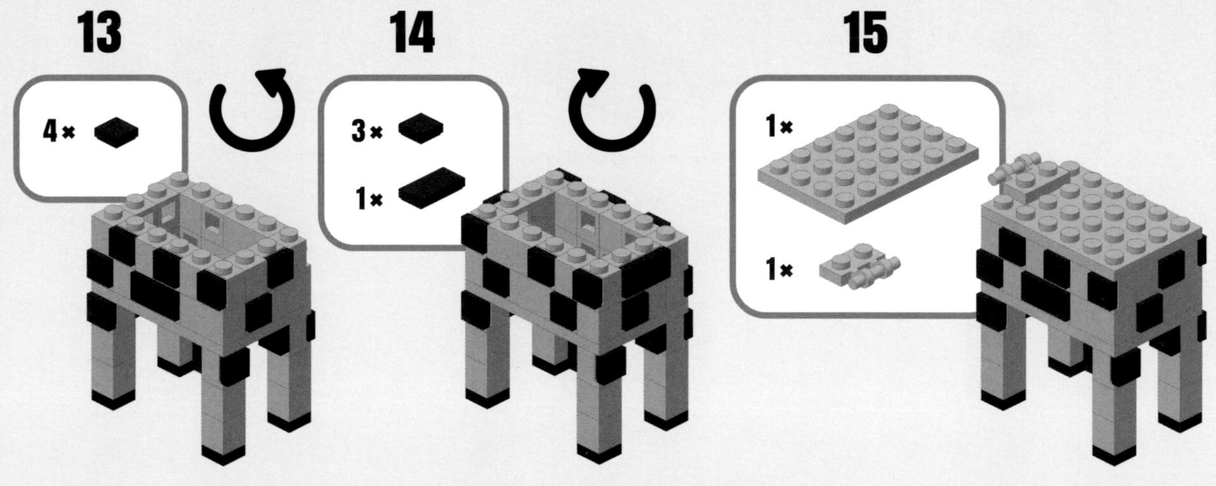
13
4×
14
3×
1×
15
1×
1×

16
1×
2×
2×
17
1×
1×
1×
1×
1×
1×
18
1×
1×
1×

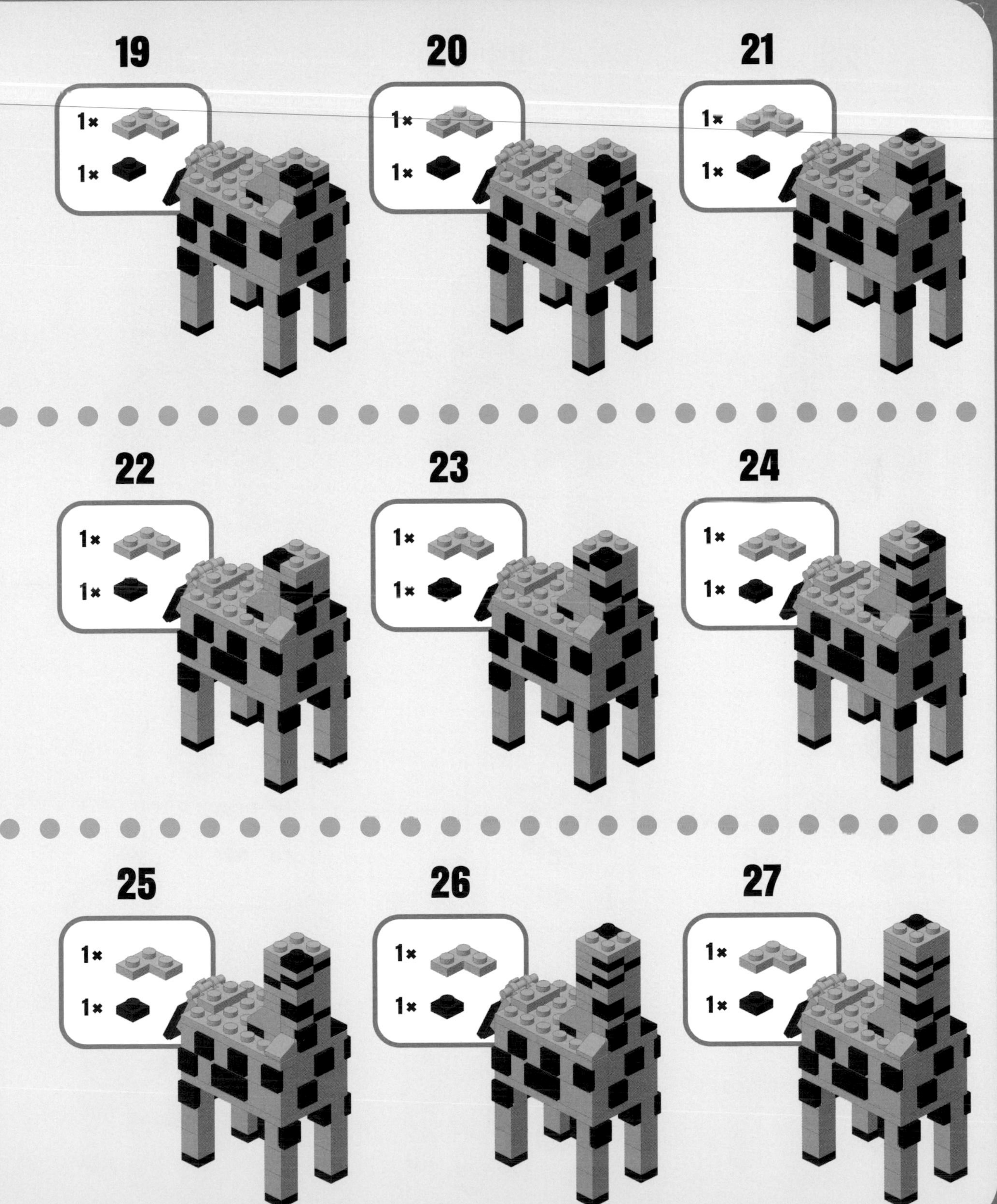
19
1×
1×
20
1×
1×
21
1×
1×
22
1×
1×
23
1×
1×
24
1×
1×
25
1×
1×
26
1×
1×
27
1×
1×

28

29

30

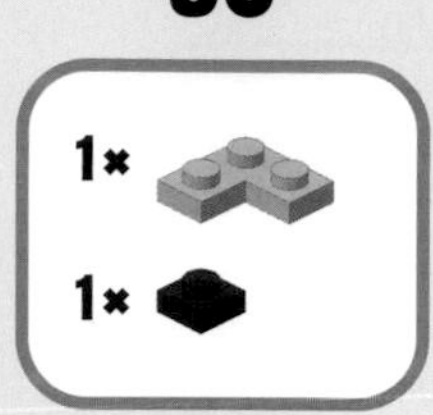

31

32

33

34

35

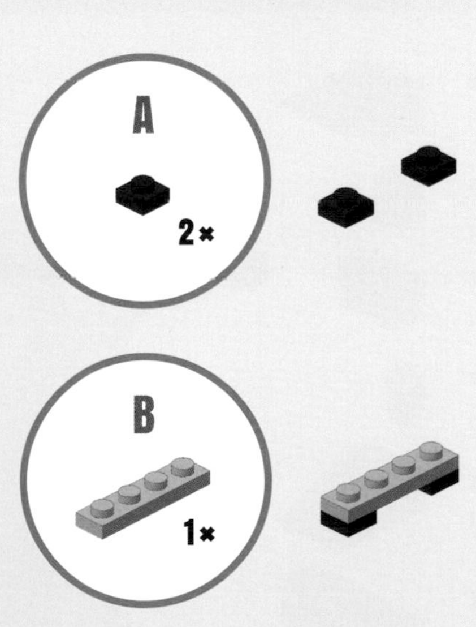

36

SEAHORSE

Seahorses get their name from their elongated horse-like face and because they live in the sea. This model uses a special trick to create its curly tail.

This is the only example in the book that uses a shaft to keep the nose parts in place.

PARTS LIST

DIFFICULTY

Qty	Part
2×	6029156
2×	4114306
11×	4624086
1×	4118866
1×	4566275
2×	303928
4×	6000071
1×	379428
4×	302328
2×	4629678
1×	4106356
4×	302428
1×	4188820
3×	302128
1×	302228
3×	4142717
1×	302028
2×	4113071
22×	4187334
2×	4107736
2×	306228
2×	329828
2×	4208191

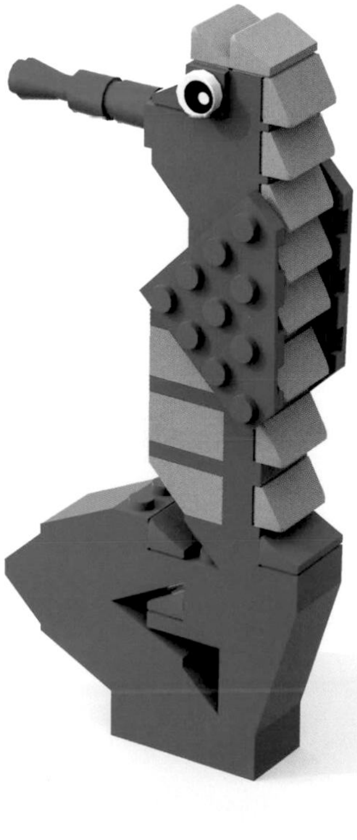

1
1×
2
1×
1×
2×
3
1×
1×
1×
A
1×
B
3×
C
1×
1×
1×
4
1×
1×
1×
5
1×
1×
1×
1×
2×
6
1×
1×
7
1×
1×
1×
2×

8
1×
1×
2×
1×
The body is made up of the same few parts.
9
1×
4×
10
1×
2×
11
1×
1×
2×
1×
12
1×
2×
1×
13
4×

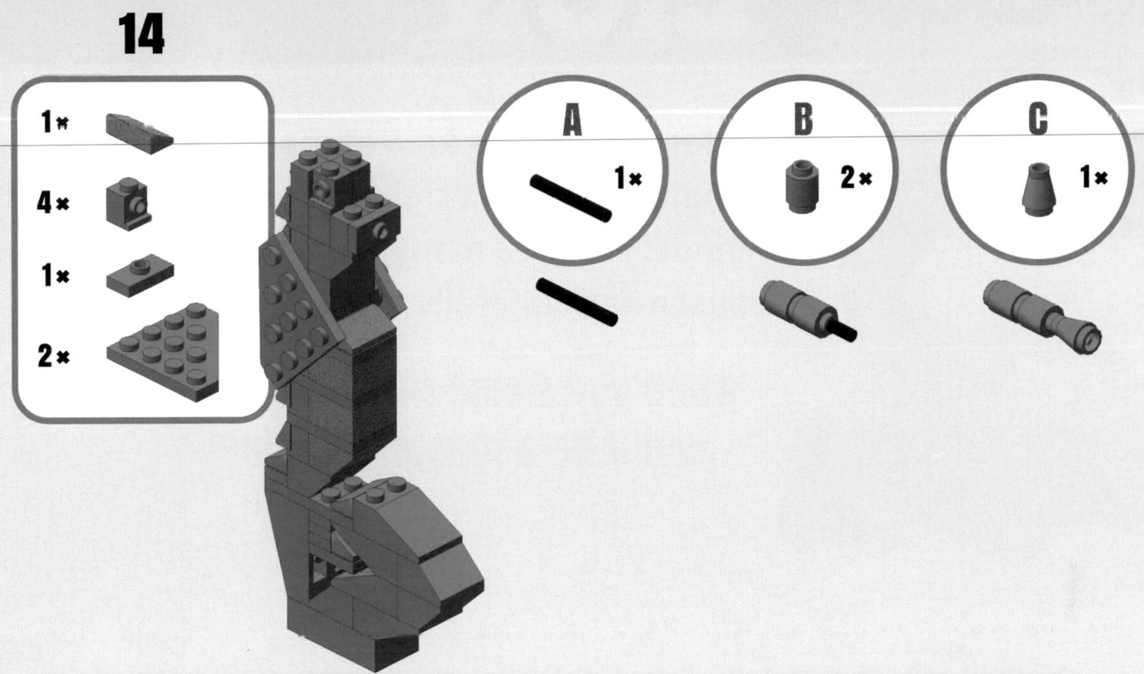
14
1×
4×
1×
2×
A
1×
B
2×
C
1×

15
1×
2×
1×
16
2×
3×

Here comes the king of the jungle! The majestic lion is a sight to behold. This model requires many parts that you must attach laterally.

When you finish this model, you'll be a master builder!

PARTS LIST

DIFFICULTY

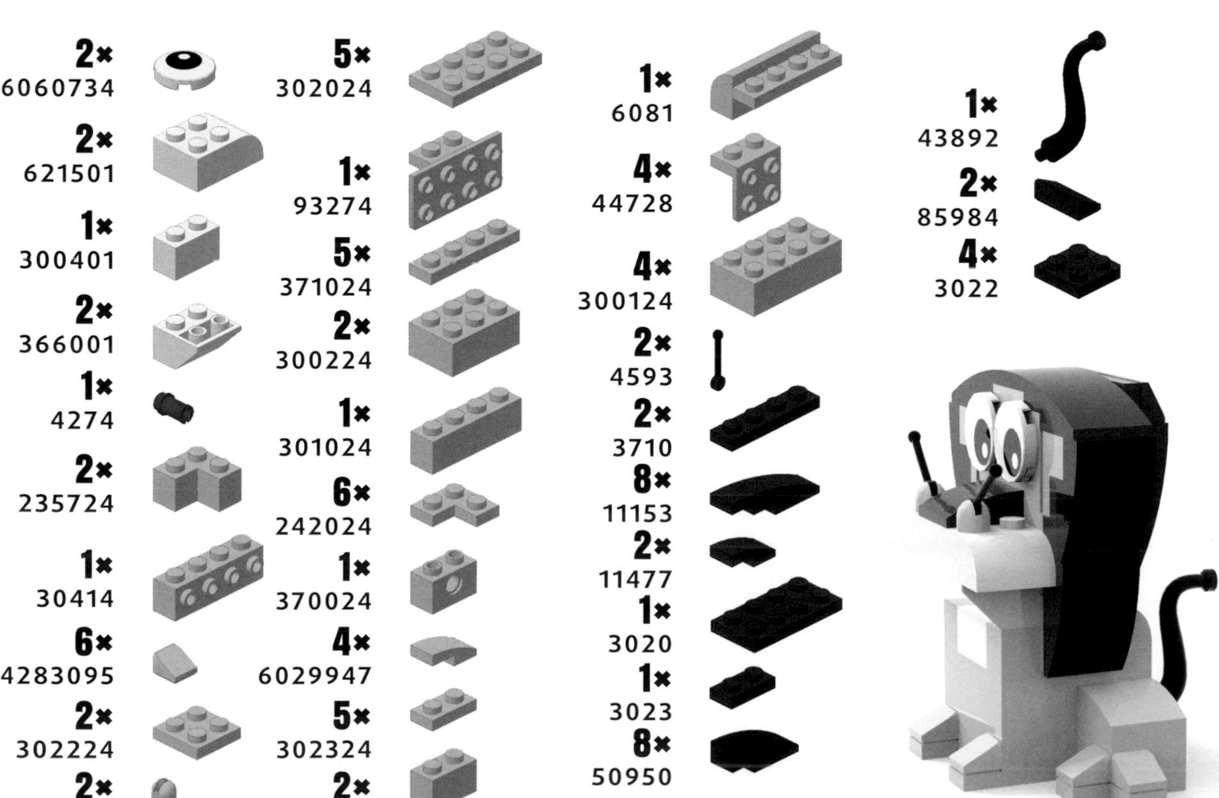

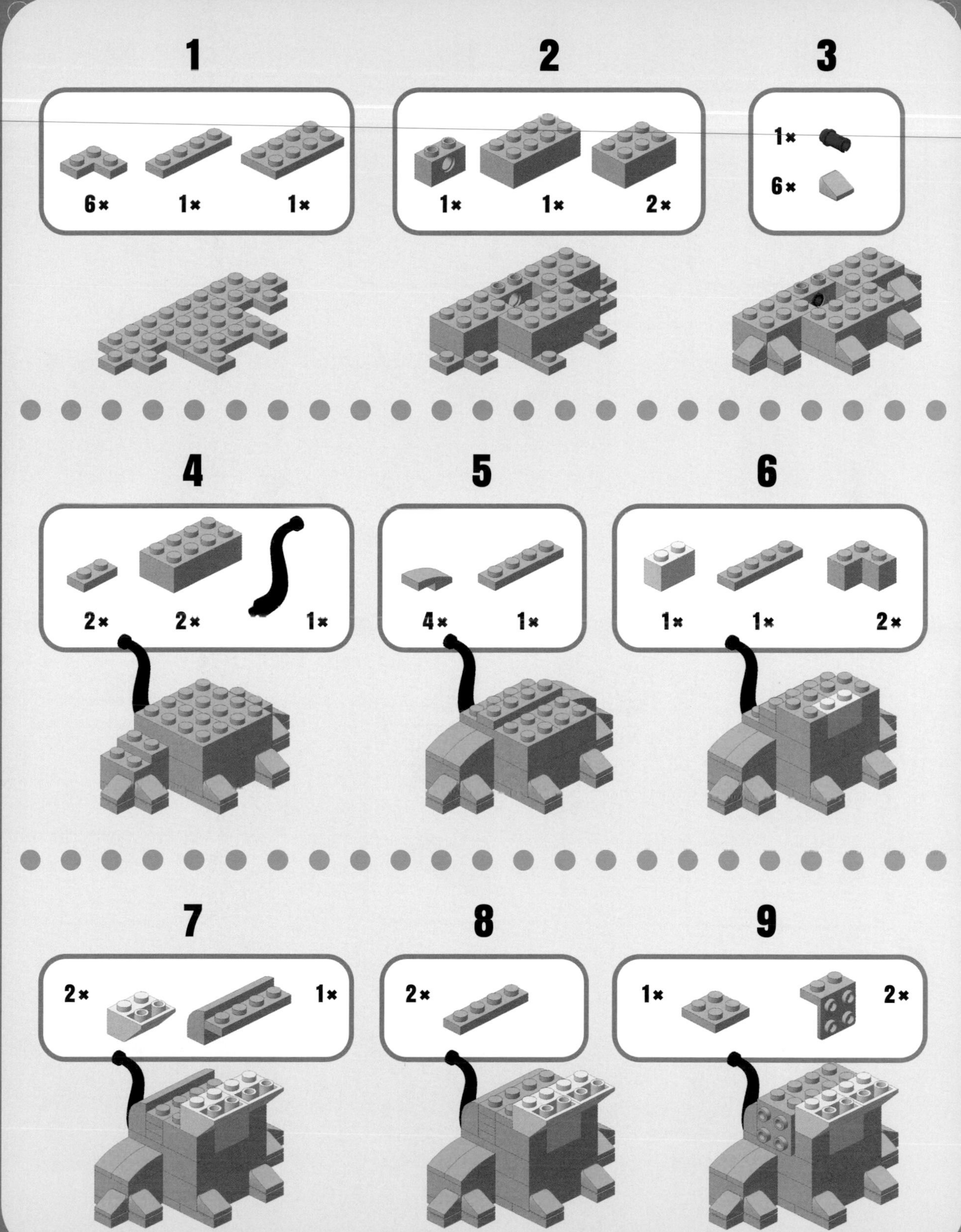

1
6×
1×
1×
2
1×
1×
2×
3
1×
6×
4
2×
2×
1×
5
4×
1×
6
1×
1×
2×
7
2×
1×
8
2×
9
1×
2×

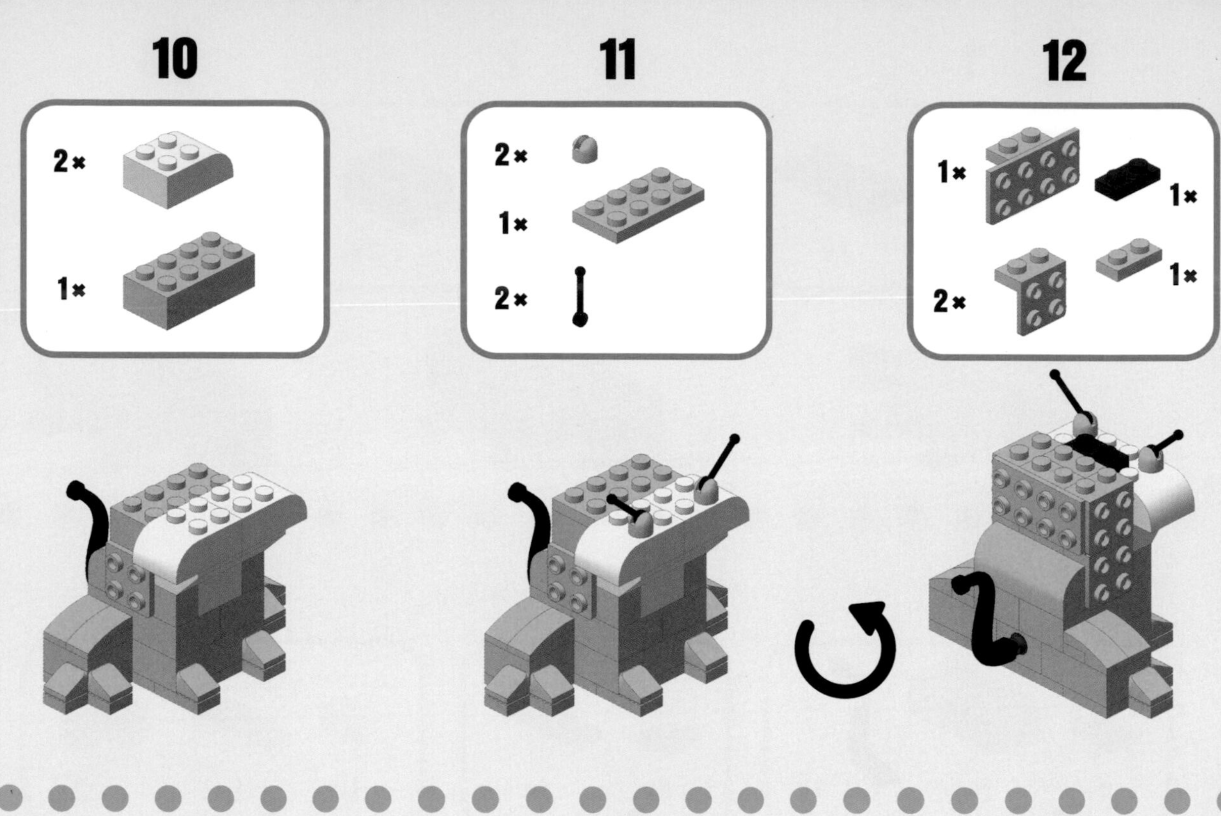

13

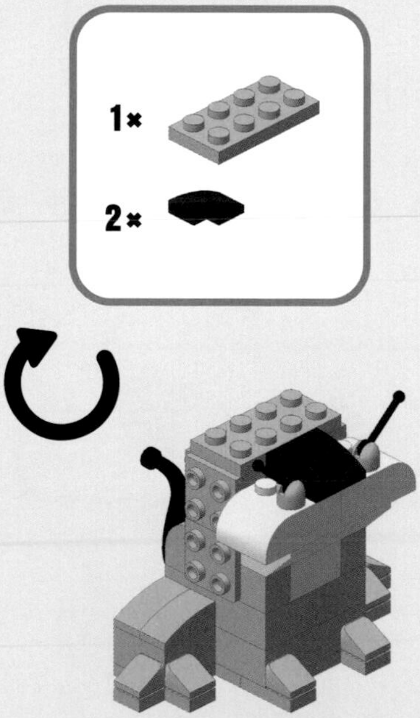

1×

2×

14

1×

1×

15

2×

1×

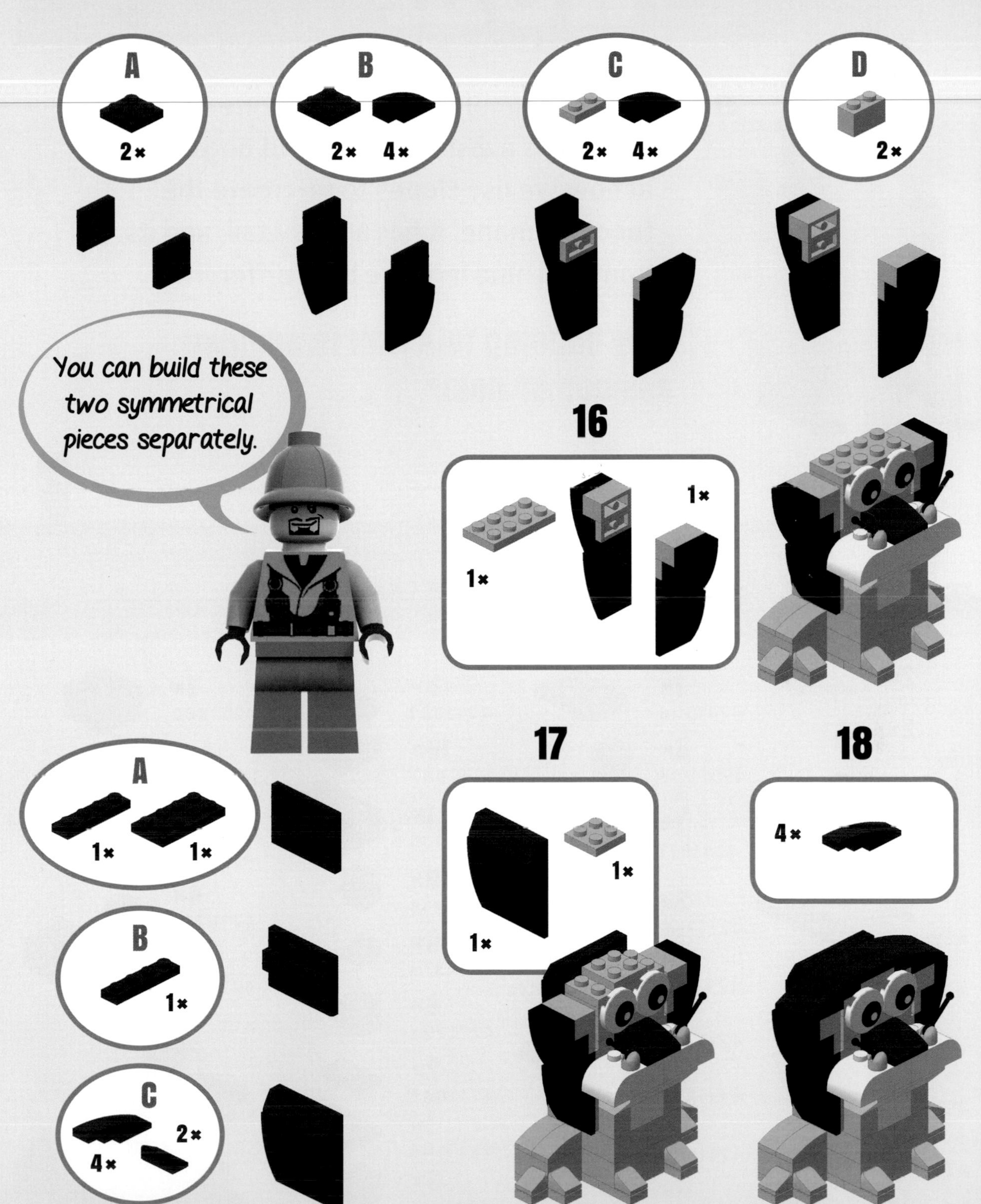
A
2×
B
2× 4×
C
2× 4×
D
2×
You can build these two symmetrical pieces separately.
16
1×
1×
A
1× 1×
17
1×
1×
18
4×
B
1×
C
2×
4×

WOLF

The wolf is an animal that can live alone or in packs, and is a distant relative of dogs. Look at how we use slopes to re-create the fur on its mane. It has a fluffy tail, and its front and hind legs are built differently.

Try building this wolf in another position or color.

PARTS LIST

DIFFICULTY

2× 4224792
2× 6029156
1× 614126
2× 4211387
2× 4211445
1× 4211414
6× 4211389
6× 4521921
1× 4211398
1× 4558169

1× 4211396
6× 4558953
1× 4211811
2× 4211760
1× 4211451
2× 4211399
3× 4211395
6× 4211436
4× 4211388
8× 4211054

5× 4211001
10× 4567887
1× 4211105
20× 4558955
16× 4244373
8× 4211096
2× 4211063
1× 4211043
6× 4211135
12× 4211098

1× 4211060
1× 4211088
2× 4211109
4× 4210719
2× 4211085

1
1×
2×
2×
Watch the distances between these parts; they're important!
2
1×
2×
2×
3
1×
2×
1×
1×
4
1×
4×
5
1×
2×
1×
1×
6
1×
4×

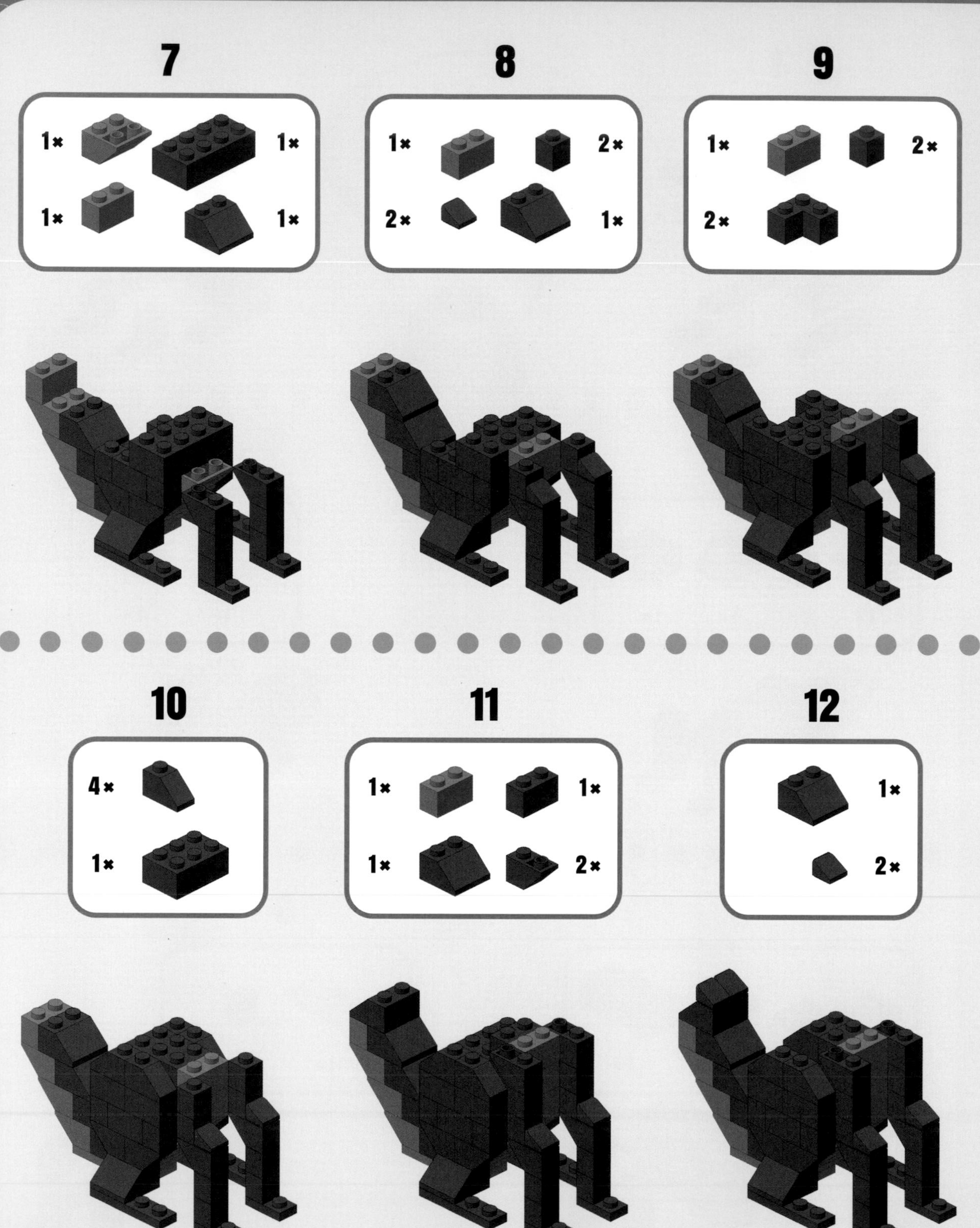

7
1×
1×
1×
1×
8
1×
2×
2×
1×
9
1×
2×
2×
10
4×
1×
11
1×
1×
1×
2×
12
1×
2×

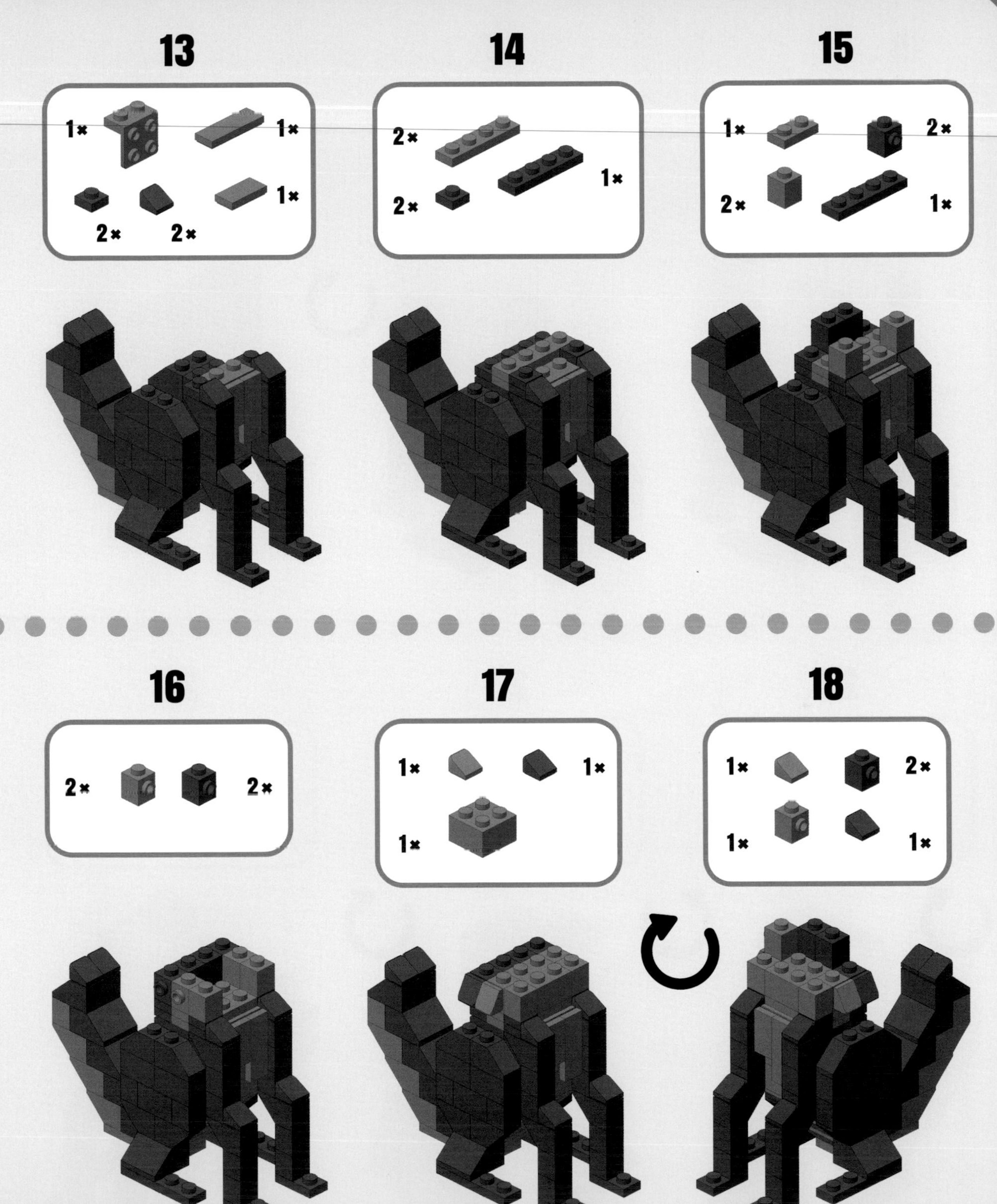
13
1×
1×
1×
2×
2×
14
2×
1×
2×
15
1×
2×
2×
1×
16
2×
2×
17
1×
1×
1×
18
1×
2×
1×
1×

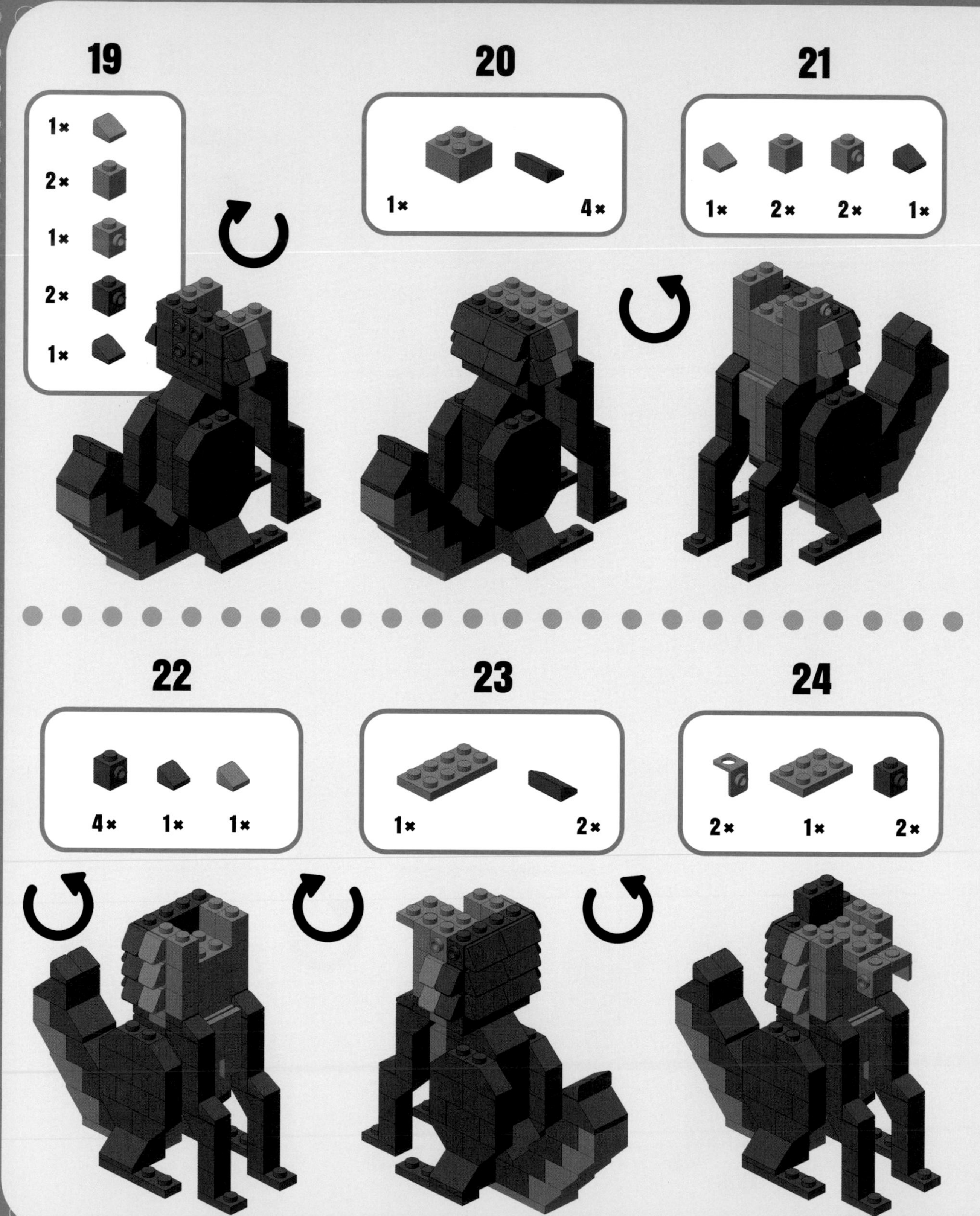

19
1×
2×
1×
2×
1×
20
1×
4×
21
1×
2×
2×
1×
22
4×
1×
1×
23
1×
2×
24
2×
1×
2×

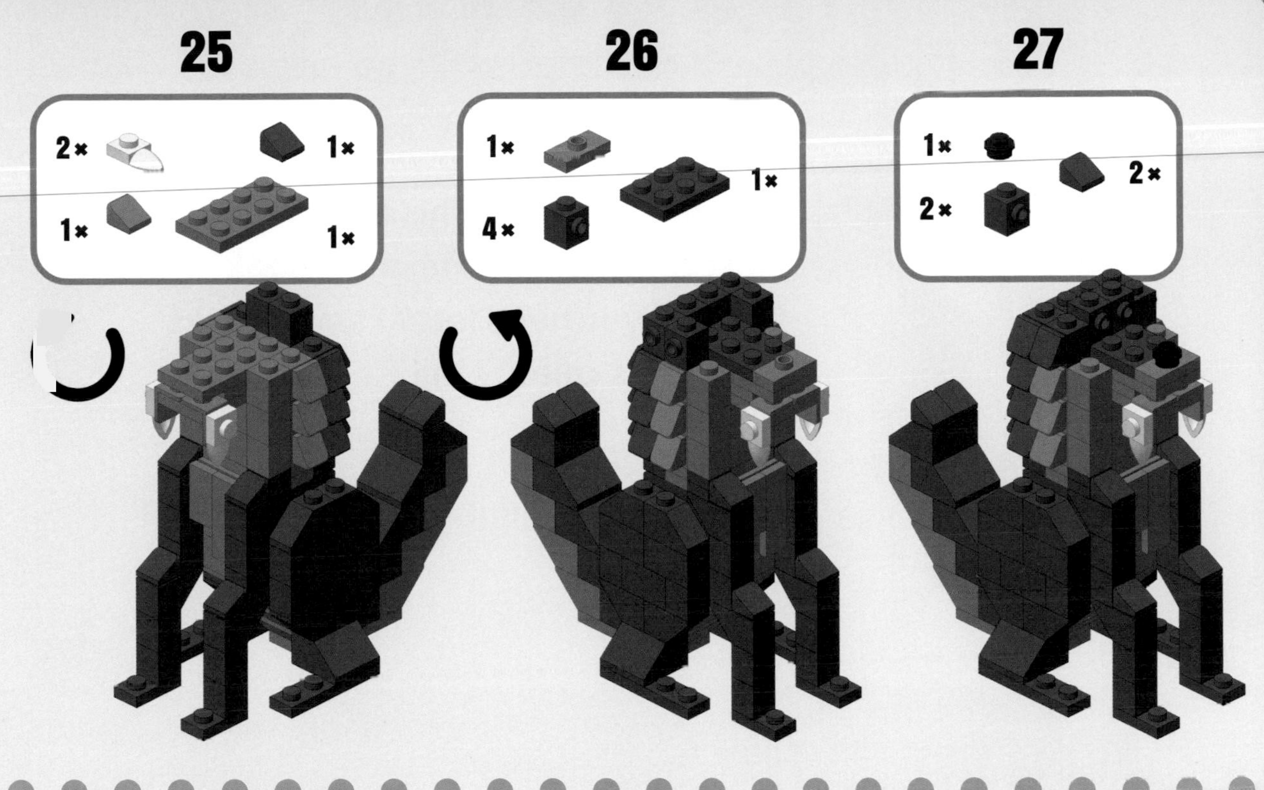
25
2×
1×
1×
1×
26
1×
1×
4×
27
1×
2×
2×

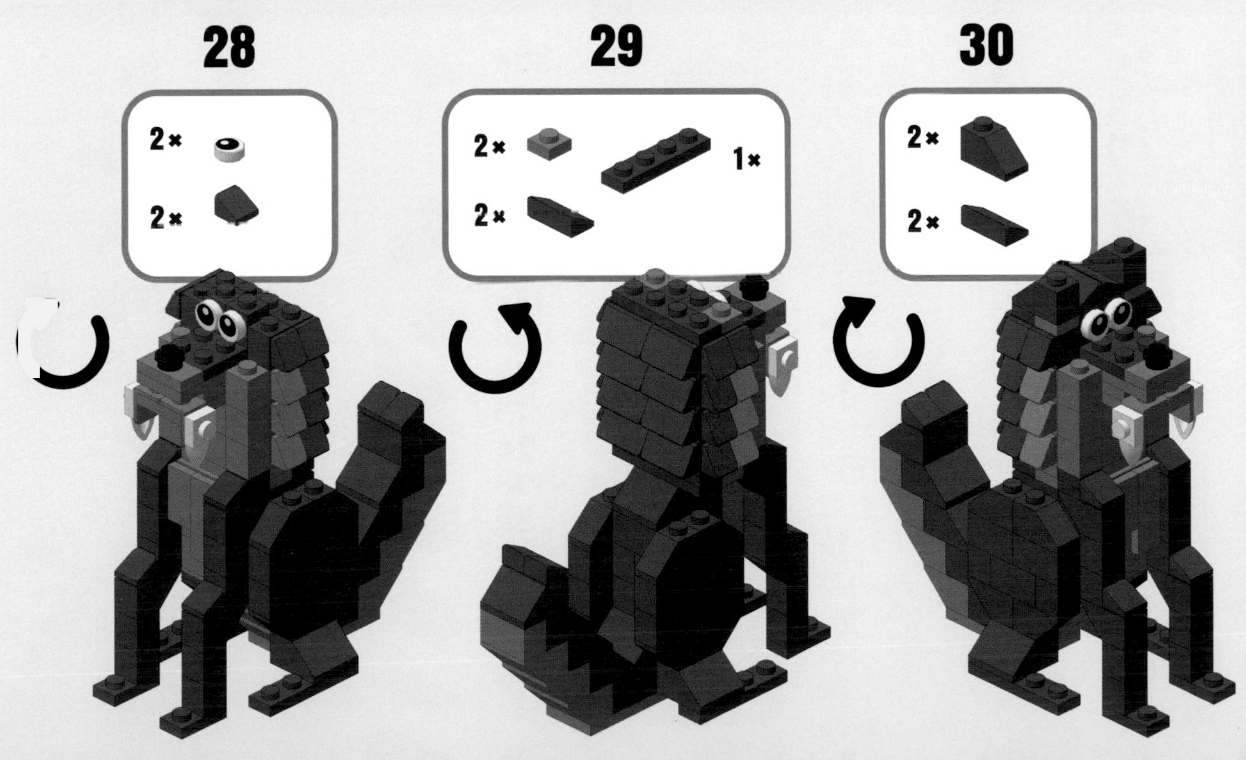
28
2×
2×
29
2×
1×
2×
30
2×
2×

PEACOCK

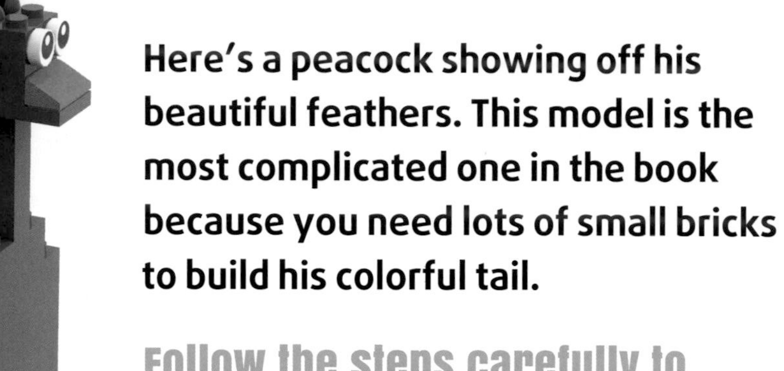

Here's a peacock showing off his beautiful feathers. This model is the most complicated one in the book because you need lots of small bricks to build his colorful tail.

Follow the steps carefully to build this charming animal!

PARTS LIST

DIFFICULTY

2× 6029156
1× 235723
1× 379423
42× 302423
4× 302223
3× 302023
5× 362323
1× 301023
6× 371023
1× 3935

6× 300223
4× 4583862
4× 304023
3× 4592
3× 300523
10× 302123
1× 300423
2× 362223
1× 3936
2× 300323

38× 302424
3× 4593
8× 4121969
13× 300528
4× 302428
2× 4107758
8× 4142989
19× 4107736
4× 302328
9× 4109679

2× 4546705
2× 6037389
2× 4173805
1× 4648855
2× 4188450
38× 6096942

1
2×
2×
2
2×
2×
3
2×
2×
3×
Make sure you get the positions right!
4
3×
2×
5
4×
6
1×
2×
2×
7
1×
2×
1×
8
1×
3×
2×
1×
9
1×
3×
1×

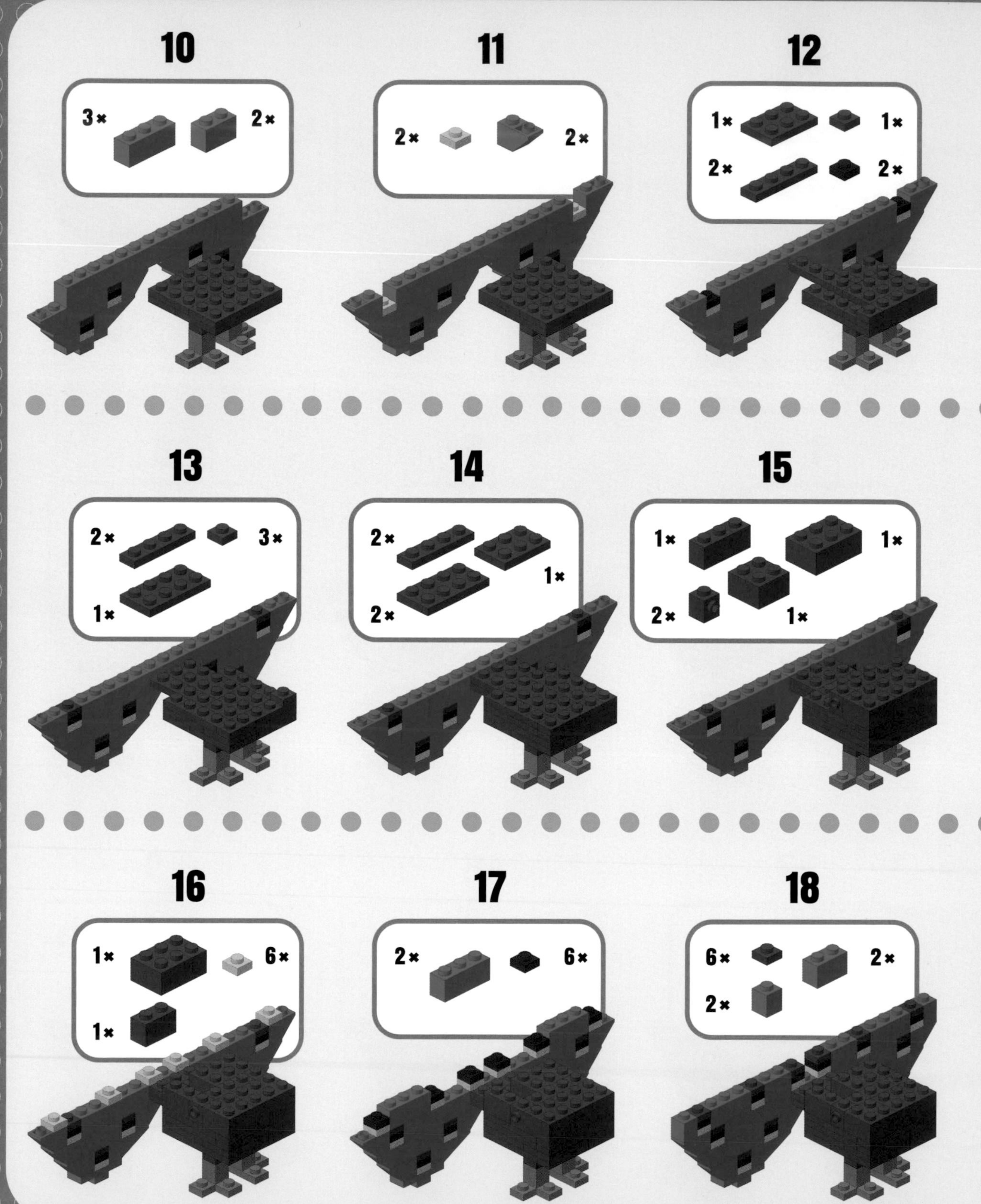
10
3×
2×
11
2×
2×
12
1×
1×
2×
2×
13
2×
3×
1×
14
2×
1×
2×
15
1×
1×
2×
1×
16
1×
6×
1×
17
2×
6×
18
6×
2×
2×

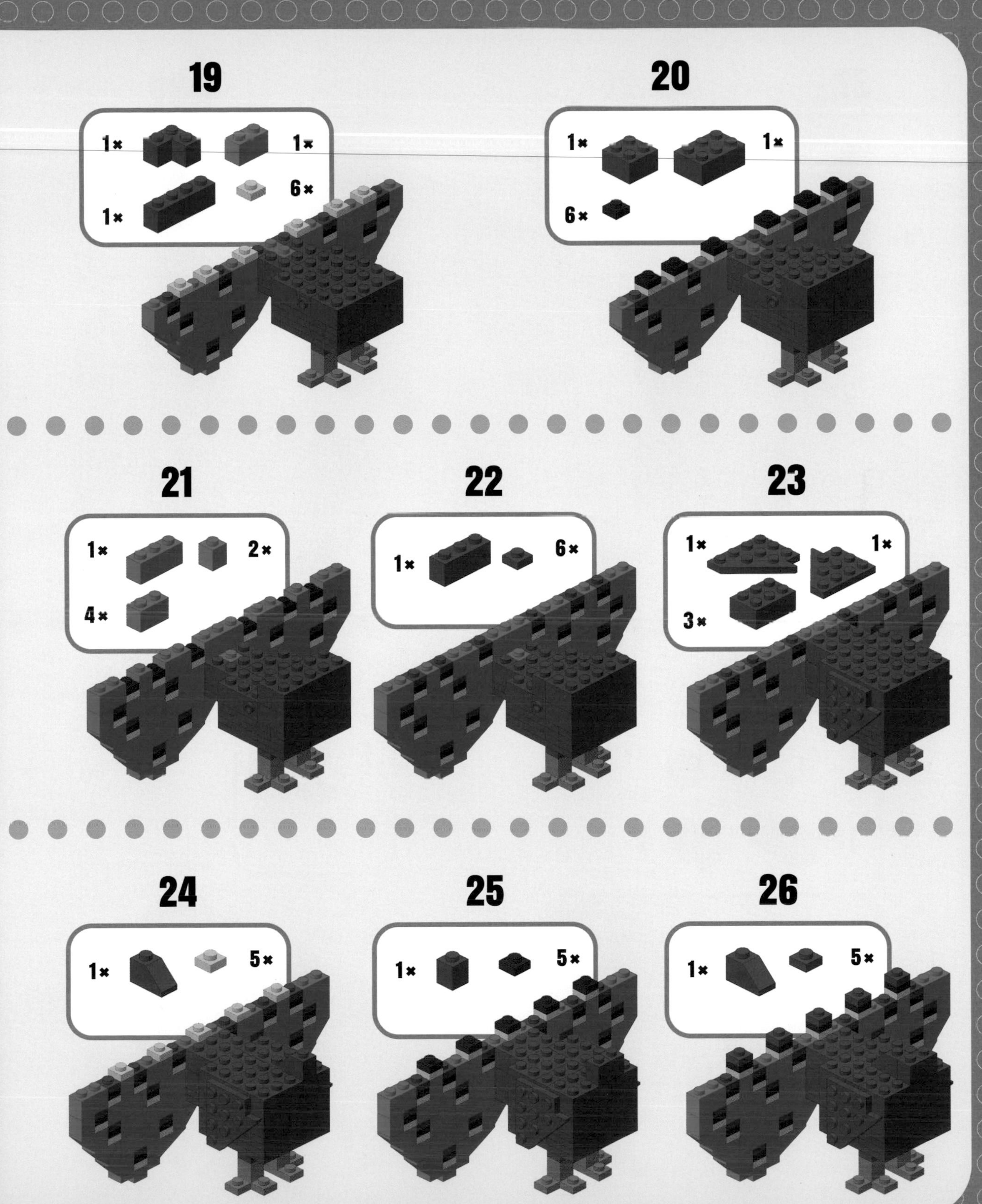
19
1×
1×
1×
6×
20
1×
1×
6×
21
1×
2×
4×
22
1×
6×
23
1×
1×
3×
24
1×
5×
25
1×
5×
26
1×
5×

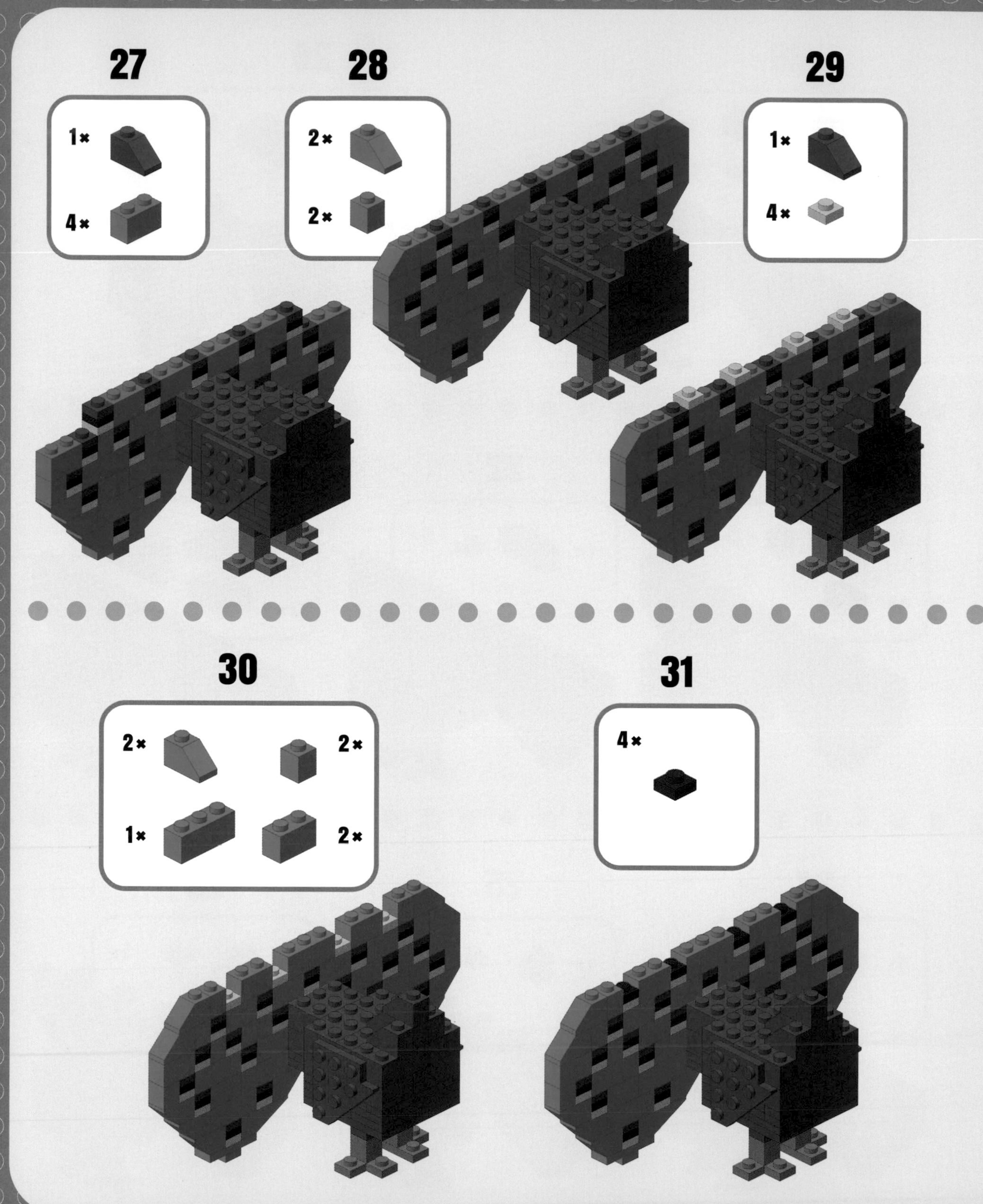
27
1×
4×
28
2×
2×
29
1×
4×
30
2×
2×
1×
2×
31
4×

32

4×

33

1×

4×

34

4×

38
2×
2×
2×
39
3×
40
3×

41
1×
4×
Make sure you get the positions right!
42
2×
1×
4×

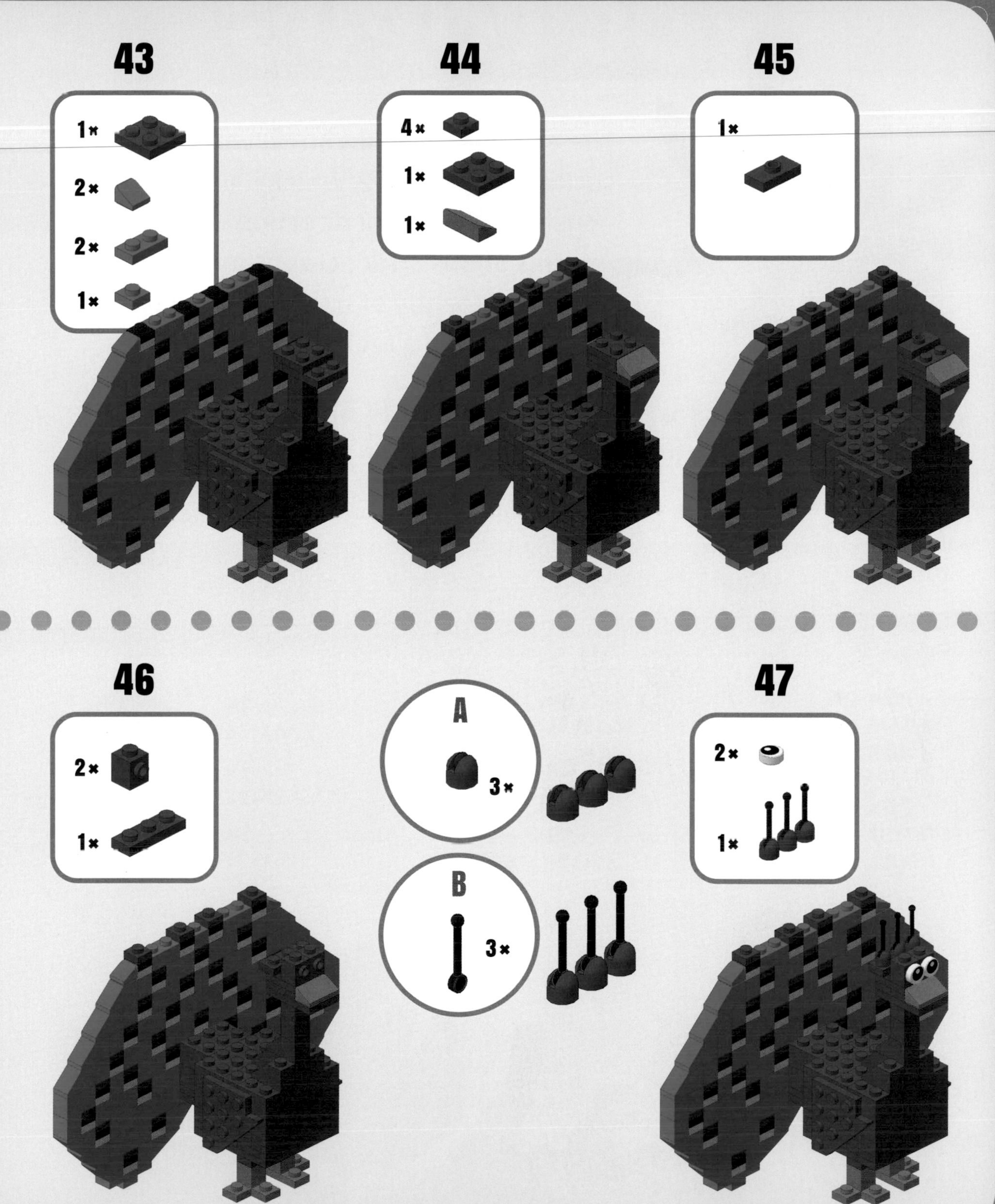
43
1×
2×
2×
1×
44
4×
1×
1×
45
1×
46
2×
1×
A
3×
B
3×
47
2×
1×

OCTOPUS

The octopus has eight arms, with suckers on each one, which it uses to push itself in every direction. The arms of this brick octopus move independently of each other, just like those of a real octopus!

You can use the base of the octopus to build another sea animal like a cuttlefish or a squid!

PARTS LIST

DIFFICULTY 

2× 6060734
48× 614101
24× 4535739
16× 4515368
4× 300126
2× 300226
1× 4162443

1× 6018805
4× 367626
1× 614326

1× 303126
1× 302426
1× 4565323

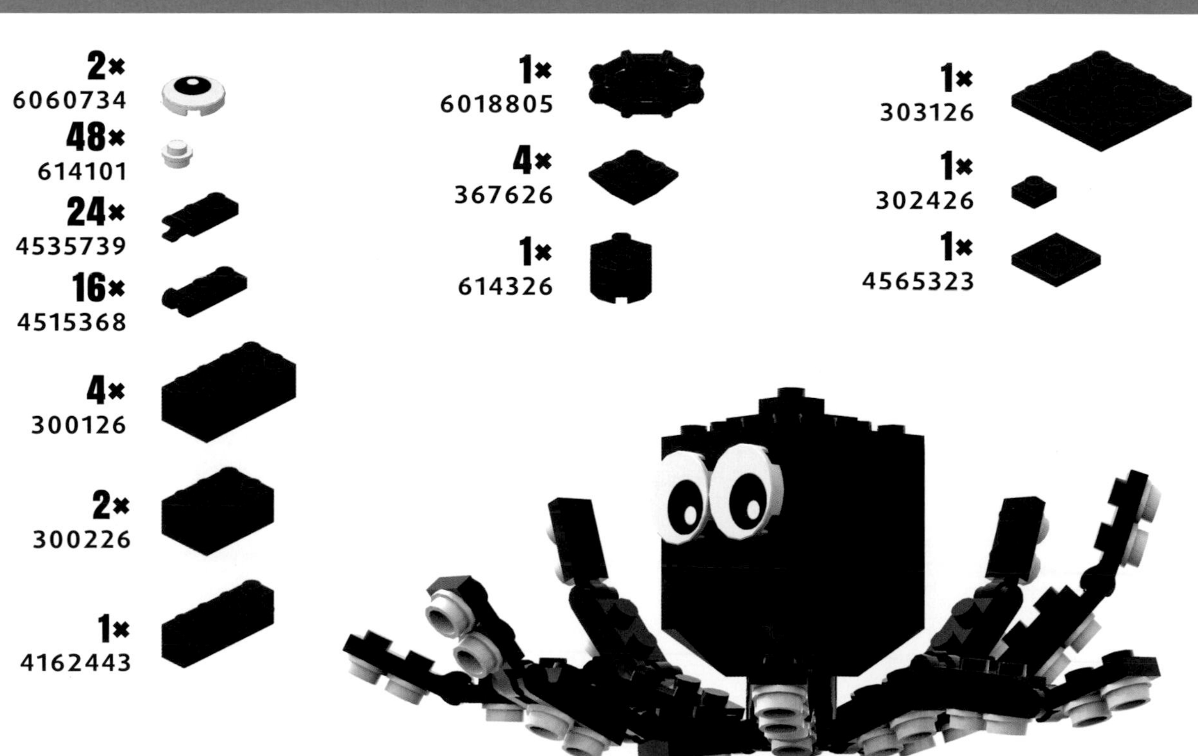

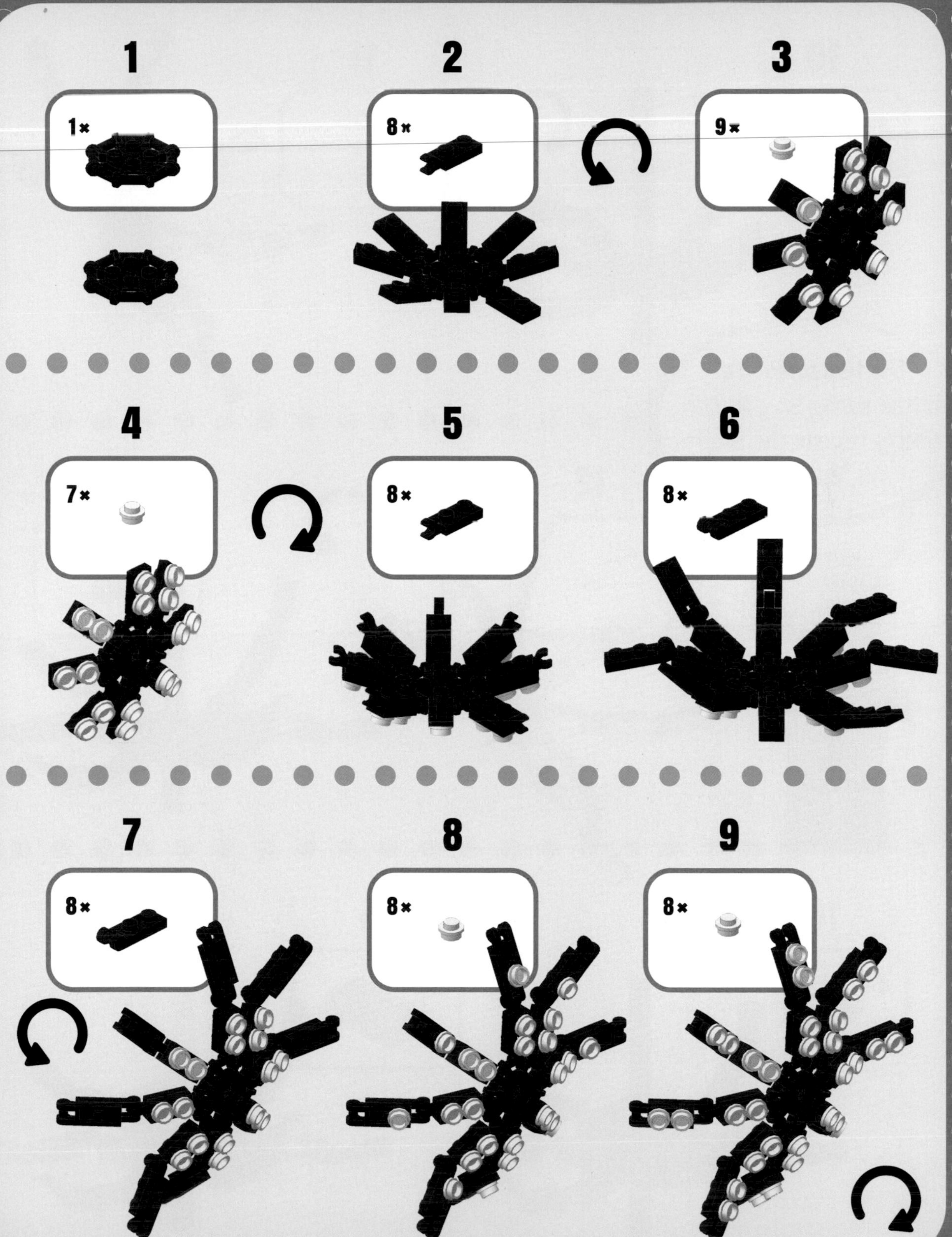
1
1×
2
8×
3
9×
4
7×
5
8×
6
8×
7
8×
8
8×
9
8×

10
8×
11
8×
The tentacles are all the same, so you can simply repeat the steps for each one.
12
8×
13
1×
14
4×
15
2×

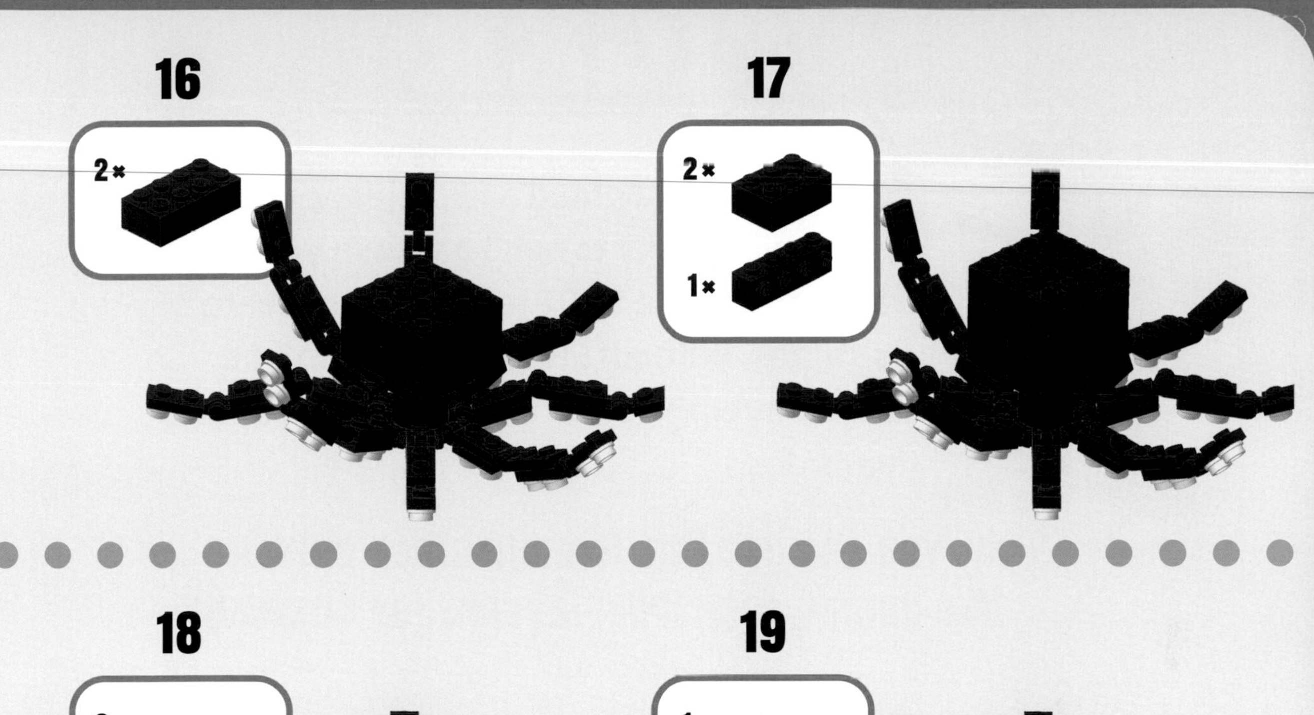
16
2×
17
2×
1×

18
2×
19
1×

20
1×
21
1×

TIGER

This tiger is a proud and majestic feline. It can be tricky to build because you have to use the SNOT technique to create its stripes. Without SNOT, we wouldn't be able to layer the black and orange plates on their sides.

You can use this to build other animals like pumas, leopards, jaguars, or cheetahs.

PARTS LIST

DIFFICULTY

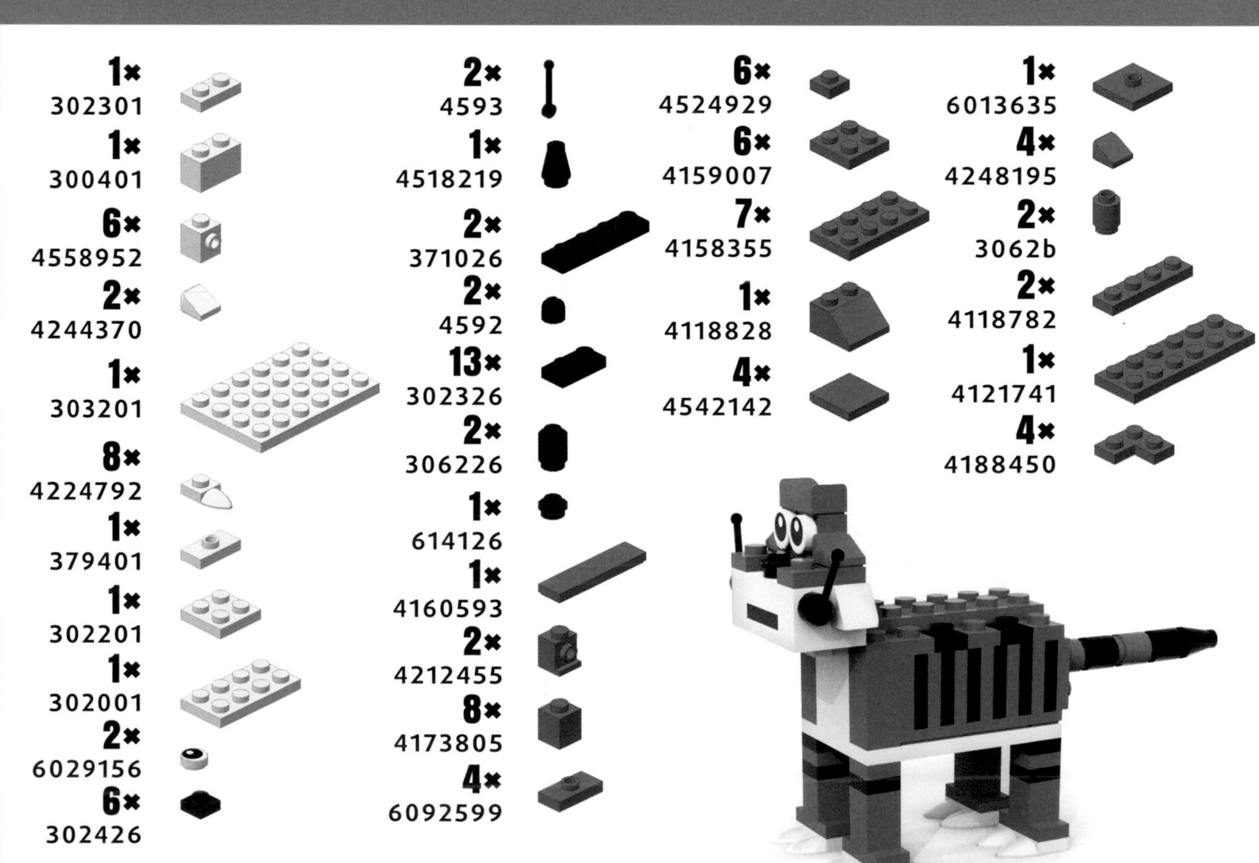

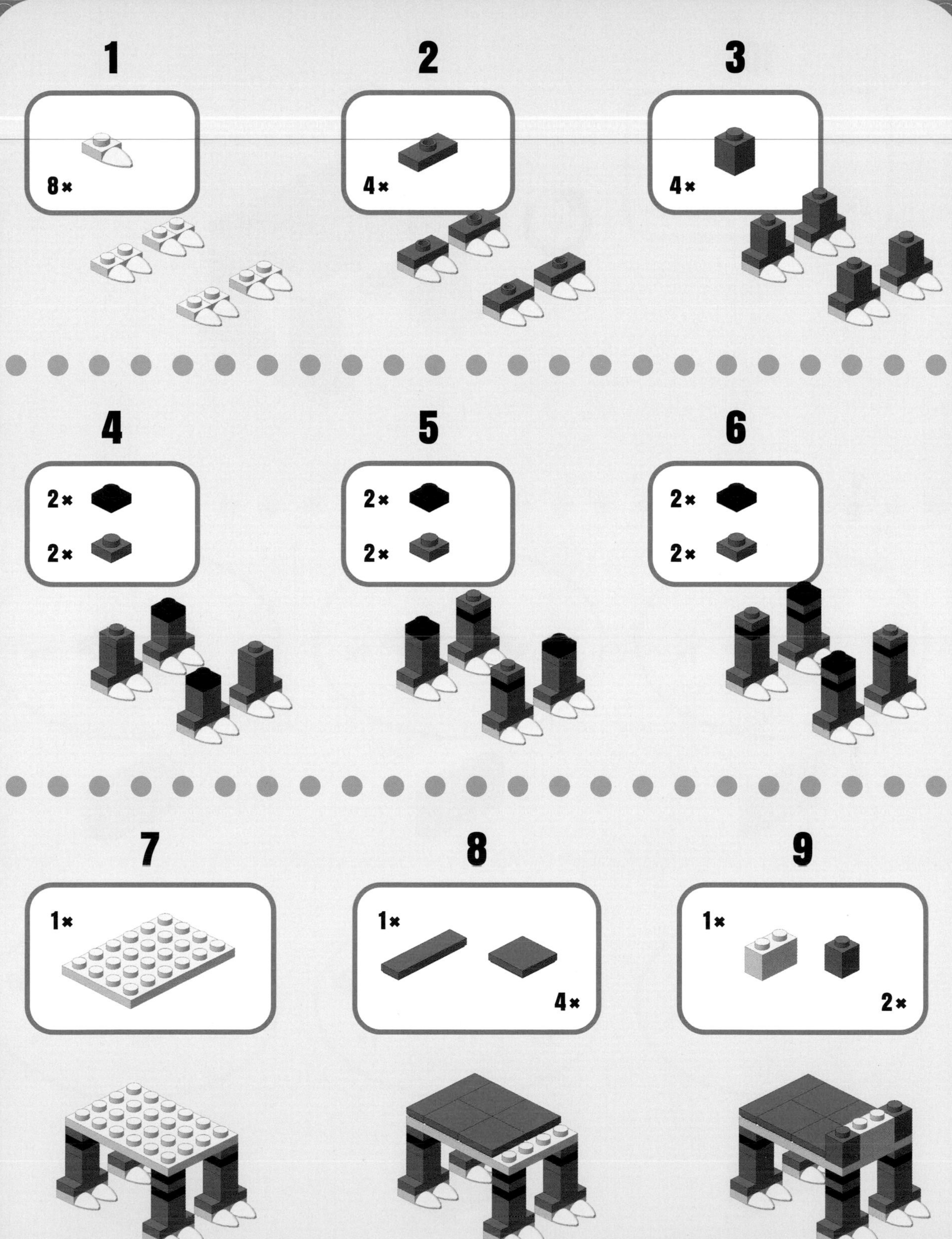

1
8×
2
4×
3
4×
4
2×
2×
5
2×
2×
6
2×
2×
7
1×
8
1×
4×
9
1×
2×

10

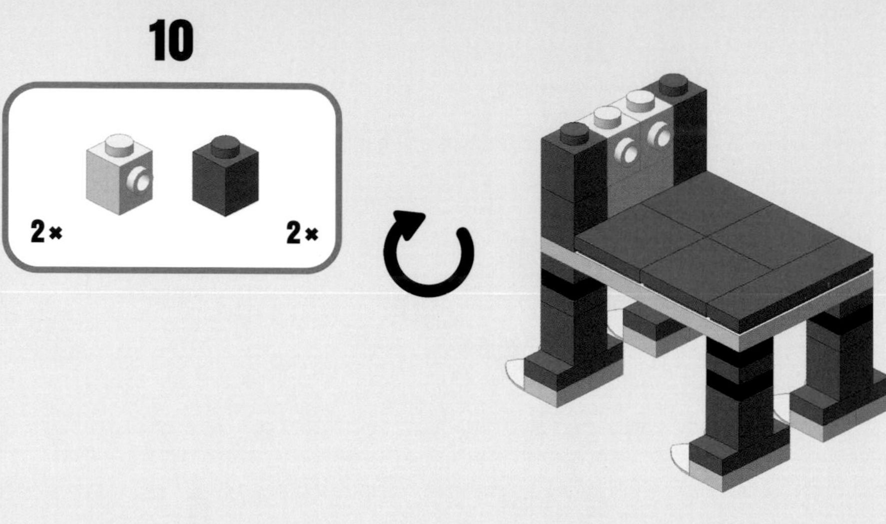

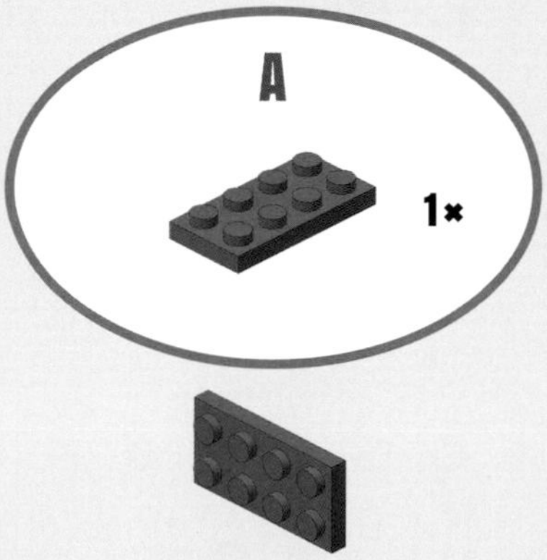

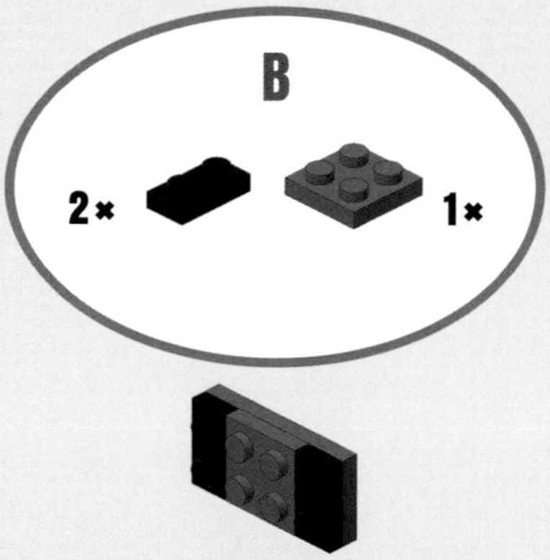

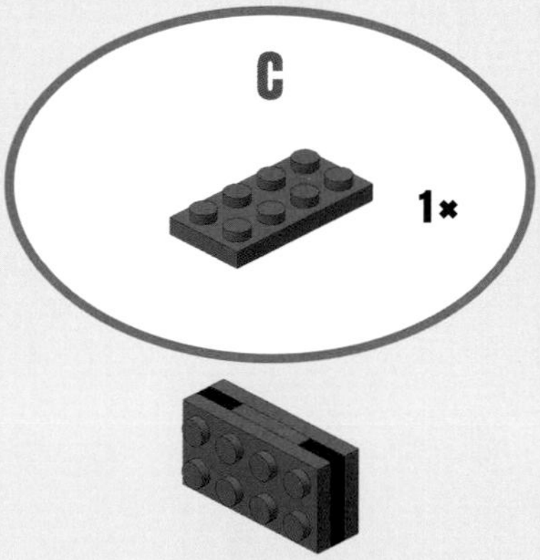

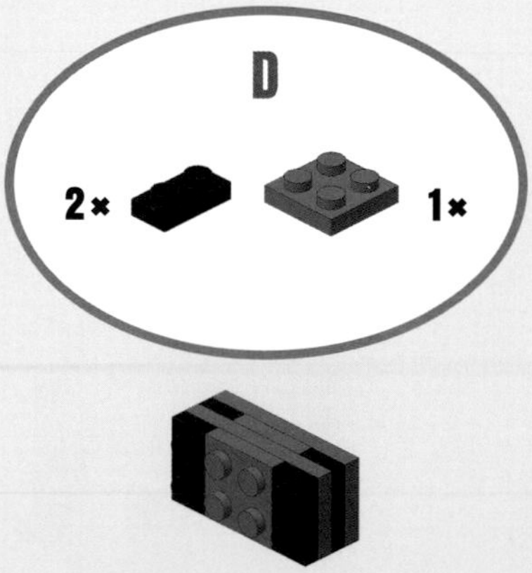

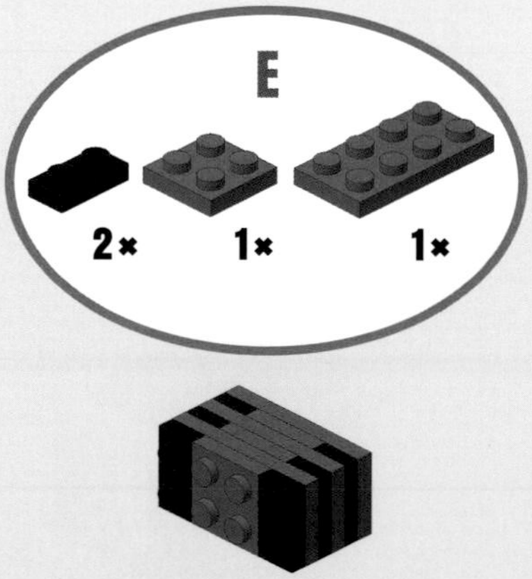

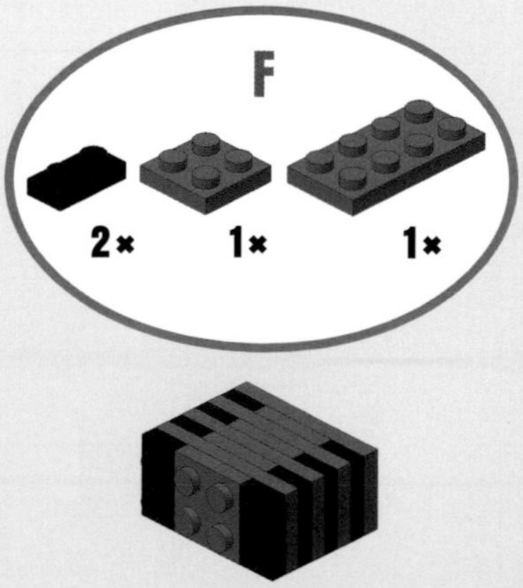

A

1×

B

2× 1×

C

1×

D

2× 1×

E

2× 1× 1×

F

2× 1× 1×

G
2×
1×
1×
H
2×
1×
1×
I
1×
J
1×
1×
K
1×
1×
L
1×
1×

11
1×
Congratulations, you've built the tiger's body!

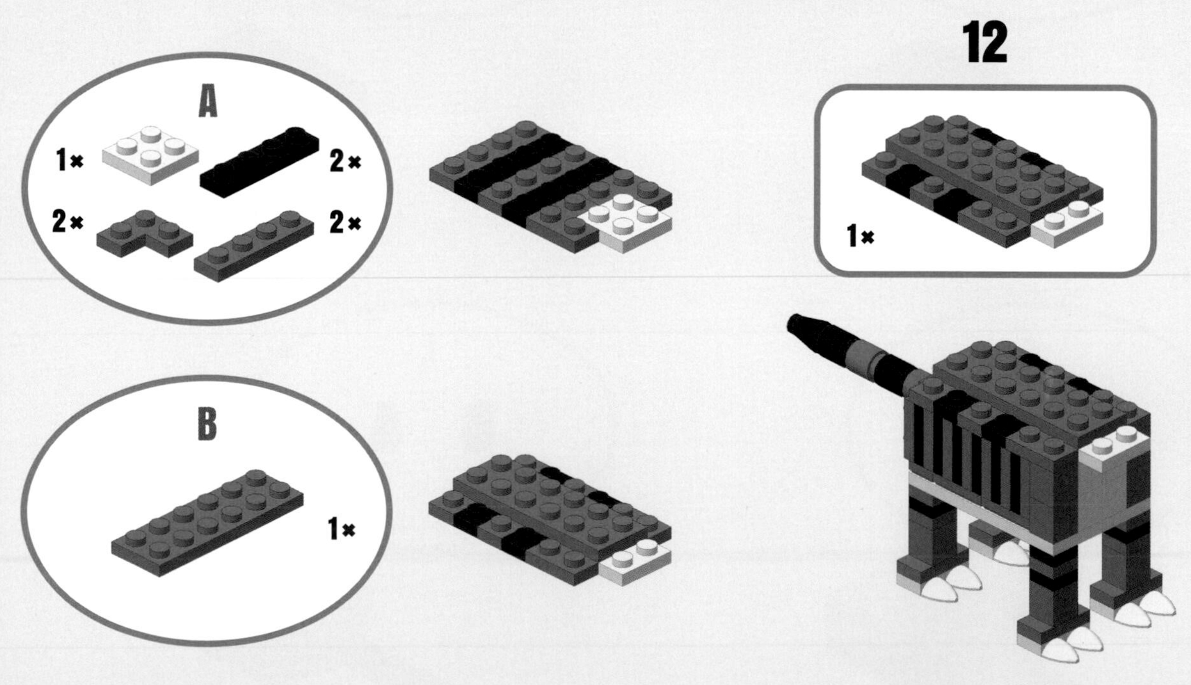
12
A
1×
2×
2×
2×
B
1×
1×

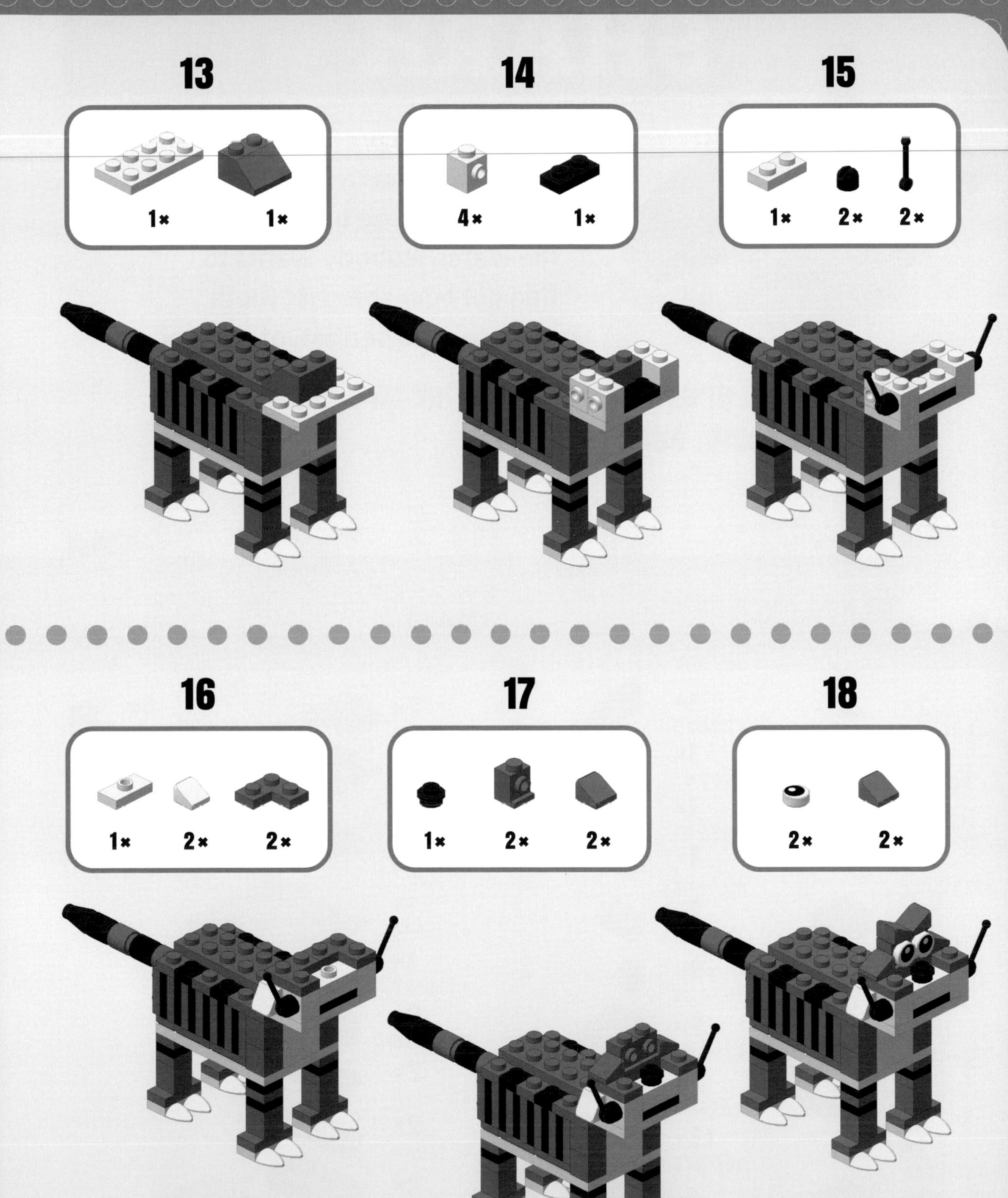
13
1×
1×
14
4×
1×
15
1×
2×
2×
16
1×
2×
2×
17
1×
2×
2×
18
2×
2×

SHARK

One of the scariest predators of the sea, the shark has a fin on its back that you can see poking out of the water. Nobody wants to find out how sharp its teeth are—except its dentist, of course!

Try building a gray shark instead, or use other pieces to build its teeth. Good luck!

PARTS LIST

DIFFICULTY

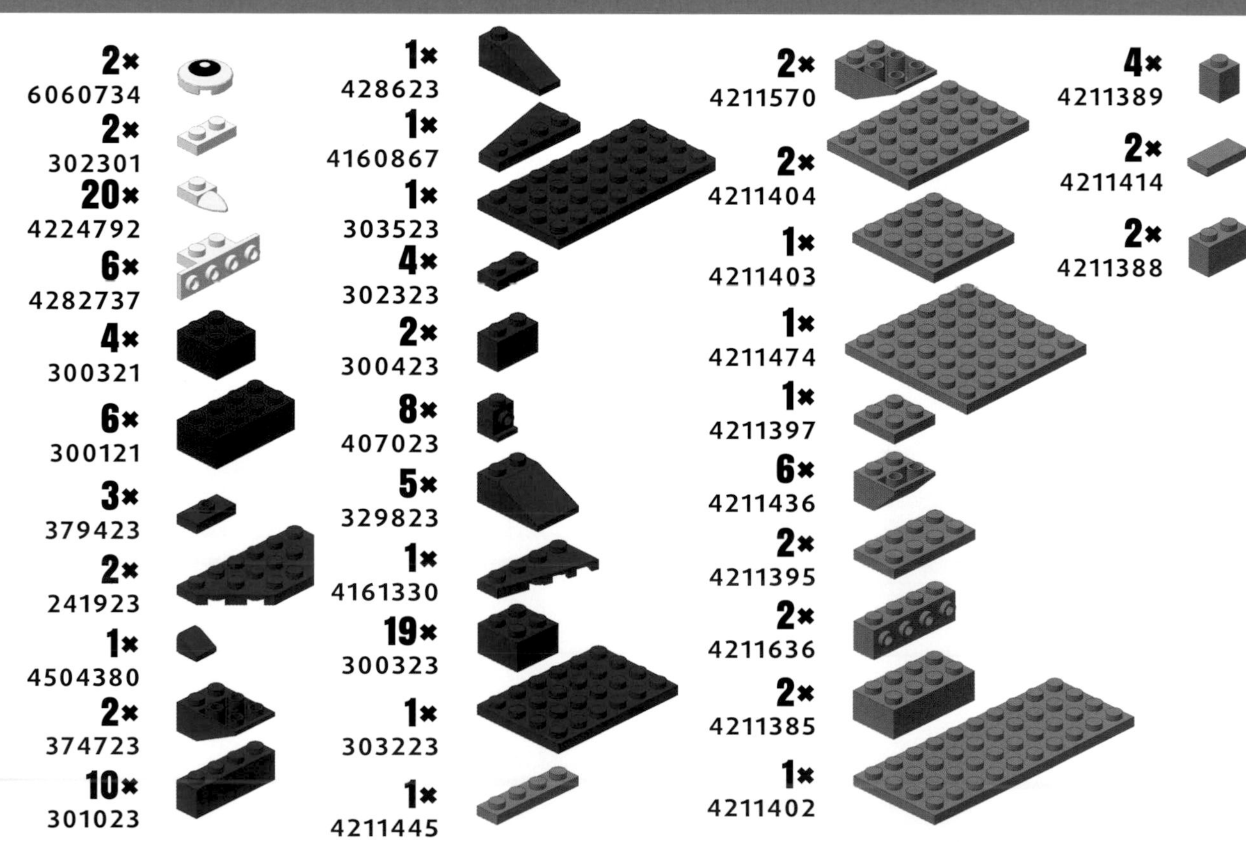

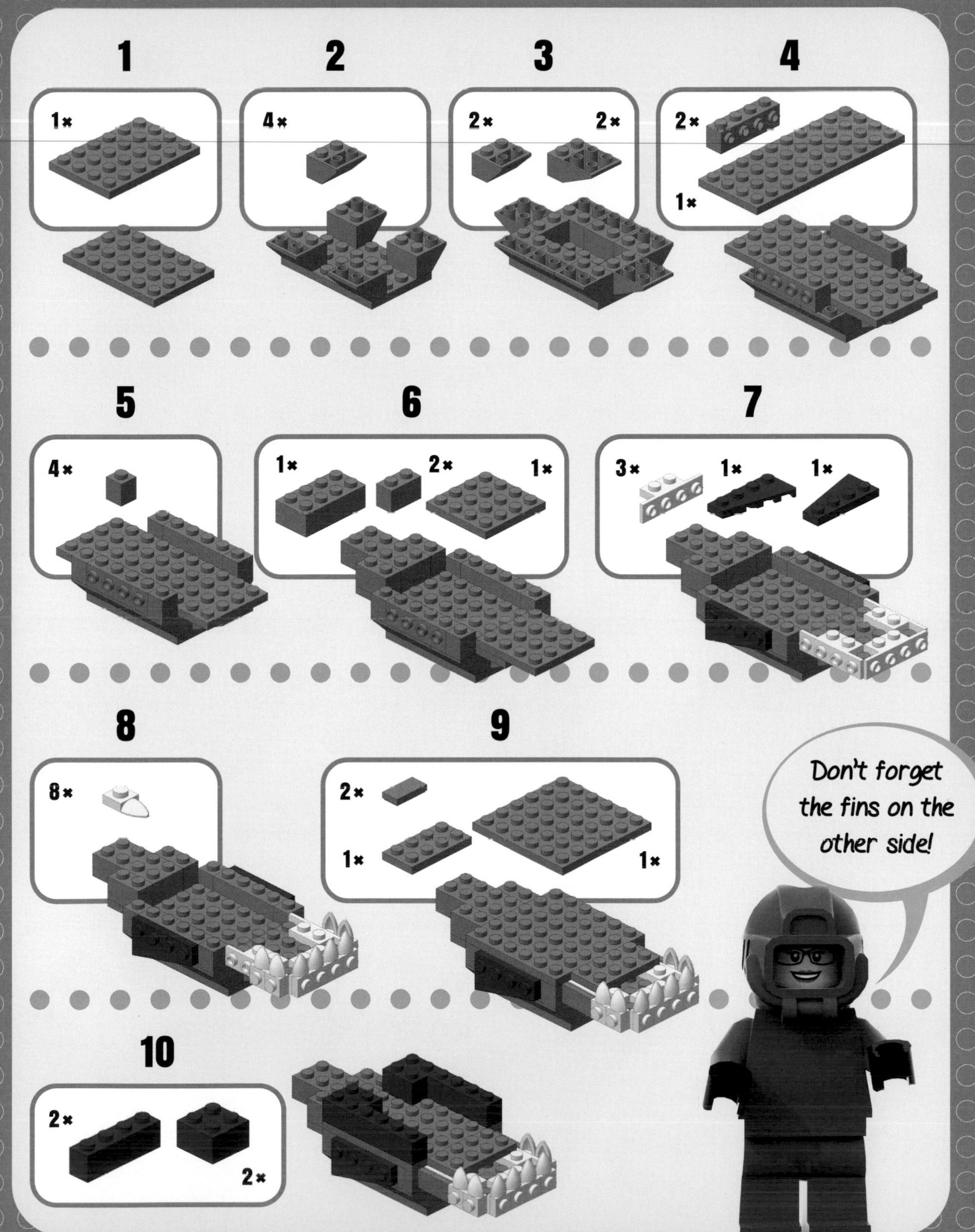
1
1×
2
4×
3
2×
2×
4
2×
1×
5
4×
6
1×
2×
1×
7
3×
1×
1×
8
8×
9
2×
1×
1×
Don't forget the fins on the other side!
10
2×
2×

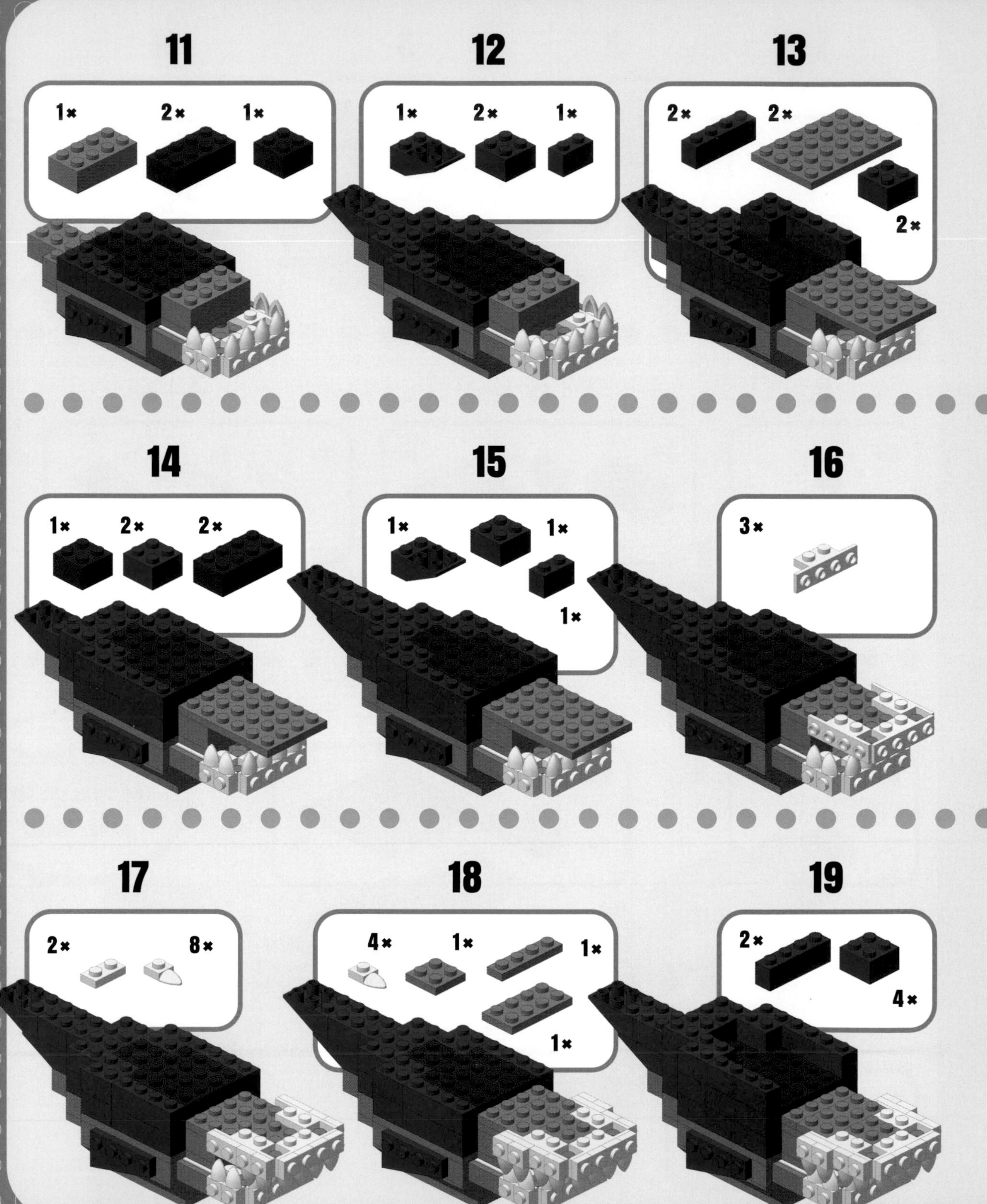
11
1×
2×
1×
12
1×
2×
1×
13
2×
2×
2×
14
1×
2×
2×
15
1×
1×
1×
16
3×
17
2×
8×
18
4×
1×
1×
1×
19
2×
4×

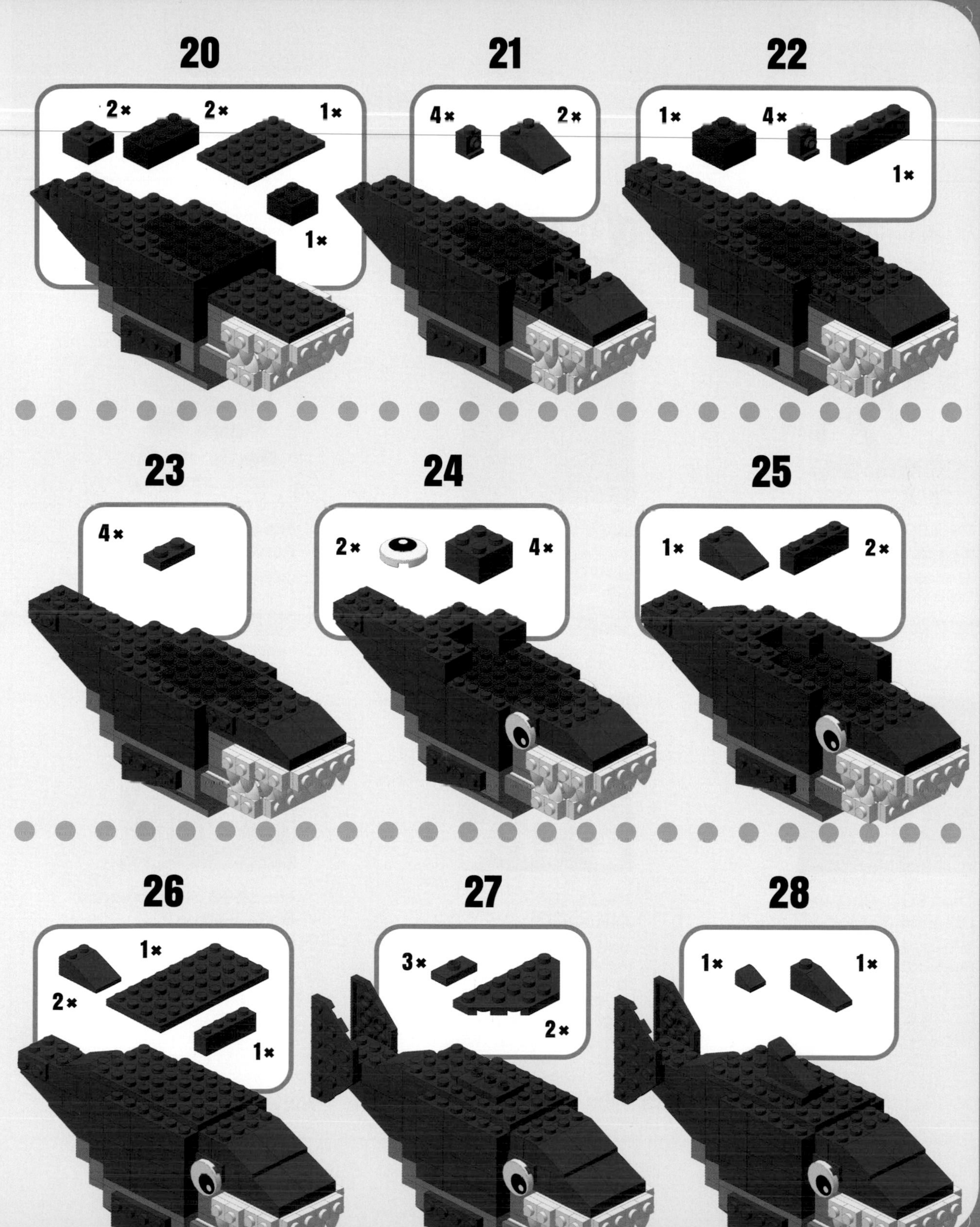
20
2×
2×
1×
1×
21
4×
2×
22
1×
4×
1×
23
4×
24
2×
4×
25
1×
2×
26
1×
2×
1×
27
3×
2×
28
1×
1×

Updates

Visit *https://nostarch.com/legozoo/* for updates, errata, and other information.